Human Sexuality in the Catholic Tradition

Human Sexuality in the Catholic Tradition

Edited by
Kieran Scott and
Harold D. Horell

A SHEED & WARD BOOK

ROWMAN & LITTLEFIELD PUBLISHERS, INC.
Lanham • Boulder • New York • Toronto • Plymouth, UK

A SHEED & WARD BOOK

ROWMAN & LITTLEFIELD PUBLISHERS, INC.

Published in the United States of America
by Rowman & Littlefield Publishers, Inc.
A wholly owned subsidary of The Rowman & Littlefield Publishing Group, Inc.
4501 Forbes Boulevard, Suite 200, Lanham, Maryland 20706
www.rowmanlittlefield.com

Estover Road
Plymouth PL6 7PY
United Kingdom

Copyright © 2007 by Rowman & Littlefield Publishers, Inc.

British Library Cataloguing in Publication Information Available

Library of Congress Cataloging-in-Publication Data

Human sexuality in the Catholic tradition / edited by Kieran Scott and Harold
  Horell.
    p. cm.
  Includes bibliographical references and index.
  ISBN-13: 978-0-7425-5240-1 (cloth : alk. paper)
  ISBN-10: 0-7425-5240-3 (cloth : alk. paper)
  ISBN-13: 978-0-7425-5241-8 (pbk. : alk. paper)
  ISBN-10: 0-7425-5241-1 (pbk. : alk. paper)
    1. Sex—Religious aspects—Catholic Church. 2. Catholic Church—Doctrines.
  I. Scott, Kieran. II. Horell, Harold Daly.
  BX1795.S48H87 2007
  241'.66—dc22   2006036906

Printed in the United States of America

∞™ The paper used in this publication meets the minimum requirements of
American National Standard for Information Sciences—Permanence of Paper
for Printed Library Materials, ANSI/NISO Z39.48-1992.

Dedicated to Carl C. Landegger
for his generosity in support of this project

Contents

I

FOUNDATIONAL ISSUES OF HUMAN SEXUALITY

1

Moving Beyond the Sound of Silence

Kieran Scott

Questions of sexual morality are among the most volatile issues in the Roman Catholic Church today. They are also among the most vital. The official teaching on a wide array of issues—contraception, sterilization, artificial insemination, masturbation, abortion, premarital sex, homosexuality, celibacy—is generally well known among Catholics and the public at large. Equally well known is the great discrepancy between official Catholic teaching and Catholic practice.

Patrick T. McCormick writes, "Since the mid-sixties there has been mounting discord within Catholicism over its teachings on sexuality and gender. Disagreements with and dissent from official positions on some or all of these questions has long been widespread among American Catholic laity, clergy, theologians, and perhaps even bishops."[1] Only a tiny fraction of American Catholics (10–13 percent) supports the church's ban on birth control. Pope Paul VI's 1968 encyclical, *Humanae Vitae*, seems to be a dead letter on the level of most individual Catholics. A steady stream of polls, spanning nearly forty years, indicate that a large majority disagree with official teaching on sterilization, masturbation, premarital sex, abortion, celibacy, and divorce.

There is only one prevailing consensus: a serious rift exists between official teaching about sex and the lived reality of Catholics. Peter Steinfels notes that this rift has produced a spider's web of small cracks and fissures— dissimulations, denials, evasions, hypocrisies—that threaten the church's integrity.[2] A deep and pervasive legitimation crisis exists. Elevating the level of this crisis in recent years has been the sexual abuse scandal traumatizing the American Catholic Church. This has sent its credibility into a free fall. And the response of officials to the scandal has merely served to reinforce the very problems that they purport to solve. This is tragic, both for the institutional church and its people: a church seemingly bereft of sexual wisdom, and its people left rudderless without credible sexual guidance.

This book seeks to repair the rift and bridge the gap between official teaching and the lived reality of Roman Catholics. Church officials have sought to bridge the divide by requiring public affirmation of their teachings, without qualification, at all levels of Catholic life. Some Catholic moral theologians and scholars, however, have sought to reopen these teachings to examination and to the test of the lived experience of Catholics. This book chooses the latter approach. It seeks to open a conversation between the realm of scholarship and the life of the church, and between the church's teaching office(s) and "the sense of the faithful."

"Catholic efforts to rethink sexual morality," Peter Steinfels observes, "operate in a slightly obscure zone of academic theology that may at best influence private pastoral counseling but is carefully fenced off from the church's public speech—in pulpits, religious education, church publications, or official statements."[3] This book is our modest effort to remove some of the fences that currently hem in discourse in the Roman Catholic community.

The initial inspiration for the book emerged from a pastoral conference titled "Human Sexuality in the Roman Catholic Tradition," which Dr. Harold Horell and I cochaired, October 28–29, 2004, at Fordham University. For the conference, we invited leading experts to address major issues of human sexuality from a Christian faith perspective. Multiple perspectives were offered to provide a holistic understanding. Each of the keynote addresses had a pastoral dialogue response. This dialogical structure frames part I of the book. Part II includes some seminar presentations from the conference. However, we have also included in this section additional material that addresses some key specific issues that our Christian communities care passionately about today.

While there has been a significant loss of institutional credibility on sexual matters among contemporary Roman Catholics, this credibility, we believe, can be restored. In the depths of our tradition a treasure of wisdom awaits to be rediscovered. The purpose of the book is to reclaim the deep wisdom within our religious tradition and make it accessible for the life of the church, its pastoral ministers, scholars, and church leaders.

However, formidable obstacles remain. A healthy sense of ecclesiastical realism is required. Sex and sexuality are controversial, difficult, and dangerous to tackle on every level of church life. Careers can be put in peril, sanctions dished out, and sacraments denied. In spite of the growing chasm dividing what the official church teaches from the community of scholars, and from parishioners, the church's magisterium refuses to engage in meaningful conversation. Efforts at dialogue have fallen on deaf ears or are met with a stony silence. "Discussion has not come to a halt," notes Peter Steinfels, "but like a jam-up on the highway when all the vehicles have to squeeze around a wreck, discussion about sexual morality has slowed to a crawl."[4]

Time and again attempts at dialogue have failed. They have been sabotaged, Patrick McCormick claims, by a fourfold silence in the Catholic Church. "This silence," he writes, "has kept bishops from speaking openly, punished or intimidated dissenting theologians, rendered pastors mute, and ignored women's experiences and voices. And along the way it has wrecked immeasurable damage."[5] McCormick's analysis is worth noting in some detail.

First, there is the self-imposed silence of bishops on disputed sexual issues. Most do not feel free to speak their mind. Their public pronouncements ring tinny and forced—masking their own doubts and disagreements. Bishop Kenneth Untener of Saginaw, Michigan compares the situation to a dysfunctional family—(bishops) fearful to speak about things that are on everyone's mind, but which are unmentionable.[6]

Second, attempts to bridge the sexual chasm in Roman Catholicism have been undermined by the silencing of theologians. "Most U.S. Catholic theologians, especially clergy, vowed religious or faculty in Catholic universities," McCormick writes, "know that sexual issues represent the third rail in Catholic theology—touch it at your peril."[7] Since *Humanae Vitae*, Rome has refused to engage the critical voices of theologians in open dialogue. Instead, it responds to dissent by silencing the critics—forbidding public debate, investigating and sanctioning theologians, and making dissent from certain sexual teachings a canonical offense. This has had a chilling effect on Catholic scholarship and retarded the growth and development of a mature, integrated sexual ethic in Roman Catholicism.

A third level of silence is found on the pastoral level. This is where the vast majority of Catholics encounter the church, its ministers, and its teachings in the concrete. This is also where the chasm is the widest—as every opinion poll indicates. "In this context," McCormick notes, "a large number of pastors have felt squeezed between a set of official teachings that neither they nor their congregations find persuasive or helpful and a bevy of questions and concerns for which they have few useful answers. All too often this results in a form of sexual silence."[8] Don't ask, don't tell is the unofficial operating policy on many sexual matters. Parishioners are encouraged—as a pastoral solution—to follow their own consciences. Pastoral ministers are rendered mute on controversial sexual issues facing their parishioners.

Finally, there is the silencing of women. Patrick McCormick declares, "Women have experienced the sexual silence of the church by being ignored and oppressed . . . traditional Catholic teachings on sex and gender were formulated without attending to the voices or experience of women."[9] This silencing continues to show up in the magisterium's unwillingness to engage in open conversation about issues critical to women, especially in its absolute proscription of certain sexual practices. The voice and scholarship, particularly of women theologians, have been ignored on sexual matters or treated as if they were mute.

These attempts at stifling dialogue and debate about sexuality in contemporary Catholicism are counterproductive. They have brought with them a heavy cost. McCormick lists four: first, it has contributed to significant erosion in the church's moral authority to teach about sex and gender; second, it has deprived many Catholics of a useful and persuasive sexual ethic to guide and instruct their children; third, it has deprived the church of the dialogical space needed to wrestle with complex sexual moral questions; and finally, it has resulted in the marginalization of anyone willing to speak the truth on the host of critical sexual issues facing our lives and demoralizes those who feel they cannot speak the truth.[10]

This book, with its rich array of essays, aims to move us beyond the sound of silence. It not only seeks to reopen dialogue, its style and format is itself dialogical. Such a dialogue, we believe, is vital to the health of our tradition and the holiness of our lives.

From 1940 through mid-1960, the official teaching of the Roman Catholic Church on sex was remarkably consistent and severe. Practicing Catholics wore their rigorous sexual code as a badge of honor. The teachings had a totalizing character—extending in sets of attitudes and actions impacting aspects of everyday life. There was a certain countercultural element to the official teachings on sexual ethics. They were out of step with postwar affluence and freedom in the United States. Practicing Catholics obeyed the strict sexual teaching. There was coherence between official pronouncements and the practices of the people.

Today, the official teaching retains an inflexible continuity. There has been no substantial modification of position on artificial birth control, premarital sex, masturbation, adultery, homosexuality, celibacy, and so forth. "In important ways," Luke Timothy Johnson writes, "the church's teaching on sexuality can be regarded as prophetic. It stands for a vision of the world defined by God over and against practices that distort creation."[11] This may be particularly true in relation to current U.S. culture. Peter Steinfels observes, "American culture . . . remains at war with itself in the absence of any cultural consensus on sexual norms. Billions of dollars and immense talent are expended in stirring sexual longings and promoting sexual fantasies. Billions of dollars and immense talent are devoted to repairing the damages of impulsive, irresponsible, or exploitative sexual conduct. . . . American society is desperately in need of moral analysis beyond the level of bumper stickers, sitcoms, and rock lyrics."[12] Official church teaching may offer some of that analysis in demanding fidelity in marriage, restricting licit sexual activity to marriage, its unwavering stance against abortion, and even in its insistence that vowed religious and clergy be celibate. In our current situation, these teachings can be legitimately regarded as a prophetic voice within US culture.

However, Luke Timothy Johnson notes, "Only to the degree that moral teaching is expressed by the attitudes and actions of Catholics themselves can it challenge anyone. . . . Teaching is real and convincing only to the extent that it is actually embraced by believers, embodied in their practices, coherently and consistently expressed by the community of faith."[13] In other words, "reception" by Catholics themselves—both clergy and laity— is an essential element of authentic teaching. This is the profound change that has occurred in the last forty years. We have experienced a seismic shift in the practice and perception of Catholic sexual teaching by Catholics themselves. The formerly monolithic Catholic sexual ethos has all but disappeared. Many Catholics today either don't believe the official teachings on sex and sexuality or don't consistently practice them. "Within the span of a decade," Johnson observes, "American Catholicism went from a clear and confident sense of sexual morality to a state of confusion and loss of confidence."[14] No longer do we have a coherent, consistent and clear sexual morality. While the words may have stayed the same, the actual content of Catholic sexual morality in the United States has not.[15] This has compromised—if not discredited—the prophetic voice of the church in matters of sexual morality. It is our hope that this book, with its holistic understanding of sexuality, will contribute in some small way to the construction of a clear, consistent, and internally coherent sexual morality for the Roman Catholic community.

To achieve this noble purpose, however, the book takes seriously the critical observations of Susan A. Ross on a deep-rooted problem the church faces. A major flaw, she says, is the official church's uncompromising approach. "I would label this," she writes, "a striking lack of tolerance of any ambiguity, particularly when it comes to sexuality."[16] Ross names four areas in particular where this lack of sensitivity to the complexities and ambiguities of life are manifest in church teaching and discipline—namely, the church's teaching on divorce and remarriage; the requirement for celibacy for vowed religious and clergy; the church's lack of a theology of sexuality that includes pleasure; and, the neuralgic issue of abortion. In the latter case, the church's failure to see any moral ambiguity in a woman's decision whether or not to continue a pregnancy is seen as theologically and pastorally problematic. Ross declares, "When it comes to sexuality, the church's default mode has been to resort to legalism. So while I would agree that there is a prophetic dimension to this situation, it is a picture in black and white, almost in silhouette, and it does not allow for complexity here, whereas it does in other areas."[17] The church is cognizant of this complexity when it comes to social justice. As a result, its social teachings have greater credibility.

Susan Ross, then, asks officials of the church, church ministers, and parishioners to think long and hard, and with patience, about the sexual issues that confront us. "We need, on the part of the church's public voices," she says, "both more sensitivity to the complexity of moral decision making and a clearer and more consistent voice."[18] As I understand her position, Ross is advocating a deeper appreciation for the constructive side of postmodernity (ambiguity, complexity, and plurality) and honoring these sensibilities in our experience of sexuality. To a significant degree that is also the purpose of our book.

Human Sexuality in the Roman Catholic Tradition is written with a broad audience in mind. Most of the chapters are relatively brief and the language is accessible. Every effort has been made to minimize esoteric technical scholarly language. However, the book attempts to combine academic rigor and pastoral sensitivity. We see it as suspension bridge between the academy and the ecclesia. The book may be of particular value to clergy and lay ecclesial ministers and those preparing for ordained and nonordained ministry in the church. It may also be of particular interest to committed Christians seeking to develop a more holistic sense of human sexuality from a Christian perspective. Finally, the Roman Catholic scholarly community may find the book valuable in its effort to establish a "double voice" discourse with the tradition.

No attempt has been made here to present a systematically complete account of human sexuality from a Roman Catholic perspective. Rather, major issues of sexuality are addressed by leading experts in their fields. Multiple perspectives are offered toward a holistic understanding of human sexuality. In particular, human sexuality is explored from the perspective of pastoral care and counseling, moral theology/Christian ethics, spirituality, pastoral ministry, and religious education. Most of the perspectives offered complement each other. On occasion, however, the authors take differing standpoints. Our goal has been to move beyond the sound of silence in the ecclesia and raise up a community of critical discourse.

Our book, *Human Sexuality in the Roman Catholic Tradition*, forms a kind of pathway through the many topics and ramifications of human sexuality viewed from a Roman Catholic perspective. The book falls neatly into two major parts. Part I (chapters 2 through 5) addresses fundamental issues of human sexuality. The angles of vision here are spirituality, pastoral care and counseling, moral theology/Christian ethics, and pastoral ministry. Part II (chapters 6 through 13) attends to specific issues of human sexuality. Specifically, the section explores John Paul II's theology of the body and human sexuality, sex and marriage, celibacy, the pastoral care of homosexual persons, adolescence and sexuality, a reevaluation of cohabitation, and discernment on the future of sexuality.

Part I: Foundational Issues of Human Sexuality comprises the four keynote presentations and the pastoral responses to each at the pastoral conference in October 28–29, 2004 at Fordham University. We begin with a chapter, "Tender Fires: The Spiritual Promise of Sexuality," by Fran Ferder, F.S.P.A., and John Heagle. Ferder and Heagle seek to demonstrate the need for a renewed theology and spirituality of human sexuality. The authors point out how we have often strayed from our deepest roots into a shame-based dualism. Frequently, this negative dualism has been "the background music" for the church's teaching regarding sexuality. Ferder and Heagle analyze the causes of our crisis and then dig deep into our religious heritage for riches to reclaim and re-envision the spiritual promise of sexuality. Their chapter concludes with some pastoral tasks and personal implications.

Harold D. Horell offers a pastoral response. His response affirms Ferder and Heagle's analysis of the current crisis in discussing sexuality and the way they have drawn from the resources of Christian faith traditions in addressing this crisis. Horell proceeds to discuss how we might begin to use the new approach offered by Ferder and Heagle to enrich our faith communities.

In chapter 3, "Toward Christian Sexual Maturity: Growing in Wisdom, Age and Grace," John Cecero offers a reflection on the processes of sexual maturity using a psychological lens. The broad psychological context within which he considers developmental tasks is the lifelong challenge to balance connection with autonomy. On the one hand, Cecero shows how Christians can draw from psychological sources in developing an understanding of the meaning and purpose of human sexuality. On the other hand, mainstream psychology's nascent interest in spirituality, he notes, can contribute to sexual maturity. Cecero draws out the pastoral implications for fostering self-knowledge, maintaining professional boundaries, and balancing prophetic and reconciling action.

My pastoral response to Cecero affirms in particular his embodied starting point and in general the contribution of his psychological perspective. I, however, suggest a larger framework for the discussion of sex and sexuality. I propose that we approach it politically and institutionally, as well as biologically and psychologically. Here I focus on the political dimension of sexuality and illustrate how it flows over into U.S. foreign policy and the politics of academia.

Christine Gudorf follows with chapter 4. She calls for a new moral discourse on sexuality. First, she lays out a number of traditional teachings that must be abandoned and provides evidence to support alternative teachings. The latter half of her chapter draws from contemporary scientific and theological resources to support her alternatives. The chapter is a tour de force and challenges us to envision a new paradigm for sexual morality.

In his pastoral response, Harold Horell applauds Gudorf for courageously raising difficult questions about sexuality. He suggests that the
church needs to confront these questions if we are to develop truly life-
giving understandings of human sexuality. Horell, then, raises two issues
for further reflection. Specifically, he questions Gudorf's analysis of maleness and femaleness and suggests we explore more fully the implications of
Gudorf's recommendation that we abandon the idea that personhood begins at conception.

In the concluding chapter in part I (chapter 5), "Sexuality and Relationships in Ministry," Sidney Callahan explores how a new, integrated, and coherent view of sexuality can be of service to the pastoral life of the church.
There is good news to affirm about sexuality in our tradition. However, she
cautions us with regard to the dark side of sexuality. It can be distorted, misused, and can blind our conscience. She calls for a more balanced approach
in addressing the topic of sexuality as we move into the future.

In my pastoral response, I fundamentally affirm Callahan's analysis,
highlighting her incarnational approach to sexuality and her warnings
against sexual naiveté. Once again, however, I place the question of sexuality in a broader framework. This time I set it in an institutional context. The
institution of the church, with its political design, is the focus of my attention. I call for a new framework for understanding, a new language for understanding ourselves, and new ecclesial structures to facilitate human sexual flourishing.

Part II (chapters 6 through 13) of the book takes up an array of concrete
issues that passionately engage our Christian communities today. This section begins with an incisive analysis, from two quite distinct perspectives,
of the theology of the body and human sexuality put forward by Pope John
Paul II. John Paul's writings have been the subject of much attention and
debate. These two initial chapters by Jennifer Bader and Luke Timothy
Johnson, when read and placed in conversation with each other, yield rich
insight into the corpus of John Paul's writings.

Bader (chapter 6) discusses prepapal and papal writings as she explores
how John Paul's understanding of personhood provides the theological and
philosophical foundation for his views about the human body, sexuality,
and sexual difference. Bader argues that the pope's views on the body and
human sexuality are grounded in his tireless and uncompromising call to
safeguard the dignity of the human person. At the same time, Bader discusses
how a body/soul dualism, rigid senses of masculinity and femininity, and an
inability to be open to dialogue create serious limitations in his thought.

Johnson (chapter 7) questions the conceptual framework of John Paul's
writings. A theology of the body, he claims, is reduced to a consideration of
sexuality. For Johnson, the pope's paradigm is distressingly narrow: human
love and sexuality appear in only one approved form; sexual pleasure and

passion seem mainly an obstacle to authentic love; there is little awareness of the bodily rhythm of ordinary life and ordinary people. If we are to reach a better theology of human love and sexuality, Johnson insists, we must be receptive and willing to learn from the bodies and stories of those involved in sexual love.

In chapter 8, Christine Gudorf takes up the question: "Graceful Pleasures: Why Sex is Good for Your Marriage." She begins by historically tracing the anti-sexual attitudes that have dominated the Christian perspective. Gudorf focuses on the sacramental significance of marital, sexual union. Sexual loving is central to marriage. It is as vitally important to the vocation of marriage as reception of the Eucharist is to membership in the church community. At the same time, Gudorf cautions against developing an overly romanticized understanding of the place and importance of sex in marriage.

The focus and content of the material shifts with Evelyn and James Whitehead's chapter on "The Gift of Celibacy" (chapter 9). In any discussion of Catholics and sexuality, the authors claim, a consideration of the lifestyle of vowed celibacy is essential. Celibacy is one of our faith's paradoxes. The authors discuss how sexual energy can be directed in healthy, life-giving ways in living a celibate life. They call for a renewed vision of celibacy as an authentic Christian way of life. This renewed vision, they propose, will come from an emerging theology that understands celibacy as a charism, a choice, and a call.

Homosexuality is one of the most hotly debated and divisive issues in our Christian churches today. As I write, the Episcopalian Church in the United States is on the verge of splitting apart on the issue. In Roman Catholicism the question is no less contentious. In chapter 10, Barbara Jean Daly Horell focuses on "Always Our Children: A Pastoral Message to Parents of Homosexual Children and Suggestions for Pastoral Ministers" issued by the USCCB Committee on Marriage and Family. The chapter is based upon a survey and discussion groups with Catholic pastoral leaders and young people. Daly Horell offers a reflection on the adequacy of the U.S. bishops' pastoral response to homosexuality, and raises questions about how the church can support the efforts of homosexual persons to integrate sexuality and spirituality in their everyday lives.

In chapter 11, "A Tortured Trio: Sexuality, Adolescents, and Moral Theology," Julie Collins, a seasoned high school religion teacher, describes how she addresses issues of sexuality in the classroom by placing them in the context of love and eternity. Specifically, she invites students to imagine dying and going to heaven and being asked by God, "What was the quality of your love life?" Collins shows how we can draw from the richness of Christian faith traditions to address issues of sexuality with adolescents.

The final two chapters are by my coeditor and me. In "Cohabitation: A Reassessment" (chapter 12), I take a fresh look at cohabitation. I set the discussion in the framework of a stage theory of marriage. Recent social science research describes how widespread the phenomenon is. I describe some of the traditional pastoral solutions of our churches before proposing a moral reassessment of the issue in light of tradition and contemporary needs.

Harold D. Horell concludes the book with his reflections on "Sexuality and the Church: Finding Our Way" (chapter 13). Changing views of sexuality, he claims, place Christians at a crossroads today. On the one hand, we can allow the currents of contemporary culture to dictate the ways sex and sexuality are understood in church and society today. On the other hand, we can examine the profound perspectives on human sexuality emerging from the riches of our religious traditions. Horell discerns the negative and positive attitudes on sexuality operative in church and society. He then proposes a new sexual ideal. This new ideal, he advocates, integrates sexuality with spirituality, and sexuality and social justice.[20] He concludes with a call for a renewed pastoral response to our complex and pluralistic sexual lives. This pastoral response should enable us to discern our way into the future by directing us toward a truly life-giving and life-sustaining sexual way of being in the world.

The trauma revolving around the sexual abuse crisis in Roman Catholicism during the last few years seems only to highlight the tip of the iceberg. The issues of sexuality are wide and deep in our tradition. And we have only begun to address them. The crisis, in a way, could be a blessing in disguise— pushing us back to rethink the basics and repair the damage. It is our hope that this small volume will contribute to this endeavor.

The spirit of our book pleads for a strategy of persuasion rather than canonical or sacramental penalties with regard to sexual matters in our church. We are very much aware of the lack of channels for listening and speaking on important sexual questions on every level of the church's life. Some of the voices raised here are critical of official church teaching on sex and sexuality. But there is a vital need at this time to move beyond the sound of silence. Many of the church's critics speak out because they love the church and are eager for it to grow beyond the present tragic events. "Ironically," Robert Maloney writes, "critics are sometimes the church's most loyal members."[21]

NOTES

1. Patrick T. McCormick, "Catholicism & Sexuality: The Sound of Silence," *Horizons* 30, no. 2 (2003): 191–207, quote from 193.
2. Peter Steinfels, *A People Adrift* (New York: Simon & Schuster, 2003), 275.
3. Ibid., 274.

4. Ibid., 270.

5. McCormick, "Catholicism & Sexuality," 197.

6. Ibid.,198.

7. Ibid., 200.

8. Ibid., 203–4.

9. Ibid., 204–5.

10. Ibid., 206–7.

11. Luke Timothy Johnson, "Abortion, Sexuality, and Catholicism's Public Presence," in *American Catholics, American Culture: Traditions and Resistance,* ed. Margaret O'Brien Steinfels, 27–38, quote from 27 (*American Catholics in the Public Square,* vol. 2) (New York: Rowman & Littlefield, 2004).

12. Peter Steinfels, *A People Adrift,* 268.

13. Johnson, "Abortion, Sexuality, and Catholicism's Public Presence," 28.

14. Ibid., 35.

15. Ibid., 38.

16. Susan A. Ross, "The Complexities and Ambiguities of the 'Prophetic Dimension': A Response," in *American Catholics, American Culture,* ed. Margaret O'Brien Steinfels, 43–48, quote from 43.

17. Ibid., 45.

18. Ibid., 48.

20. On justice as an indispensable element in marriage, see Pauline Kleingeld, "Just Love? Marriage and the Question of Justice," in *Mutuality Matters: Family, Faith and Just Love,* eds. Edward Foley, Bonnie Miller-McLemore and Robert Schreiter, 23–41 (New York: Sheed & Ward, 2004).

21. Robert P. Maloney, "Critics from Within," *America* (October 4, 2004): 12.

2

Tender Fires: The Spiritual Promise of Sexuality

Fran Ferder, F.S.P.A., and John Heagle

INTRODUCTION

For more than thirty years we have had the privilege, as Catholic ministers and psychotherapists, to listen to the love stories of our sisters and brothers. In the context of counseling sessions, university classes and seminars, parish missions and retreats, national and international conferences and workshops, people have shared their deepest personal experiences and convictions about human love and relationships.

They have been women and men of all ages, ethnic backgrounds, and states of life. Some of them have been married, others single, separated, divorced, or remarried, and still others in committed same-gender partnerships. They have been priests and members of religious communities. They have been persons who are gay and straight, those involved in faith communities and others who have been alienated from them.

We have been profoundly moved by their openness, honesty, and courage as they struggled with sexuality in their lives and relationships. Some of them have playfully teased us about being "a nun and a priest who write books about sex." Most of them have thanked us for our ministry.

And, of course, there are some who have been angered by our message—those who have picketed us, reported us to ecclesiastical authorities, or sent us e-mails that are sometimes so mean-spirited that we could only assume that their motivation was not that of gospel values or authentic Catholic teaching. But most of all we have been *inspired*, especially by those Catholics who struggle with tensions between church teachings about sexuality and the "sacred core and sanctuary" of their own conscience.

We begin, then, with three foundational assumptions: first, the church—as an institution and a community—has a right and a responsibility to teach about the meaning and value of human sexuality. Second, that teaching is open-ended and dynamic; it isn't finished yet. Third, all members of the faith community deserve to have their love stories heard, respected, and taken seriously in the quest to articulate a contemporary Catholic sexual ethic.

HUMAN SEXUALITY IN CRISIS

For the last half-century, human sexuality has been undergoing what might best be described as a "sea change"—a major historical transition—in our culture and in our religious institutions. The most recent manifestation of this upheaval or crisis for the Roman Catholic Church is the scandal of clergy sexual abuse and its painful aftermath for victims, their families, and for the entire believing community. But even as we continue to confront this urgent crisis in the church, we believe that we are also facing an even deeper challenge, namely, *the need for a renewed theology and spirituality of human sexuality.*

In our society, what came to be known as the "sexual revolution" brought a much needed forthrightness and honesty to human sexuality, but it has not been able to provide us with a viable vision for responsible and reverent relationships. For the majority of our culture, the only ethical question left to discuss regarding sex is the issue of consent. In its contemporary societal images, sexuality is increasingly reduced to genital behavior. It is also exploited by the media and increasingly connected to interpersonal violence.

What about our churches? How have they responded to this time of upheaval and change? To what extent can we look to them for vision and guidance? Certainly, we can be grateful for the nourishment of our sacred writings and traditions, our unfailing source of wisdom and hope. When the Judeo-Christian tradition speaks from it deepest roots about love, mutual respect, the goodness of the body, and the sacredness of relationships, there is no more powerful source of spiritual guidance. Sadly, we have not consistently spoken from our deepest roots, but instead have been influenced over the centuries by a shame-based dualism. Too often this negative dualism has been the background music for the church's teaching regarding sexuality.

However affirming our tradition might be, we continue to be haunted by a quiet, pervasive ambivalence toward sexuality and human loving. With the clergy sexual abuse scandal, this lingering suspicion and ambivalence has evolved into a major crisis of credibility for the institutional church. We are convinced that the Catholic community will not be able to move through the clergy sexual abuse scandal unless it is willing to confront the institutional misuse of power, to reclaim the affirming roots of its tradition, and to listen more attentively to the love stories of all the people.

THEOLOGICAL AND CULTURAL CAUSES OF THE CRISIS

What are some of the cultural and theological reasons for these shame-based attitudes toward sexuality? What is the source of the ambivalence, the anxiety, and the fear that often surrounds sexual feelings and images?

From our years of listening to individuals, working with couples, and exploring this topic in classes and workshops, we have become convinced that one of the major reasons for our cultural and religious ambivalence toward sexuality is rooted in the *fear of eros*. Obviously, this statement demands some clarification. What do we mean by eros? How does it impact and shape our lives? How is it imaged and understood by cultural and institutional traditions?

On the popular level, the term "erotic" carries various meanings. For some, eros simply describes the realm of sex drives—the animal magnetism evoked by the rites of fantasy, seduction, and sexual liaisons. It implies those stimuli associated with sexual arousal and pleasure in the limited physical sense. For others, eros relates to the classic romance myth as portrayed in gothic novels or popular media. Here the drama of human passion is played out against a backdrop of personal quest, chance encounters, heroic struggles, and tragic love narratives. These two understandings of the erotic—what we might describe as the *recreational* and the *romantic*—are probably the most prevalent images of eros in the popular media.

The popular culture successfully promotes these images of eros, perhaps because, at first glance, they leave us with the illusion of being in control of our private pleasures. What the popular media does not tend to address is what we might describe as the vulnerable face of eros. Our culture tends to keep this deeper dimension of eros at a distance, since it evokes something mysterious and transcendent, something beyond our power to control or manipulate. What is this more profound meaning of eros? Most of us probably experience it as a kind of restlessness in our daily lives. As creatures, we are essentially unfinished, and we confront this radical openness in different ways. We know it in loneliness and relationships; we taste it in our salty tears and hear it in our laughter. We feel it in our physical weariness and the times of emotional exhaustion. We know its goodness when we hold the hand of our beloved or go for an evening walk with one of our children. It is far more than the raw material for sitcoms and popular films; it is the mystery that envelops our lives and relationships.

In the history of Western theology, eros has taken on other, additional layers of meaning, many of which reveal another form of fear or anxiety related to human sexuality. In Greek, the language of the Christian scriptures and the Septuagint version of the Hebrew writings, there are several words for love. The most familiar of these are *eros, philia,* and *agape.* Most of us would welcome a variety of words to describe something as rich and diverse in its expression as human loving. But in our spiritual tradition, this has been a mixed blessing. Although there are advantages to clarity in language, we forget that precision can also become an instrument—even a weapon— for our fears and for the anxiety surrounding the human condition, especially our sexuality.

In the Western Christian tradition, this desire for conceptual clarity combined with our fear of the human condition (otherwise known as dualism) has resulted in the creation of what might be described as the "hierarchy of loving." Although there are variations on the theme, depending on the century and philosophical mindset of the times, spiritual commentators usually articulate the hierarchy of loving along the following lines:

- *Agape* is considered to be the highest form of love, since it embodies God's way of loving: it is generous, other-centered, and disinterested in control and possession.
- *Philia* is the love of friendship and mutuality, in which self-interest is tempered by the care we have for our family members, friends, coworkers, or neighbors.
- *Eros* is ranked as the "lowest" form of loving, since, from this spiritual viewpoint, it seeks to satisfy our physical and emotional needs instead of those of the other person.

In the more extreme versions of this perspective, such as Anders Nygren's twentieth-century work, *Agape and Eros,* there is an immense gulf between eros and agape: God is the only source of true agapic love; eros is of human origin and is, in Nygren's words, inherently "acquisitive and egocentric."

The assertion that there is no eros in God has grave consequences for how we view sexual desire and human longing. If the restlessness of our hearts and the physical desires of our bodies are not rooted in God's life and creativity, then our eros has no source outside ourselves. But this leaves us vulnerable—as the history of Christian spirituality attests—to finding our erotic selves alienated from God. Such estrangement and fear of our bodies is certainly not part of God's creative intention, as it is expressed in Genesis and the Song of Songs. At the very least, we can say that creating a hierarchy of love seems to run counter to the affirming vision of sexuality in the Judeo-Christian tradition.

THE PATH TOWARD RENEWAL:
RECLAIMING THE SPIRITUAL PROMISE

"The spiritual promise of sexuality." Unfortunately, many Catholic believers would consider this phrase to be, at best, an oxymoron. In their moral formation, becoming spiritual was usually identified with leaving behind or at the very least severely controlling sexuality in order to explore the purer realms of the soul. In similar fashion, sexuality, far from carrying a promise of closeness to God, was often understood to be a danger or threat to holiness and virtue.

Perhaps the first step toward a renewed theology of human sexuality is that of reclaiming this inherent, incarnational bond between God and creation, between the holy and the human. In the biblical tradition, the language of eros and the language of mysticism are remarkably parallel. The Song of Songs has been understood as both erotic love poetry and as an allegory of the soul's quest for divine union. It is replete with the language of passionate yearning, longing, and seeking; with metaphors of ecstasy and union; with images of abandonment, consummation, and surrender.

The popular media and images of contemporary culture perpetuate the assumption that in order for someone to have "good sex," it must be "naughty"—that is, in a context outside of an exclusive, permanent commitment. In this view, commitment supposedly takes the "fun" out of sex. The poet/author of the Song of Songs certainly doesn't see life and relationships this way! The love between the Shulamite woman and her soul mate is passionate, celebratory, joyful, and sensuous; but it is also committed, faithful, monogamous, and covenantal.

There is an ancient Buddhist saying that reflects this more integrating approach to human love. The proverb states: "Sex is the seed. Love is the flower. Compassion is the fragrance." What if we were to understand *eros*, *philia*, and *agape* in a similar way? A renewed theology of human sexuality will reclaim sacred eros as the passionate center of all human loving. It will give us the discipline to transform the fire of eros into friendship, compassionate service, and, of course, the joyous self-gift of making love.

REIMAGINING HUMAN SEXUALITY

Reclaiming the vital connection between God and creation, between the holy and the embodied, is the first step toward renewal, the path toward understanding sexuality as a blessing and a gift.

The second step involves expanding our vision of sexuality itself. The church's hierarchical leadership has persistently condemned human culture for reducing the mystery of human sexuality to its biological, instinctual function. But when we view history with balanced realism, we recognize that the same criticism can be leveled against the institutional church: it has also tended to focus on the external physical behaviors that surround bodily arousal and procreation. Reading the moral manuals that were used for seminary formation in the 1940s and 1950s, one gets the distinct impression that the hierarchical church was focused on—if not obsessed with—the biological dimensions of the human sexual response. It seemed to have little interest in or appreciation for the interpersonal, mutual aspects of human relationships.

Sexuality is, in the first place, *energy*—energy for relationships. It is grounded in the encompassing inner dynamic of every creature that unites, draws, and compels it into a relational field-of-force—from the *élan vital* of subatomic matter to the vast galaxies that populate our universe, from the mystery of DNA to the complex psychology of human loving. Sexuality can best be understood when it is rooted in this communion-making energy that is close to the heart of creation.

Some may object that this makes human sexuality too diffuse and undifferentiated, but we believe that a more comprehensive vision is a necessary counterbalance to the narrow, reductionist perspectives of the past. In one of its more remarkable statements, the Catechism of the Catholic Church pursues a similar inclusive understanding: "Sexuality affects all aspects of the human person in the unity of body and soul. It especially concerns affectivity, the capacity to love and to procreate, and in a more general way the aptitude for forming bonds of communion with others" (#2332).

From our perspective, there is the quiet stirring of a more affirming vision of sexuality in this brief phrase: "the aptitude for forming bonds of communion." It provides a context in which human relationships can be celebrated in their diversity, complexity, and beauty—encompassing the love of spouses, the warmth of friendship, the bonds of family, colleagues, soul mates, and generous service.

It likewise invites us to reimagine the deeper meaning of *arousal* in our lives. We cannot fully appreciate the beauty and power of physical, sexual arousal, unless we are attentive to the many other ways in which we are "awakened"—cognitively, intuitively, emotionally, and compassionately. "Our arising," writes John of the Cross, "is God's arising within us, and our awakening is God's awakening within us." What difference would it make, if we began to view the "arousals" of our daily lives from this incarnational perspective when we are stirred by a symphony or moved by the fading colors of a sunset? When we hug a dear friend goodbye, or snuggle next to our beloved by a fireplace in winter? When we encounter God as "the song in our silence," a wordless presence in our loneliness?

In our teaching and in our recent writing we propose the following "working description" of human sexuality:

Human sexuality is the divine energy of creativity and love,
as it is manifested in wondrously diverse forms in the cosmos,
and as it becomes conscious and intentional in human relationships,
for the purpose of giving life and deepening communion.

UNDERSTANDING SEXUALITY IN
THE CONTEXT OF THE NEW COSMOLOGY

The emerging creation story that comes to us from contemporary science reaffirms the encompassing vision of sexuality that we are proposing here. Today's cosmologists now recognize that carbon elements from the original fireball—that first burst of cosmic energy propelling the universe into being—live on in every exchange of human passion, every expression of relational energy, and every display of light in the heavens. Brian Swimme refers to this pervasive energy of attraction as "cosmic allurement," an image that goes beyond the language of science to embrace the world of mystery.

There are profound theological and spiritual consequences for such a view of creation. More than a passing physical urge or a gender category, sexuality is grounded in and part of a unique form of attraction-energy that pulsates at the heart of the universe. Tender enough to communicate non-possessive love, and yet powerful enough to keep the planets from spinning out of control, when this sacred force is directed toward connections that create and sustain life, we call it "sexuality." When it becomes conscious in human persons and when it is intentionally directed toward relationships of care, we call it love.

Dante may have been using poetic metaphor when he said that love is the force that moves the stars and the planets, but contemporary science tells us that this is more than poetry. Dante's words describe the inherent qualities of the universe. The love that continues to create stars and to shape the sprawling galaxies is the same energy revealed in the gaze of our beloved and in the affection of our friends. It is the same quiet passion that stirs in our blood and quickens our heartbeat when we are in the presence of someone whose energy sparks something deep and joyous in us.

RETURNING TO THE PRIMAL BIBLICAL VISION

The creation stories of Genesis invite the human community to see that we all share a common calling. We are *imago Dei*—creative images of the divine—in two fundamental ways: each of us is called to be a *life-giver* and a *lover*. The first creation story (Genesis 1–2:4, the Priestly account) gives us images of light bursting forth and oceans teeming, of plants and animal life in abundant array, and human persons as the culminating high point of God's creative intention. It is literally a "song of creation," filled with mandates to increase and multiply, to deepen and expand life, to till and to keep, to be fecund, creative, and generous. The second creation story (Genesis 2:5ff., the Yahwist account) focuses on the centrality of love and mutuality. Its poetry reminds us that it is not "good for the earth-creature to live in destructive isolation," but rather in the joyous mutuality of relationship.

When we return to these epic descriptions of human meaning, we find renewed passion and purpose. We reclaim the authentic qualities and questions surrounding our sexuality. Thus, the central question regarding our sexuality is not about our gender, ethnic background, age, vocation, sexual orientation, faith tradition, or even our religious and moral convictions, though each of these helps define our uniqueness. The core issue is not whether we are married or single, divorced or remarried, celibate or sexually active, gay or straight, wounded or well, old or young, male or female. The central question is: How can I—in the unique circumstances of my life and with God's help and grace—become a more responsible lover and life-giver?

CONCLUSION: SOME PASTORAL TASKS AND IMPLICATIONS

What are some personal and pastoral implications in what we have been sharing? We bring this chapter to a close by sharing what we believe to be four vital pastoral tasks.

1. Reuniting spirituality and sexuality in ongoing faith-formation.

The first challenge facing us as a Catholic community is that of reconnecting sexuality and spirituality. This is a vision that impacts all ages and stages of psychosexual development, and all phases of faith formation. Those who have the primary responsibility of preaching, teaching, and catechesis will need to study, pray, and integrate this renewed vision into all of their interactions with parishioners and spiritual seekers.

But this is not just a responsibility for those in pastoral leadership; it is also a task that involves the entire parish community. In the past, "sex education"—if it was permitted at all—was usually limited to a controlled environment in Catholic schools, with an emphasis on the church's moral teaching and rules. Given the groundswell of concern about sexuality, our faith communities have a prophetic opportunity to change this situation for the better. The challenge for the future is to reimagine "sex education" as something more than a cautionary program for adolescents, and to see it instead as "relational formation" for a lifetime. A renewed theology of human sexuality must be young enough to engage children, open enough to be taken seriously by teens, credible enough to challenge young adults, seasoned enough to understand the needs of those in their middle years, wise enough for the elderly, and sufficiently compassionate to embrace all of us over a lifetime.

2. Listening to the love stories of all of God's people.

When the Catholic Church prepared to celebrate the beginning of the third millennium of Christianity, it chose the motto, "Open Wide the Doors to Christ." In the years before and following that event, our church placed a strong emphasis on becoming welcoming communities. The opening paragraph of *Gaudium et Spes*, the Pastoral Constitution on the Church in the Modern World, describes a community in solidarity with other human pilgrims: "The joys and hopes, the grief and anguish of the people of our time, especially those who are poor and afflicted, are the joys and hopes, the grief and anguish of the followers of Christ as well. *Nothing that is genuinely human fails to find an echo in their hearts"* [emphasis added].

Here is a description of the disciples of Jesus as listening communities, people of openness and compassion. Gratefully, we have experienced this listening spirit in parishes, retreat centers, and other small faith communities. We have found it in Protestant congregations and gatherings. We have seen this compassionate stance in many communities of sisters, brothers, and priests. But we recognize—somewhat sadly—that this is not always the case. Our experience over the last decades tells us that many people do not feel safe bringing their search for love, their struggles and failures with relationships to their communities, their pastoral leaders, or other ministers in the churches.

In each of our parishes, there is a wide diversity of backgrounds, life experiences, and love stories. In our church, we have tended to speak of and listen to only two of those love stories: marriage and consecrated celibacy. But consider for a moment all of the people who do not fit neatly into either of those categories: single adults, the separated and divorced, those who are celibate not by choice but circumstance, gay and lesbian persons, together with all the other people who wonder if there is a place for them at the table.

As difficult as it is, we need to raise the question about who is invited and who is welcome at the banquet table of love. To what extent can the Eucharist be *both* a sign of a communion already achieved *and* a source that brings about unity and reconciliation? Can our churches hold up the value of marriage *and* at the same time welcome those who do not fit the official norms? Can we continue to affirm our belief in permanent commitments *and* at the same time create a welcoming space for divorced persons? Can we offer opportunities for healing after divorce without necessarily burdening people with the complex and sometimes humiliating process of annulments? Can we believe in traditional family life, *and* also set a table where people in other experiences of family will find a place card with their name on it?

The challenge before us is a daunting one. It involves our ability to hold the values of the Gospel in a creative tension. In practice, this means that we must find a way to honor both our ethical vision and our summons to compassion, our call to moral responsibility and the demands of inclusivity.

3. Reclaiming the bond between sexuality and justice.

Many older Catholics recall the sermons they heard growing up about the evils of sexual immorality. The warnings were quite explicit: Don't read books about sex. Don't look at impure pictures. Don't go to bad movies. Don't "go too far" with your boyfriend or your girlfriend. Don't engage in impure actions with yourself. Don't have sexual thoughts or feelings. The impression was given that sins against sex were the worst forms of immorality.

In contrast, this same generation of Catholics heard little, if anything, preached about the evil of sexual abuse, forced sex, and domestic violence. The institutional church seemed preoccupied with sex, but apparently not as concerned about abuse or sexual violence. In the wake of the current clergy abuse scandal, many Catholics are wondering why our church doesn't appear to care as much about sexual injustice as it does about what is traditionally called the "sins of the flesh."

The biblical word for promoting and protecting the dignity of persons in relationships is *justice*. Because of our social conditioning and religious formation, we may not immediately associate sexuality and intimacy with issues of power and justice. But they are profoundly interrelated. Alice Walker's novel, *The Color Purple*, is the story of the young woman, Celie, and her search for healing in her life. The opening words of the book relive the scene in which Celie is raped by her stepfather, followed by his warning: "You better not tell nobody but God." So, Celie turns to the only safe presence left in her life. In a series of letters that become the literary framework for the novel, she tells her story to God. It was her only form of resistance at a time when Christian churches had little to say about sexual violence. She recalls that when she cried out in pain, her stepfather choked her and said, "You better shut up and get used to it." Celie writes, "but I don't never get used to it."

For as long as human beings can remember, vulnerable people—most of them women and children, like Celie—have been told by their abusers and by unjust social systems to "shut up and get used it." And for just as long, most of the victims had only their own broken hearts and God to whom they could turn. Sexual violence is the silent scream in the unfolding dream of humanity; it is the multitude of invisible faces hidden in the canvas of recorded history. In our emerging global society, sexual abuse continues to be a tragic way of life for millions of women and children around the world. It is the predictable aftermath of war and terror; it is taken for granted as an instrument of political and military strategy. It is a social reality in impoverished countries, where families sometimes sell their young daughters into prostitution for economic survival. But it is also the unspoken reality in many middle class and affluent families in more developed countries. Interpersonal violence is an equal opportunity perpetrator; it is not limited to any national identity, economic class, racial category, or religious preference.

In contemporary spirituality, the antiquated and unhealthy preoccupation with illicit pleasure is being replaced with a more person-centered ethic based on mutual respect in relationships. Sexual morality is reclaiming its roots in biblical justice as the call to restore right relationships.

4. Rediscovering the fire of love.

Our final reflection is less a pastoral task than it is the inner "soul work" of the whole church—indeed of the entire human family. There is perhaps no more difficult or complex question facing our churches, our families, and our personal lives than that of human sexuality. Certainly, there are more urgent global issues to be addressed: ongoing wars, international terrorism, ethnic cleansing, massive starvation, global poverty, and the growing ecological crisis on our planet. But on the most personal level of our lives—in the daily search for meaning and connection—our relationships with other people are often uppermost in our minds and hearts. The challenge of how to embrace and live our sexual energy in a creative and responsible manner is a quiet, deeply personal concern for just about everyone.

The challenge of loving responsibly and well is one of the most pressing spiritual tasks of our age. The title of our recent book and this chapter are both references to the words of Pierre Teilhard de Chardin, a Jesuit priest, paleontologist, and mystic. Teilhard concluded an essay on "The Evolution of Chastity" in 1934 with the following prophetic statement. In his memory and in his spirit, we can find no better way to conclude:

Some day after we have mastered the winds,
the waves, the tides, and gravity,

we will harness for God the energies of love,
and, then, for the second time in the history of the world,
we will have discovered fire.

SELECTED BIBLIOGRAPHY

Avis, Paul. *Eros and the Sacred*. Harrisburg, PA and Wilton, CT: Morehouse Publishing, 1989.

Cahill, Lisa Sowle. *Sex, Gender, and Christian Ethics*. Cambridge: Cambridge University Press, 1996.

Catechism of the Catholic Church. Second ed. Libreria Editrice Vaticana, 1994; United States Catholic Conference, 1997.

Collins, Raymond F. *Sexual Ethics and the New Testament: Behavior and Belief*. New York: Crossroad, 2000.

Conlon, James. *Earth Story, Sacred Story*. Mystic, CT: Twenty-Third Publications, 1994.

Countryman, L. William. *Dirt, Greed and Sex: Sexual Ethics in the New Testament and Their Implications for Today*. Philadelphia: Fortress Press, 1988.

Downey, Michael. *Altogether Gift: A Trinitarian Spirituality*. Maryknoll, NY: Orbis Books, 2000.

Eiseley, Loren. *The Immense Journey: An Imaginative Naturalist Explores the Mysteries of Man and Nature*. New York: Vintage Books, 1946.

Ferder, Fran, and John Heagle. *Partnership: Women and Men in Ministry*. Notre Dame, IN: Ave Maria, 1992.

———. *Tender Fires: The Spiritual Promise of Sexuality*. New York: Crossroad, 2002.

———. *Your Sexual Self: Pathways to Authentic Intimacy*. Notre Dame, IN: Ave Maria, 1992.

Flannery, Austin, O.P., ed. *Vatican Council II: A Completely Revised Translation in Inclusive Language*. Northport, NY: Costello Publishing Company, 1988.

Fox, Thomas C. *Sexuality and Catholicism*. New York: George Braziller, 1995.

Green, Lorna. *Earth Age: A New Vision of God, the Human and the Earth*. New York: Paulist Press, 1994.

Guindon, Andre. *The Sexual Language: An Essay in Moral Theology*. Ottawa: University of Ottawa Press, 1976.

John Paul II, Pope. *The Theology of the Body: Human Love in the Divine Plan*. Boston: Pauline Books and Media, 1997.

Liebard, Odile M., ed. *Official Catholic Teachings: Love and Sexuality*. Wilmington, NC: McGrath Publishing Company, 1978.

Liuzzi, Peter J., O. Carm. *With Listening Hearts: Understanding the Voices of Lesbian and Gay Catholics*. New York: Paulist Press, 2001.

Michael, Robert T., John H. Gagnon, Edward O. Laurmann, and Gina Kolata. *Sex in America: A Definitive Survey*. Boston: Little, Brown and Company, 1994.

National Conference of Catholic Bishops (NCCB). *Human Sexuality: A Catholic Perspective for Education and Lifelong Learning*. Washington, D.C.: United States Catholic Conference, 1990.

Nelson, James B. *Between Two Gardens: Reflections on Sexuality and Religious Experience*. New York: Pilgrim Press, 1983.

———. *Embodiment: An Approach to Sexuality and Christian Theology*. Minneapolis: Augsburg Publishing House, 1978.

Nelson, James B., and Sandra P. Longfellow, eds. *Sexuality and the Sacred: Sources for Theological Reflection*. Louisville: Westminster John Knox Press, 1994.

Nygren, Anders. *Agape and Eros*. New York: Harper and Row, 1969.

Rolheiser, Ronald. *The Holy Longing: The Search for a Christian Spirituality*. New York: Doubleday, 1999.

Swimme, Brian. *The Universe is a Green Dragon: A Cosmic Creation Story*. Santa Fe, NM: Bear and Company, 1995.

Swimme, Brian and Thomas Berry. *The Universe Story: From the Primordial Flaring Forth to the Ecozoic Era—A Celebration of the Unfolding of the Cosmos*. San Francisco: Harper, 1992.

Teilhard de Chardin, Pierre. *The Human Phenomenon*. Edited and translated by Sarah Appleton-Weber. Portland, OR: Sussex Academic Press, 1999.

———. *Toward the Future*. Translated by René Hague. New York: Harcourt Brace Jovanovich, 1975. (Includes "The Evolution of Chastity," 60–87.)

Walker, Alice. *The Color Purple*. New York: Simon and Schuster, 1982.

A Pastoral Response to Fran Ferder, F.S.P.A., and John Heagle, "Tender Fires: The Spiritual Promise of Sexuality"

Harold D. Horell

Fran Ferder and John Heagle have made tremendous contributions to the pastoral life of the church. Through their counseling practice at Therapy and Renewal Associates (TARA) they have mentored hundreds of persons seeking to integrate Christian faith with a sense of psychological/mental health. In their individual writings and jointly authored work, they have addressed pressing pastoral issues and made a significant contribution, in particular, to helping us as a church come to a clearer understanding of human sexuality and the relationship between sexuality and spirituality. In this brief response I affirm three ways in which their work provides new categories for thinking about sexuality and for aligning church teaching and practice more fully with Christian spirituality. I then offer one suggestion for further exploration, and conclude with some questions for reflection.

REALISM, BALANCE, AND HOPE

Ferder and Heagle are realists. They understand the harsh realities of the scandal of clergy sexual abuse, the institutional misuse of power within the church in the failure to address clergy sexual abuse, the reduction of sexuality to genital behavior in much of popular culture, the exploitation of sexuality by the media, and the connection between sexuality and interpersonal violence. They have walked with those who have suffered because of the distorted and distorting senses of sexuality sometimes found in our church and society today. Yet, Ferder and Heagle resist the temptation to adopt a negative or pessimistic attitude as they discuss all the ways sexual energies are misused.

28

Rather, Ferder and Heagle focus on the positive resources in church and society for helping us understand human sexuality, and they emphasize the great promise of our sexuality for contributing to human flourishing. At all times they achieve a balanced view, commenting on the negative in the light of the positive. For example, in discussing church sexual teaching they note that "when the Judeo-Christian tradition speaks from its deepest roots about love, mutual respect, the goodness of the body, and the sacredness of relationships, there is no more powerful source of spiritual guidance. Sadly, we have not consistently spoken from our deepest roots."[1]

The realistic yet balanced tone that Ferder and Heagle adopt enables them to address sexuality insightfully. This is one of the many strengths of the chapter. In both church and society we have too often adopted an overly negative view of sexuality that has led, in some cases, to a fear of sexuality. At the same time, the naïve embrace of sexuality in the "sexual revolution" sometimes led to the exploitation of sexuality and the reduction of sexuality to genital behavior. Ferder and Heagle avoid the pitfalls of both overly negative and naïve views of sexuality. While recognizing the possibilities for the misuse of sexual energies, they explore positive understandings of human sexuality and strive to offer a vision for "responsible and reverent relationships."[2] They suggest how our understanding of sexuality can be wholly transformed so that we can envision more clearly the potential for our sexuality to be integrated with our spirituality.

A PERSONAL, COMMUNAL, AND COSMIC FRAMEWORK

On the personal level, Ferder and Heagle are concerned with reclaiming "sacred eros as the passionate center of all human loving." They suggest that "the core issue is not whether we are married or single, divorced or remarried, celibate or sexually active, gay or straight, wounded or well, old or young, male or female. The central question is: How can I—in the unique circumstances of my life and with God's help and grace—become a more responsible lover and life-giver?"[3] Today, discussions about birth regulation, homosexuality, and other sexual issues too often become bitter and divisive. Ferder and Heagle show how we may be able to move beyond current impasses in the church in addressing sexual issues by reframing these issues in terms of *the* central issue of being responsible lovers and life-givers. In essence, they suggest a new way of approaching issues of sex and sexuality that is grounded within our Christian faith traditions and that, at the same time, provides a perspective for moving beyond present-day controversies.

However, Ferder and Heagle do more than provide a healthy framework for helping us to understanding sexuality as an important part of our personal lives. They encourage us to see the personal in the light of a broader cosmic framework. They note that carbon elements from the original cosmic energy burst that created the universe live on in every person and that because of this "sexuality is grounded in and part of a unique form of attraction-energy that pulsates at the heart of the universe." Moreover, Ferder and Heagle, in emphasizing the communal and relational dimensions of human sexuality, note that we need to address "the evil of sexual abuse, forced sex, and domestic violence." Then, they call us to reclaim "the bond between sexuality and justice."[4] Overall, they offer a helpful framework for developing a personal sense of sexuality and discussing personal choices concerning the expression of sexuality. At the same time, their analysis fosters greater sensitivity to the ways sexuality can contribute to or detract from the ongoing creation of more just relations among people.

A WEALTH OF RESOURCES

Ferder and Heagle identify and draw insight from Christian resources that have often been underused in the past; specifically Genesis, the Song of Songs, *Gaudium et Spes*, *The Catechism of the Catholic Church*, and the work of John of the Cross and Pierre Teilhard de Chardin. It is fairly common in discussing sexuality from a Christian faith perspective to note the distorting views of sexuality found in the work of influential theologians such as Augustine, Thomas Aquinas, and Martin Luther. While it is necessary to reflect critically on the past and to discern how unhealthy views of sexuality may still have a negative influence in the present, it is just as important to remember the numerous resources from Christian faith traditions that have contributed and still have the power to contribute to positive and healthy views of sexuality. Ferder and Heagle's analysis shows how we can draw upon the resources of our faith traditions to renew and even expand our understanding of sexuality and the spiritual promise of sexuality. It is also worth noting that Ferder and Heagle turn to insights from the work of Alice Walker's novel *The Color Purple*, Buddhism, and other sources. Hence, they remind us of the rich resources in other faith traditions and in the broader culture to which we can turn in striving to construct life-affirming and life-giving understandings of sexuality today.

A SUGGESTION

Ferder and Heagle call for the reuniting of "spirituality and sexuality in ongoing faith-formation." They contend that "the challenge for the future is to reimagine 'sex education' as something more than a cautionary program for adolescents, and see it instead as 'relational formation' for a lifetime."[5] As I reflected on this challenge, I wondered: Where might we begin? How, within the everyday rhythms of pastoral life, might we reimagine sexuality education as ongoing faith formation?

I suggest that we reimagine sexuality education as ongoing faith formation by focusing on existing programs and parish leadership. For example, many parishes and dioceses already have programs for marriage preparation and enrichment. One practical way to contribute to a renewed theology of sexuality is to focus on renewing or enhancing the sexuality education provided within these programs. Similarly, college and university campus ministry and parish young adult programs could include forums for young persons to discuss the question: "How within the context of our lives, can we be responsible lovers and life-givers?" (During the years after college many young adults experience the loss of a "place" in the church. By providing young Catholics with forums to wrestle openly with questions about sexuality, we may help them to recognize that our faith communities welcome them and are interested in them.)

Another way to renew sexuality education in our parishes is to focus on parish leadership. Specifically, pastoral and lay ecclesial parish ministers could identify couples and single persons of all ages and stages of life (including both heterosexual and homosexual persons and couples) and invite them to form leadership groups to discuss their love stories with one another. The leadership groups could then reflect upon how greater opportunities could be provided for sexuality education within their faith community. They could also be asked to take on part of the responsibility for inviting people to attend sexuality education programs.

FOR FURTHER CONSIDERATION

To embrace the core insights of Ferder and Heagle's analysis more fully, I suggest that we reflect on the following questions: How can we create opportunities in our faith communities for all God's people to tell and reflect upon their love stories? How might greater opportunities to tell and reflect upon our love stores contribute to the ongoing development of church sexual teaching? Then, how might a renewed sexual teaching provide greater credibility to the church's efforts to address issues of sex and sexuality today?

NOTES

1. Ferder and Heagle, "Tender Fires: The Spiritual Promiste of Sexuality," in this volume, 16.

2. Ibid.
3. Ibid., 19, 22.
4. Ibid., 21, 24.
5. Ibid., 22–23.

3

Toward Christian Sexual Maturity: Growing in Wisdom, Age, and Grace

John J. Cecero, S.J.

At a recent conference that I was giving on sexuality and professional boundaries to Dominican superiors, all dressed in their white habits around a boardroom table, one person asked, "How do you define sex?" It felt a bit like the Inquisition! I was hard-pressed to generate a neatly packaged answer. After all, sexuality is complex and multidimensional, with biological, psychological, social, and spiritual components. This chapter will address each of these components and comment, specifically, on opportunities for wisdom and grace as one matures along each of these dimensions.

From a Christian perspective, sexuality continually challenges us to acknowledge the divine mystery that we are as human beings. Because sexuality is so complex, we (individuals and institutions) can be tempted to reduce it to a set of behaviors that can be governed by universal principles and rules. However, to do so would ignore the broader, richer, and essentially more authentic context for human sexuality. Gabriel Marcel spoke of this temptation in the history of philosophy—where the great questions of the meaning of humanity, God, and freedom have often been reduced, in his language, to problems to be solved rather than appreciated as mysteries to be lived. Courses in the "problem" of God betray such an orientation. Instead, to truly know ourselves, God, and one another, we must participate in a relationship that is always larger than our preconceived ideas and rational categories, and that always opens us up to something larger, often unanticipated, and closer to the truth.

Our sexuality opens us to the divine mystery within us. As Pope John Paul II writes, "The body, and it alone, is capable of making visible what is invisible, the spiritual and the divine. It was created to transfer into the visible reality of the world, the invisible mystery hidden in God from time immemorial, and thus to be sign of it."[1]

So, our body, our sexuality, is not an accident, nor is it simply a wrapping (and tainted at that) for our pure and immortal souls (Platonic). No, our bodies are the medium of God's Presence in Jesus today (Teresa of Avila, committed more recently to song: "Christ has no body now but yours . . . no hands, no feet on earth but yours") and of the very Trinity alive and loving through us in this world. In his *Theology of the Body*, John Paul II uses the metaphor of the body as in the "image and likeness of God," (most fully expressed in our way of loving) and of our sexuality as a *communion* between persons that gives expression to another person through the "blessing of fertility," explicitly reflecting the community and generativity of the Trinity. As I describe the characteristics of true adult sexual maturity, I will be using these exact descriptors: intimate communion and generativity. Our mature sexuality, then, mirrors that of the Trinity. What a refreshing approach to sexuality!

This is the reason for the title of this chapter: "Growing in Wisdom, Age, and Grace." Because if we are to appreciate our sexuality as a mystery reflecting the divine mystery, then we always need to resist attempts to reduce it to one and only one dimension (an urge, a thought, a feeling, a behavior). Our sexuality is always all of these—and much more!

DEVELOPMENTAL TASKS AND CHALLENGES TOWARD CHRISTIAN SEXUAL MATURITY

While the complexity of Christian sexuality certainly deserves the attention of multiple disciplines—theology, philosophy, anthropology, history, among others—as a clinical psychologist I confine these reflections to the psychological lens on the processes of sexual maturity. One broad psychological context within which to consider the tasks and challenges involved in growing toward Christian sexual maturity is the lifelong challenge to balance connection with autonomy. This is a lifelong task, so all attempts by developmentalists to neatly categorize and linearly present this challenge by stages that are "gone through" are inherently misleading. We are always struggling to strike this balance, sometimes more successfully than at other times!

Margaret Mahler identifies the separation and individuation phase, where the child who had been securely connected to mother/caregiver now (at roughly two years old) tries to establish independence and at the same time stay connected (practicing and rapprochement). Peter Blos describes adolescence as the "second individuation," where adolescents try again to negotiate the necessity for connection with family of origin with the relentless desire for independence.

All through our lifetime, with friends, peers, colleagues, family, mates, and children, we encounter the perennial struggle to be closely connected but not smothered, independent but not isolated. And we can encounter problems on both poles of this connection/autonomy challenge. If we are not separate enough—and technology can exacerbate this problem through e-mails, cell phones, blackberries, pagers, and the like—we risk workaholism, burnout, relationship fatigue, and resentfulness. These dangers highlight the need for boundaries, to say "no" sometimes, to take time alone, to take Sabbath time. On the other hand, if we are not connected enough, we risk the danger of isolation, which is the breeding ground for all sorts of addictions and compulsive behaviors, despondency, and loss of a common vision.

STAGES TOWARD SEXUAL MATURITY

The Predisposing Stage is prenatal, where the influence of the *biological* aspects of our sexuality, that is, those aspects that are the "givens" in our lives, less amenable to pastoral intervention or change, are predominant. Specifically, our temperament is governed by our genetic predisposition (activity level, emotionality, sociability). For example, we may be "easy," "shy/withdrawn," or "irritable, difficult to soothe." Temperament will interact with the environment in the genesis of relational scripts or schemas. For example, if one is "easy" by temperament and others are excited to be around the child, then this person is more likely to develop a deep belief that the world is trustworthy, friendly, and emotionally responsive, and this person is likely to approach others more easily. On the other hand, if the child is "withdrawn" or "irritable," and others in his/her early environment are less interested or even actively avoiding him/her, this person is likely to feel less comfortable or even very distressed in the company of others and to develop lifetraps or early maladaptive schemas such as abandonment, emotional deprivation, and mistrust, which are core thoughts/beliefs/emotions/body sensations which endure through life and cause emotional distress and interpersonal problems.

Gender, being male or female, will also influence our capacity for, and ease with, intimacy. Carol Gilligan and Nancy Chodorow have made significant psychoanalytic contributions to understanding the role of gender in identity development. They emphasize that for females, identity is achieved by remaining connected with the primary attachment figure (mother), whereas for males, identity is achieved by becoming separate from her, so that for males, autonomy is more prized. In adulthood, male intimacy is often characterized as "doing things together"—each from his separate space—whereas women are more comfortable expressing feelings to each other.

Another obstacle to intimacy for men is the role of competition (as more important than self-disclosure). Again, from a psychoanalytic perspective, boys have phallic urges to compete, surges of testosterone (aggression), and cultural reinforcers for competition (sports, business). The danger of over-competitiveness, however, is that it can breed superficial relationships where one makes narcissistic demands on "friends" to keep oneself going by becoming over-controlling and manipulative.

As a result, it is necessary to underscore the value of discussing feelings and relational needs, especially for boys without appropriate male role models. The danger for girls and women, of course, lies in overemphasizing connection and relationality at the expense of appropriate competitive strivings. This is breeding ground for resentment!

The Childhood Stage (0 to 12 years old) places more emphasis on the psychological and social influences on sexuality. Attachment styles develop in infancy and are elaborated upon in early childhood in response to the quality of the relationship with the parent/caregiver. And these attachment styles remain stable throughout our lifetimes, and are very resistant to change. With consistent emotional responsiveness by the parent, the child develops a secure attachment style: appropriate separation anxiety, the ability to self-soothe in the absence of the loved one, and joy at the reunion.

An adult who has developed this secure attachment style seeks relationships where the other is free to pursue his or her own interests and is not threatened by the other's independence. The person feels comfortable in his/her own skin, and the vulnerability fostered by intimate sharing of emotions is not overly threatening.

Inconsistent or unpredictable parenting, on the other hand, breeds anxious attachment: high separation anxiety, the inability to self-soothe, and a preoccupied style of relating to others. Adults who have an anxious attachment style have low self-esteem. That is, they do not believe that they can take care of themselves on their own, and at the same time they tend to exaggerate the strengths of others, believing that only the power/status/presence of these "powerful" others can guarantee their happiness and competence in the world. They will become preoccupied with their partners, clingy, jealous, and often end up scaring their partners away.

Abusive (emotional, physical, and/or sexual) parenting breeds an avoidant attachment style characterized by an absence of separation anxiety, a detachment from emotions, and interpersonal isolation. These are adults who live lonely lives, not enduring the lonesomeness that we all experience, for example, missing those who mean so much to us, but rather experiencing the cold emptiness—an emotional vacuum—of not missing anyone ever! Emotions are too threatening, and so these people become detached, cold, distant, aloof. They protect themselves from others by isolating themselves through excessive TV watching, compulsive masturbation, cybersex addictions, eating, drinking, gambling, or shopping, to name some common isolation behaviors.

Children begin to develop a relationship with their own bodies as a source of pleasure. Boys are often born with erections, and they smile when their parent touches their genitals while changing them! Some claim that boys have erections prenatally. Masturbation starts between six and twelve months, and it is important for the parent not to shame or punish the child as a result of untrue inferences about this behavior, for example, my child is sinful, dirty, going to be punished.

Around three to seven years old, children engage in "playing doctor" and other games intended to promote the experience of pleasure in mutual exploration. Again, these activities should not be punished or shamed, but may be opportunities to educate the child about differences and respect for privacy. These are opportunities for parental empathy and emotional attunement to the feelings of their children, which are cornerstones of healthy self-esteem and emotional self-regulation as adults. Children who grow up to be ashamed of their sexual feelings are more prone to "act out" their sexual desires by translating sensations/impulses immediately into action without filtering them through the lens of reflection on values or moral standards.

Another task of childhood is gender-role identification, where the emphasis is on the social/cultural influences of sexual maturity. The child begins to feel like a boy or girl and develops a clear sense of what it means to be a boy or girl in his or her own culture. Confusion here may lead to significant problems with sexuality in later years, characterized by a sense of deficiency, deviance, and related defensive styles. The person might avoid relationships altogether, become asexual, and experience depression and even suicidal thoughts and desires. It is important to emphasize to the child that gender roles are not as rigid as might be communicated by our culture which often dictates that, for example, boys must like sports and girls must like playing with dolls.

As adults, those men and women who grow up with rigid senses of masculinity and femininity according to established cultural norms are less likely to achieve a more adaptive sense of balance, in the Jungian sense of the *animus* and *anima*. They are more likely, instead, to deny the opposite sides of themselves, and in so doing to close themselves off to sexual maturity. In empirical studies with dependency styles, men are far less likely than women to endorse the need for emotional warmth, support, and nurturance on self-report measures; but on projective measures—where they don't realize what they are endorsing—they are just as dependent. So, why are men not allowed to acknowledge openly this emotional need? Think about the implications of this finding for religious and spiritual practice. In a recent study with undergraduates at Fordham University, I explored the relationship between healthy dependency (that is, striking a balance between connection and autonomy) and religiosity (spiritual well-being). Much to my delight, I found that they were positively correlated. From a pastoral perspective, the implication is that we must challenge cultural norms about gender role rigidity if we are to foster healthy spiritual awareness and practice.

Adolescence (13 to 19 years old) is marked by biological hormonal surges as well as psychological and social/cultural influences. The key developmental task during this stage of psychosexual development is self-mastery, developing the capacity to achieve a balance of pleasure and self-control over one's needs, desires, wishes, and cravings. Problems with self-mastery can lead to superficial pleasure-seeking relationships.

Some adults are chronologically in their thirties, forties, even fifties, yet emotionally and relationally are stuck in this adolescent struggle for self-mastery. This is marked by self-absorption (the mark of adolescence) where relationships with others are "used" to achieve a sense of identity. "I'm just in this 'til it stops working, then I'll move on. . . . It's a learning experience." What about fairness to the other person? There is a blatant lack of empathy and accountability demonstrated by these statements and beliefs. Erik Erikson had a key developmental insight, that identity must precede intimacy. Not that we must completely know ourselves before we get into an intimate relationship—otherwise, we'd be rather lonely creatures!—but that we must at least be far enough along in identity formation, including the achievement of this task of self-mastery, before we can engage in a mature relationship. In the words of Henri Nouwen, "We must have a home to invite someone else into."

Sometimes, when people go through midlife crises, where identity is questioned and a period of self-absorption may ensue, they re-engage this adolescent struggle and for a period of time seek relationships that are immature and self-serving. What is the voice of pastoral counseling for these people? Perhaps to remind them (confront them?) that such relationships ignore the reality and mystery of the other person, and as such fall short of the Christian vocation to love in the manner of Jesus, in the manner of the Trinity, as discussed above. Better to start with one's own identity and becoming more at home with oneself, rather than relationship shopping, often extramaritally. And the place of prayer and pastoral counsel can be enormously helpful here.

During adolescence, heterosexual behavior is in full swing. Fifty percent of high school students are sexually active. There are cultural variations to this statistic: 78 percent of African Americans; 58 percent Latinos; 50 percent European Americans. The earlier intercourse begins, the less likely the use of contraceptives, and the more likely teenage pregnancy (10 percent of American girls each year). When surveyed for why one might abstain during adolescence, the most common responses are: (1) religious/moral values; and (2) educational and career goals.

These data emphasize the very practical need for resources to articulate a religious/moral/psychological rationale for sexual self-control. The challenge for parents and pastoral personnel, it seems to me, is how to reach the 50 percent of teens who are sexually active with a message about sexuality that emphasizes its essential connection with the divine life in our midst. It is no secret that teens are attracted by the sense of transcendence in music, drugs, sex, and other mind-altering experiences. How do we make the connection between this search for transcendence and the quest for God? Bruce Marshall, a Catholic novelist whose work is reminiscent of G. K. Chesterton, once said, "the young man who rings the bell at the brothel is unconsciously looking for God."[2] How do pastoral counselors draw connections for adolescents (and adults, for that matter) between spiritual and sexual longings? In the next section, I will address some points of convergence.

The Adult Stage witnesses the development of a sexual lifestyle (single, cohabitation, married). Of note, *singlehood* is the most common lifestyle among people in their twenties, and this represents a generational shift, much to the distaste of parents! Reasons for this shift include: taking time to pursue professional goals, less stigma attached to being single today, and difficulty finding the right person. Many are dissatisfied with this sexual lifestyle, complaining of loneliness, although this is certainly not the exclusive domain of singles. In fact, if people are attracted to the married or cohabitating lifestyle only to avoid loneliness, issues of overdependency may loom large and breed over time a strong resentment in both parties (one for feeling used, and the other for feeling so dependent).

Cohabitation is much more tolerated today, especially among those who are less affluent and less well educated. Some argue that it's better to cohabitate before marriage, to get to know someone so that there are no surprises/disappointments after the wedding. Research suggests, however, that cohabitators are more likely to divorce.

Marriage arguably permits a full expression of mature intimacy and generativity, not designed primarily to legitimize lust, as St. Paul would have it, but instead, in words of John Paul II, so that married people may see that their marital sexual union "bears in itself the great mystery of creation and redemption."

Len Sperry, M.D., author and clinical professor of psychiatry, defines mature intimacy as the capacity for expressing the self fully in a close relationship with a minimum of anxiety or fear of rejection. This assumes a secure attachment style and an adequate sense of identity and self-mastery.

There are various types of intimacy, and a mature relationship (married or otherwise) will include any one or a combination of the following expressions of intimacy.

- *Sexual intimacy*: includes physical closeness, contact, and interactions intended to be sexually arousing and satisfying
- *Physical nonsexual intimacy*: involves body contact, e.g., hugging, back rub, that is not a prelude to genital sexual activity.
- *Psychological intimacy*: communicating personal thoughts and feelings with a significant other
- *Intellectual intimacy*: communicating important ideas and beliefs
- *Emotional intimacy*: exercising *empathy* for a significant other
- *Social intimacy*: engaging in playful experiences (sports, meals)
- *Spiritual intimacy*: sharing beliefs about God, praying together

For married persons, it is imperative to engage in some combination of these types of intimacy, in order to avoid "marital burnout" when the honeymoon is over. In addition, it is important to rely on other sources of intimacy, namely, family, friends, and colleagues, so that the married partner does not become the sole source of intimacy on all these levels. That is too much responsibility for any one individual.

For celibates (priests, sisters, and others who may choose this state of living out their sexuality), mature sexuality also involves engaging these types of intimacy, with the exception of sexual intimacy. This sacrifice of sexual intimacy necessitates the cultivation of deep and close friendships in which the other types of intimacy outlined above may be shared. In a study published by the NCEA, "Grace Under Pressure," a national survey of "successful" priests— religious and secular, ordained ten years or more, who were selected to join regional focus groups on the basis of being perceived as happy and successful in their lives and ministries—these priests identified twelve factors that account for their well being. Among them, they labeled a "life of multiple intimacies." Without such intimacies, celibacy can be a haven for sexual immaturity and a breeding ground for acting out behaviors. And we are all too well aware of this!

Generativity is the second marker of mature adult sexuality, and it may be defined as "the capacity to show concern for and interest in others, particularly in guiding and encouraging those in younger generations."[3] Unlike earlier developmental stages (childhood and adolescent sexuality), mature adult sexuality in marriage is marked by the openness to life and love that is generative—fully modeling that life of the Trinity to which John Paul II compares it in *Theology of the Body*. Perhaps as never before, the parent truly lives for another, putting the needs of the child above one's own and those of the couple.

Again, mature sexuality for celibates—while not marked by parenthood—also entails responsibility for others, a community, or for the next generation. This direction of sexual energy into responsible and productive concern for others has been labeled as sublimation, a healthy direction of sexual energy. Celibates who lose this generative focus tend to become overly self-absorbed and passionless. And without an appropriate passion, religious celibates may succeed in keeping themselves immune from sexual improprieties, but they will fail at preaching the realm of God, which is the very purpose of their celibate vocation.

SPIRITUAL INFLUENCES ON SEXUAL MATURITY

While mainstream psychology would certainly endorse the reflections offered thus far, on the developmental tasks and challenges toward sexual maturity, the specific focus on spirituality and its contribution to sexual maturity is relatively recent and empirically, at least, in its infancy.

Sperry has made great strides in formulating a bio-psycho-social-spiritual perspective on sexuality. The stages of spiritual development correspond to the stages of psychosexual maturity outlined above. In this section, I will point out how spiritual growth is related to psychosexual maturation, stage by stage.

But first, what is "spirituality"? As distinct from (although not necessarily in place of) religiosity—which is understood as adherence to certain creeds, religious beliefs, and practices— spirituality may be defined as a personal orientation to the sacred, i.e., an attachment to God, a way of coping with life stressors, a heightened awareness of the transcendent in everyday life, and a real relationship to God that sometimes brings comfort and peace and at other times discord and struggle.

Now, how does this spiritual focus or orientation to God inform—that is to say, enhance or impede—healthy sexual development?

As the first school in spirituality and sexuality is the family, the spiritual atmosphere of the home will create a climate of openness to the child as a gift of God, allowing the child to experience a deep and abiding acceptance of his or her temperament, gender, and nascent sexual expressions (e.g., seeking pleasure in touching himself/herself). This parenting style will likely result in a secure attachment, with implications for future relating as spelled out above. It will also foster a God image that reflects this secure attachment. Research suggests that our God image mirrors our parent image—either as loving, generous, available, or else as punitive, demanding, unresponsive. Moreover, those who feel securely attached to God are more self-accepting, more able to self-soothe, and better equipped for a life of intimacy and generativity, even under conditions of stress and disappointment; those with insecure attachments to God are less able to employ the benefits of a spiritual orientation in any domain of life, sexual and otherwise.

As children grow into preadolescence and begin to deal with body-image changes and sexual exploration, religious attitudes, and prohibitions about sexuality influence how one copes with these stressors. To the extent that one has a secure relationship with God, the individual is likely to see God as a collaborative partner to whom he or she can turn for support, guidance, and direction in sexual matters. On the other hand, if there is an anxious or avoidant attachment to God, then these religious attitudes and prohibitions will be perceived as threatening and guilt inducing, or else minimized and ignored as emanating from an uncaring God. In either case, spirituality will be divorced from sexual decision-making, and this pattern is likely to endure throughout adulthood.

As the adolescent's capacity for abstract thought and analysis emerges, previously accepted religious beliefs may be questioned or discarded, and at the same time a longing for personal, subjective, mind-altering experiences may emerge as the dominant quest. As noted earlier, the adolescent is ready for spirituality, but there is an important caveat for adolescents and religious mentors alike. If spirituality is solely conceived as a subjective experience, it may all too easily ignore the broader context of the ecclesial community and foster, perhaps unwittingly, the very self-absorption that it ought to challenge, especially in sexual matters. The task is to balance this subjective experience of the transcendent God with attention to a religious tradition and its wisdom acquired over centuries. For this reason, St. Ignatius of Loyola, in the *Spiritual Exercises*, which rely heavily on personal spiritual experiences—using thoughts, feelings, fantasies, and images as the very medium of God's intention—appends to these *Exercises*, "Rules for Thinking with the Church." Authentic spiritual discernment, at least for St. Ignatius, must always include the wisdom of the larger ecclesial community.

Pastoral leadership, therefore, with adolescents, will entail helping them to appreciate in their own longings for sexual experience a spiritual, transcendental passion that is oriented fundamentally to God. In other words, this passion is holy, and needs the wisdom and direction of the larger church community to achieve its ultimately satisfying destination.

Finally, an adult spirituality is characterized by a mature, intimate relationship with God, one that endures the test of doubt, confusion, and periods of dryness, with fidelity and commitment. Ignatius in the *Exercises* distinguishes between the spiritual experience of those newly converted to God, where the experience of the divine is accompanied by sensible consolation, for example, peace, joy, and enthusiasm, with the experience of those who are more mature in the spiritual life, where divine consolation is more subtle, perhaps devoid of palpable experiences of joy (akin to John of the Cross's "dark night of the soul"), where the relationship deepens because it proceeds on faith. In Scripture, this phase of the relationship is similar to the experience of the Israelites with Moses in the desert, who, having been freed from captivity some twenty years earlier but still some twenty years away from the Promised Land, are tempted to abandon the journey.

Moses encourages them to move on in faith. This kind of relationship with God is more profound, less prone to fall apart in times of trial, and may serve as a model for the multiple intimacies of the mature adult.

PASTORAL IMPLICATIONS FOR
FOSTERING CHRISTIAN SEXUAL MATURITY

I would like to conclude this chapter by offering three specific points for consideration by pastoral leaders, as you work to promote Christian sexual maturity.

1. Foster self-knowledge.

In order to be a credible witness to others of sexual maturity, pastoral leaders must be capable of mature intimacies and authentic generativity, and so must be aware of their own personal liabilities in these domains. Earlier in this chapter, I spoke of "lifetraps." It seems to me that a thorough and ongoing self-evaluation with respect to the presence and severity of these lifetraps in one's own life would be an invaluable strategy for fostering this awareness. For example, do I have an *abandonment* lifetrap, fearing that significant people in my life will ultimately leave me in preference for others whom they may find more attractive for whatever reason (beauty, intelligence, wealth)? Or do I have an *emotional deprivation* lifetrap, fearing that others will never be able to provide me with the emotional nurturance, guidance, protection, or empathy that I need to be happy? Or perhaps *mistrust* is my lifetrap, that is, I have a difficulty believing that others will not lie, cheat, or manipulate me in some way, if given the chance. Or maybe I have a *dependence* lifetrap, where I do not believe that I can make ordinary decisions or complete ordinary tasks without considerable help from others. Lifetraps compromise one's ability for mature intimacy, and likewise make it very difficult to be truly generative, as fear always fosters self-absorption.

2. Maintain professional boundaries.

As the context for Christian sexual maturity has been framed in terms of maintaining a balance between connection and autonomy, pastoral leaders must model this balance in their own ministry. As God's representatives, pastoral leaders bear the awesome responsibility of speaking in the name of God and the Christian community, and people invest power in pastoral leaders for this reason. Sometimes, too much power. For example, a pastoral leader may be idealized, namely, "you're the best thing that ever happened to this community, etc." While this is indeed flattering, it is important to recognize that it is a distortion (this recognition often requires overcoming some powerful resistance in the pastoral leader, because the idealization feels so good). If not recognized as a distortion, the temptation may be to try to live up to the expectations imposed by these admirers, which is a path to self-destruction. Alternatively, some may denigrate the (powerful) leader, often due to early experiences with abusive or depriving parents and related images of God. While it is easier on the pastoral leader to recognize the distortion in these cases, the challenge remains to remember who one is (with realistic assets and liabilities) and to represent who one really is to the community. This is a fundamental ethical boundary, which involves a clear sense of identity as a precursor to effective ministry.

A related professional boundary for pastoral leaders centers on the exercise of care. While pastoral leaders accept the *primum non nocere* dictum of physicians, their mandate goes beyond simply doing no harm. Pastoral care is modeled on the ministry of Jesus, who actively seeks the wounded and the confused for attention, healing, and reconciliation. This other-orientation must be balanced with appropriate self-care, otherwise pastoral leaders will be tempted to expect a reciprocity of care from those whom they serve, setting the stage for resentment in ministry, entitlement, and acting out. This balance gets at the heart of the connection/autonomy framework for mature sexuality. If the pastoral leader is not taking care of himself or herself in appropriate ways, e.g. rest, exercise, balanced diet, engaging in multiple sources of intimacy, then the connection to others will be motivated more by emotional hunger than by sincere altruism.

3. Balance the prophetic and the reconciling.

In assisting others on their path to Christian sexual maturity, the pastoral leader is facing some formidable obstacles—cultural, generational, and familial, among others. Temperamentally, we are all predisposed either to be more prophetic (challenging, confrontational) or more reconciling (peacemakers, getting along is the overarching value). However, if pastoral ministry is to be truly effective, a balance of both roles must govern its exercise. For example, the pastoral leader must confront rigid or overly permissive cultural norms about sexuality, where being a man or a woman is defined in terms of certain sexual appetites and practices that permit no exception or questioning. Why must men be fiercely independent and ashamed of acknowledging their needs for emotional nurturance and support? Why must women adhere to certain gender roles in the family or at work, such that strivings for autonomy and power are ridiculed or pathologized? Are men encouraged to be promiscuous in order to prove their masculinity, and does the opposite standard apply to women? How does our culture foster sexual self-absorption as a substitute for mature sexual relationships that are characterized by intimacy and generativity? It seems to me that pastoral leaders should be opening these difficult questions for discussion.

At the same time, there is a need for reconciliation for those who are estranged from the church because of its sexual teaching about certain behaviors, such as premarital sex, contraception, and homosexuality, among others. By emphasizing that the church is struggling to comprehend the complexity of sexuality and to appreciate and uphold its sacred character as the medium of God's presence in the world, pastoral leaders might reach out to those who instead perceive that sexual teachings are punitive and intended to weed out those who do not conform. Recall the significance of attachment (to parents and to God) and its influence on religious rules and prohibitions. If one were anxiously or avoidantly attached to God, then an emphasis on the rational correctness of a religious precept would not achieve reconciliation. Instead, an emphasis on the absolute commitment of God to our growth in truth and holiness, if preached with consistency, does stand a chance of bringing back to the communion of believers those who have been estranged. And, as pointed out earlier, this connection with the ecclesial community is an essential ingredient in helping others to contextualize their personal spiritual and sexual experiences, and thereby to move toward Christian sexual maturity.

NOTES

1. John Paul II, *Theology of the Body*, 76 (February 20, 1989).
2. Bruce Marshall, *The World, the Flesh and Father Smith* (Boston: Houghton Mifflin, 1945), 108.
3. Len Sperry, *Sex, Priestly Ministry, and the Church*, 135.

SELECTED BIBLIOGRAPHY

Blos, Peter. *The Adolescent Passage: Developmental Issues.* New York: International Universities Press, 1979.
———. *On Adolescence, a Psychoanalytic Interpretation.* New York: Free Press, 1962.
Cecero, John. *Praying Through Our Lifetraps: A Psycho-Spiritual Approach to Freedom.* Totowa, NJ: Catholic Book Publishing/Resurrection Press, 2002.
Chodorow, Nancy. *Femininities, Masculinities, Sexualities: Freud and Beyond.* Lexington, KY: University Press of Kentucky, 1994.
———. *The Reproduction of Mothering: Psychoanalysis and the Sociology of Gender.* Berkeley: University of California Press, 1978.
Erikson, Erik. *Childhood and Society.* New York: W. W. Norton, 1993.
———. *Identity and the Life Cycle.* New York: W. W. Norton, 1980.

————. *Identity, Youth, and Crisis*. New York: W. W. Norton, 1968.

Erikson, Erik, and Joan M. Erikson. *The Life Cycle Completed*. New York: W. W. Norton, 1997.

Gilligan, Carol. *In a Different Voice: Psychological Theory and Women's Development*. Cambridge, MA: Harvard University Press, 1993.

————. *Mapping the Moral Domain: A Contribution of Women's Thinking to Psychological Theory and Education*. Cambridge, MA: Center for the Study of Gender, Education, and Human Development, Harvard University Graduate School of Education, Distributed by Harvard University Press, 1988.

————. *Women, Girls and Psychotherapy: Reframing Resistance*. New York: Haworth Press, 1991.

Ignatius, of Loyola. *The Spiritual Exercises of Saint Ignatius*. Translated with commentary by George E. Ganss. St. Louis: Institute of Jesuit Studies, 1992.

John Paul II, Pope. *The Theology of the Body: Human Love in the Divine Plan*. Boston: Daughters of St. Paul, 1997.

Mahler, Margaret. *The Psychological Birth of the Human Infant: Symbiosis and Individuation*. New York: Basic Books, 1975.

Mahler, Margaret, in collaboration with Manuel Furer. *On Human Symbiosis and the Vicissitudes of Individuation: Infantile Psychosis*. New York: International Universities Press, 1968.

Marcel, Gabriel. *The Mystery of Being*. South Bend, IN: Gateway Edition, 1977.

Sperry, Len. *Sex, Priestly Ministry, and the Church*. Collegeville, MN: Liturgical Press, 2003.

Walsh, James, John Mayer, James Castelli, Eugene Hemrick, Melvin Blanchette, and Paul Theroux. *Grace Under Pressure: What Gives Life to American Priests: A Study of Effective Priests Ordained Ten to Thirty Years*. Washington, D.C.: National Catholic Education Association, 1996.

A Pastoral Response to John J. Cecero, S.J., "Toward Christian Sexual Maturity"

Kieran Scott

We are all profoundly grateful to John Cecero for his reflection on the process of sexual maturity, and for incorporating into his analysis the wisdom of the Christian tradition. Throughout his chapter, I found myself continuously nodding in agreement and affirming: Yes, what a refreshing approach to sexuality. In an effort to open up and advance the conversation, I will briefly highlight three areas in Professor Cecero's chapter.

First, I deeply appreciate and affirm John Cecero's starting point: our body, our sexual body, is not an accident. It is not simply a wrapping for our soul. Our sexual bodies are the medium of God's presence. John Paul II's *Theology of the Body*, he notes, supports this position. It is very incarnational. It is the fruit of a Catholic sacramental imagination.[1]

Christianity's affirmation of and belief in the fundamental goodness and holiness of our bodies must guide our conversation about sex and sexuality. They are sacraments of God's creativity. They are sacraments of God's love. They are sacraments of God's pleasure. The God that was in Jesus dwells in our corporality. Bodiliness is where we (sexual) humans "hear" God, "see" God, and "sense" and "feel" something of God. It is sacred space.

The body is our common ground.[2] This sameness we share as embodied persons makes it possible for us to speak in common about "stirring within," "inner proddings," and "a hunger for justice." Of course differences and distinctions emerge from that common ground. But they are secondary. The Incarnation and Resurrection was/is a resounding vote for (sexual) bodily life. This is what we teach. This is what we preach. This is what we counsel. The wisdom of the Roman Catholic tradition, then, points to the wisdom of our bodies.

Our bodies, our selves, are the locus of revelation. God dwells in intimacy and love with the self, and in intimacy and love with our partners. Mature sexuality, as Cecero notes, mirrors the life of the Trinity. That is, it exemplifies intimate communion and generativity. Sex and sexuality is sacred.[3] It is our bridge to the divine. This perspective can be the basis for a rich spirituality of sexuality for men and women, adults and children, heterosexual and homosexual persons.

Second, Professor Cecero sets the discussion of Christian sexual maturity within his field of expertise—namely, clinical psychology. His lens is the lens of modern psychology. That is his chosen framework. Other angles of vision, he acknowledges, could have been employed. He utilizes his own psychological lens very well.

However, I would like to suggest that sex and sexuality, and sexual maturity, needs a broader framework for discussion. They need to be approached politically and institutionally, as well as biologically and psychologically. Here, in this political season, I will risk taking up the political.[4] Does sexuality not also have a political component, with institutional and policy implications?

Take, for example Vietnam, not the country but the war. Was it not very much a male sexual war? Nixon, Kissinger, Westmoreland, Johnson. As Robert Duvall, in *Apocalypse Now*, declared: How they love the smell of napalm in the morning!

Or again take Iraq, not the country but the war. Is it not very much a kind of male sexual war? Once more, the names sound like rolling thunder: Bush, Cheney, Rumsfeld, Wolfowitz. How they strut, how they swagger, how they sway. Are these not surges of testosterone, urges to compete, lifetraps—men frozen in rigid forms of male sexuality? Has not our whole political season been: I can be more macho than you! Slogans capture the rhetoric: Bring them on! Don't be a wimp! Mission accomplished! Stay the course!

Stephen Kinzer, in his meticulously documented and gripping new book, *Overthrow*, chronicles the history of forcible regime changes by the United States over the past 110 years. By Kinzer's count, starting with the undermining of the Hawaiian monarchy in 1893, passing through Cuba (1898), the Philippines (1898), Iran (1953), Guatamala (1954), and ending with the present-day Iraq, the United States has toppled foreign governments fourteen times in the past century.[5] Is this arrogant and unilateral exercise of power not an extension of American machismo into foreign policy?

Our social lives also are lived in the context of social institutions. For some of us, our primary social working context is academia. Academia, I believe, is a perfect illustration of sexual politics. Much of its life illustrates how the "masculine" drive for power and use of power is the essential motivating force in the functioning of academic institutions. In academia, the personal is truly political. Our professional self-concept tends to be based on power. Ideas can be used as weapons to establish power over others. And the infamous tenure process is renowned, frequently, not for assessment of competencies, but for the capacity to form political alliances.

Certain forms of contemporary pastoral psychology also direct us to the God within.[6] This inner journey to the center of the self is indispensable for human development. However, we must not overplay the subjective. And the ego is not all that counts. David Tracy cautions us: A God of psychology cannot be one more projection of the modern ego. "Our modern psychological culture," he writes, "concentrates far too much attention upon human subjectivity and personal experience . . . the authentic self, for the Christian, is never an individual in the modern individualistic sense . . . but a person constituted by her/his relationships to others, to history and the struggle for justice, to the cosmos, and above all to the God of history and the God of wisdom and love."[7] For the God of psychology to be true, then, He, She, or It must also be the God of history. The God of the authentic self is also the God in daily affairs. This is the Spirit of God in which we live and move and have our being. This is the God we experience in our historical, political struggle for justice and love. This is a political and sexual God who seeks to make all things new.

My final point is also John Cecero's, namely, the role of spirituality in sexual maturity. Modern psychology has much to teach the great religions about the nature of the self and the nature of the God experience. On the other hand, I would propose that modern psychology has much to learn from the great spiritual traditions with regard to God and the self. And one of those areas is the arena of spirituality.

However, when spirituality is added to the biological, psychological, and social perspectives on sexuality, are we simply only adding another layer or perspective? Are we tacking on a thin veneer of the spiritual severed from religion? If spirituality is to enhance our healthy sexual development it needs rootedness in our classic religious traditions and their set of practices. Otherwise, it may become a fad, a curiosity, one more consumer item for self-actualization and self-mastery.[8] Spirituality solely conceived as a subjective experience could also unwittingly foster the very self-absorption it ought to resist.

Professor Cecero, of course, is aware of this, not only as a good clinical psychologist but especially as a good Jesuit, a spiritual son of Ignatius of Loyola.[9] Spiritual discernment in sexual matters needs the context of religious communities to affirm, correct, direct, and nurture us toward responsible and just sexual relations. Contemporary psychology is, as John Cecero notes, an infant in this area. It needs to expand its horizons and get over its antipathy toward religion. Cecero is a fine example of the integration of the two. Of course, perverted forms of religion and spirituality can be barriers to sexual maturity. On the other hand, intelligent forms of religion and spirituality are indispensable on the lifelong journey toward sexual maturity.

But how do the great religious/spiritual traditions imagine that life journey? They are in one accord: It is not a linear journey of growth. It is not, contrary to Cecero, the acquisition of self-mastery. Their major theme is nearly the opposite. Let go, let go of the ego, let go of the illusion of self-mastery, let go of your prized possessions. This is St. Paul's concept of kenosis, or self-emptying. Let go of compulsive clinging is what we also learn from Buddhist practices. But how? By a disciplining of thought, as well as emotions. There is no development, sexual or otherwise, without relinquishment, without detachment.[10] No thing is G-D. Not even the all-consuming modern ego.

Christian spirituality is a protest against closure on life. It keeps open the developmental journey . . . without end. How? By inviting us to circle back and reappropriate our sexual lives at a deeper level. In a word, to slowly become a new sexual person. That is what St. Paul meant by clothing yourself with and growing up in Christ.

NOTES

1. David Tracy, *The Analogical Imagination: Christian Theology and the Culture of Pluralism* (New York: Crossroads, 1981).

2. Colleen M. Griffith, "Human Bodiliness: Sameness as Starting Point," in *The Church Women Want*, ed. Elizabeth A. Johnson, 60–67 (New York: Crossroads, 2002).

3. Evelyn Eaton Whitehead and James D. Whitehead, *A Sense of Sexuality* (New York: Doubleday, 1989).

4. On the political nature of sexuality from a social constructivist perspective, see Gayle S. Rubin, "Thinking Sex: Notes for a Radical Theory of the Politics of Sexuality," in *The Lesbian and Gay Studies Reader*, eds. Henry Abelove, Michael A. Barale, and David M. Halperin, 3–44 (New York: Routledge, 1993).

5. Stephen Kinzer, *Overthrow: America's Century of Regime Change from Hawaii to Iraq* (New York: Times Books, 2006).

6. John J. Shea, *Finding God Again: Spirituality for Adults* (Lanham, MD: Rowman & Littlefield, 2005).

7. David Tracy, "God of History, God of Psychology," in *On Naming the Present* (Maryknoll, NY: Orbis, 1994): 47–58.

8. Gregory L Jones, "A Thirst for God or Consumer Spirituality? Cultivating Discipline Practices of Being Engaged by God," *Modern Theology* 13, no. 1 (1997): 3–28.

9. See William A. Berry, S.J and Robert G. Doherty, S.J., *Contemplatives in Action: The Jesuit Way* (New York: Paulist Press, 2003).

10. Gabriel Moran, "A Grammar of Religious Development," in *Religious Education Development* (Minneapolis, MN: Winston Press, 1983), 129–56.

4

A New Moral Discourse
on Sexuality

Christine Gudorf

There can be little doubt that the Catholic Church needs a new moral discourse on sex. The framework I am about to present has, for the most part, been worked out over the last forty years through discussions among perhaps a few hundred moral theologians, both clerical and lay, and many thousands of lay Catholics, most of them during the first decades married couples, but more recently a much more sexually varied group. Many persons have taken great risks and endured great suffering at the hands of our mother church in order to contribute to a transformation toward a more human, more loving sexual theology. And there have been many millions of people—many women, gays and lesbians, clergy and religious, couples needing to control fertility, couples trapped in bitter, even violent, marriages—who have been sacrificed on the altar of anti-sexual Catholic tradition and legalism.[1] At the same time, there are resources within the tradition that can support a new moral discourse on sexuality, and there are areas in which the twentieth-century church has reformed traditional church teachings in ways that support a new moral discourse.

This is a huge topic. I will first lay out a number of traditional teachings that must be abandoned, and the emerging trends that support, even demand alternatives. Then I will turn to the specific theological resources in the church that can support alternatives. A new moral discourse, to become popular—that is successful—discourse, must first analyze the socio/political/economic trends of late modernity that affect human sexual ideation and behavior, deciding which of these can be altered in ways that better serve human needs and protect human dignity, and which probably can't. Those trends which cannot be altered must either be accepted, and teachings on sexuality must be adapted to these trends, again in ways that best serve human needs and protect human dignity, or the church must prepare to defend its stance against the larger culture. Available theological resources for a new moral discourse on sex include both many that have been around for centuries, as well as some of the twentieth-century innovations and reforms already made in official teaching.

PART I. CURRENT TEACHINGS THAT SHOULD BE ABANDONED: A LIST

- The inseparability of the unitive and procreative aspects of human sexuality
- The moral superiority of vowed virginity over marriage
- The centrality of sex/gender for personhood
- Sexual dimorphism and complementarity
- All sexual matters as grave
- Personhood as present from conception
- The limitation of all sexual activity to marriage

Inseparability of the Unitive and Procreative

Though this principle has often been understood as the central Catholic teaching on sexuality,[2] the vast majority of U.S. Catholics have been convinced that sexual intercourse and procreation are not only separable, but *that such separation has become normative.* They reject the understanding of marriage as created for the weak who cannot control sexual desire, and the understanding of children as the sacrifice that couples must accept as the price of sexual pleasure. Most U.S. Catholics want children, and believe that children should be conceived when they are wanted, when the parents are able to care for them adequately, and when they will not be a burden to their families or society. And they do not believe that when those conditions do not exist, that couples must refrain from sex. Instead, they believe that shared sexual pleasure in marriage is a good in itself, both validating the worth of the individual experiencing it and expressing—even increasing—the love between the partners. They accept the argument of Gallagher, Maloney, Rousseau, and Wilzcak in *Embodied in Love*[3] that sexual pleasure acts as a school for love, teaching partners that just as the pleasure of orgasm rewards them for opening themselves to the partner in sex and making themselves vulnerable physically and emotionally, so they can risk opening themselves to others in a variety of non-sexual relationships, expecting those others to respond with similar openness. Couples who create mutual sexual pleasure out of love produce an aura of love and warmth that overflows onto their children, their friends and neighbors, and their church.

Couples with infertility problems are often incredulous when they are told that because of the principle of inseparability of the unitive and procreative elements they should accept infertility: fertilization must take place in the fallopian tubes of the wife, not in a Petri dish. From their perspective this distinction makes no difference for either the pregnancy or the birth of the child in question. From the couples' perspective the inhumanity in most infertility treatments is not so much the separation of the unitive and procreative aspects itself, as it is that the couple themselves often come to feel objectified by the policies and demands of the clinical process, which are focused only on conception, and ignore relationship. The clinical process needs to be humanized, and the desire for conception put back within the context of marital love instead of being made a solely technical end. But let's not throw out the baby with the bathwater.

Moral Superiority of Vowed Virginity

This teaching, which many thought was made obsolete by Vatican II only to find it reinforced by John Paul II, is a relic of the suspicion of sex and the condemnation of sexual pleasure in the history of the church, which together have served to keep the laity subordinate to the clergy. Many clergy, religious, and laity reject this moral superiority, recognizing that there is no state in life which is immune to the temptation to sin by closing oneself off to the demands of love, just as there is no state in life in which persons cannot become saints. The church has argued that married persons are preoccupied with the demands of family, while celibates are free to serve the community, but the experience of the last few decades has been that many married people are as visible in time-consuming church ministries as clergy and religious. As humans live longer lives, and rear fewer children, the preoccupation argument is less and less apt. At the same time, the strong tendency in modern society to locate intimacy in sexual relationships and to subordinate, or even suspect, other locations for intimacy, disadvantages some clergy and religious in learning the gift of self in intimacy, and may even affect their ability to minister well.

Centrality of Sex/Gender for Personhood | Sexual Dimorphism and Complementarity

The late twentieth-century popes, at least Pius XII through John Paul II, have strongly argued that one's maleness or femaleness is an essential part of who one is. The characteristic form for expressing this belief has been instructions to women that they are essentially different from men, and they must take care not to become like men, which would be a betrayal of their Creator and his plan of creation.[4] This is a relatively new teaching that developed in the nineteenth and twentieth centuries within modernism. There is a certain irony here, in that the same church that condemned modernism changed its own teaching, which had long followed Augustine's (and Jerome's and others') dictate that sexuality did not touch the core of the person.[5] They were especially convinced that female sexuality did not touch the core of the person, and promoted women becoming "virile and virtuous" by renouncing sex in perpetual virginity. Sex/gender was corruption from the outside of the person, and peripheral to true personhood. This ideology began to change in the late nineteenth century to accord with early modern science's attempt to explain all human traits and roles in terms of maleness and femaleness[6]—a view which itself was seized as a tool against early feminism.

It is interesting that from pope to pope the message about the status of women changed:[7] for Pius XI, women were simply unequal to men, and those who taught differently were false prophets. For Pius XII, men and women were essentially different and women belonged primarily in the home under the headship of men, or if necessary in social work that involved care of children, the sick, and the needy, but were spiritually equal to men. For John XXIII, women had (mostly) equal rights in society but should use them carefully in accord with their different natures, and were subject to husbands in the home. For Paul VI, women were completely equal to men in society, but unable to resemble Christ enough to assume the ministries of lector, acolyte, or priest in the church (he did not deal with authority in the family).[8] Most recently, for John Paul II, women are fully equal to men in the home and in society, where they may hold any role, but in the church they are excluded from all positions of governance due to their inability to resemble Christ.[9]

Over the last seventy years, no matter what kind of equality women demanded, the papal answer was that women were equal in some other area, but not that one. First they were only equal in the eyes of God but not in the home, church, or society; later they were equal for God and in society over which the popes had no control, but not in the church. Finally under John Paul II they were equal in the family as well as society, but they remain unequal in the church—the only arena controlled by the popes!

In developed and many developing nations, women are exercising power in many responsible roles, from political leadership to technical and professional roles. In fact, in developed nations women are outperforming men at almost every educational level, so that it can no longer be argued that women are not rational, have no judgment skills, and so on. The roles of men and women in society, and increasingly in the home, have become so similar that it simply is not believable to many that there is an essential sexual difference which runs to the core of the person, deeper than racial, ethnic, national, or other cultural differences, deeper than education and training differences.

It is revealing that even as John Paul insists on sexual complementarity, he does not, as earlier popes, name masculine or feminine traits, much less social roles embodying them. The old masculine and feminine stereotypes are not believable anymore; they have been the butt of jokes and humor for too many years precisely because our economy does not provide a foundation for them anymore. Many women must work to support children either with their husbands or on their own, and to do this successfully, they have had to learn some traditionally male roles and traits, especially decisive styles of leadership. At the same time, research shows that men have changed, too, though less dramatically. More and more of men's occupations today demand not so much the muscle power of heavy lifting and carrying, but more people skills, such as those required for cooperative work in teams, or for supervising a noncaptive workforce. Husbands with working wives, especially professional wives, have been pressured to share domestic and childcare work as necessary to protect wives' salaries.

It is difficult not to suspect that the reason for hanging onto complementarity is that, together with the principle that every sexual act must be open to procreation, it constitutes the moral bulwark against homosexuality. Homosexual couples are seen as lacking this complementarity of sexual difference. A homosexual couple can reflect racial/ethnic difference, difference in training and occupation, difference in temperament and personality and many others, but these differences are not seen by the magisterium as being as deep as sexual difference.

Thus physicalism—understanding human beings in terms of biology alone—is not limited to church teaching on contraception, but pervades the foundation of church teaching on sexuality. And yet the biology on which this physicalism is based is not contemporary biology. Biologists today tell us that there are six indicators of biological sex, and that for many millions of people these indicators do not line up in any simple dimorphic pattern. Not only do many millions have ambiguous genitalia, especially (but not only) when young, but even chromosomal sex is not dimorphic: in addition to a majority of people who are xx or xy, many are xo, xxy, xyy, xxx, or more rarely, xxxx.[10] Are these people male or female? If these are the biological types, how did humans decide to reduce these seven types to two, ignoring the real differences, between say, an xy and an xxy?

We also have a number of social and medical interventions into sexual biology, such as transgendered persons and transsexuals. In addition to self-identified bisexuals, there are also large numbers of people who have changed sexual orientation—both from heterosexual to homosexual and from homosexual to heterosexual—even after decades of apparently successful function (this is especially true for lesbians, probably because eroticism in women is more diffused[11]). More than that, we have *therapies* which create sexual ambiguity. A male friend of mine from high school has prostate cancer, and for some years has received a common therapy: female hormones. Completely heterosexual, he was taken aback when he grew breasts, but now jokes that he takes his needlework to meetings with women friends and shares his stories of hot flashes between treatments. His experience of the last few years, he says, has made him aware that what we call maleness and femaleness are human traits accessible to all, that societies have arbitrarily labeled characteristic of one sex or the other.

All Sexual Acts as Grave Matter

This teaching is also clearly a leftover from the anti-sexual heritage of the church. The image of a pretty girl pops into the head of a twelve-year-old and he gets an erection—mortal sin? A fourteen-year-old girl masturbates— mortal sin? A couple who just had a baby six weeks ago uses a condom when they resume sex, lest the wife get pregnant again too soon. Or a hospital lab worker who contracted HIV uses a condom so as not to infect her husband—mortal sin? What works against the believability of all sexual sins as grave is that it is simply impossible to understand masturbation or contraception, much less an unintentional sexually arousing thought, as able to cut one off from God in the same way that mass murder, violent rape, human torture and mutilation, or any number of other horrible acts of violence do. What kind of a God would respond to a masturbating adolescent and a mass murderer in the same way? Most of us have come to believe in a God who is offended by what hurts human beings and the rest of creation, a God who created human nature with a capacity for dynamism and development that allows us to choose responsible adaptations to changes and situations in the world in which we live.

Personhood from the Moment of Conception

It was only in 1869 that the church abandoned its traditional teaching on the progressive humanity of the fetus in favor of this current teaching that the fetus is a person from the moment of conception. In fact, the very science that the church was rushing to adopt in 1869 when it identified personhood with conception now undermines that teaching, for according to modern science, there is no "moment" of conception. Conception is a process—it takes twelve to sometimes more than twenty-four hours for a sperm to penetrate the ovum and fertilize it. Thus conception never takes place simultaneously with intercourse. Furthermore, the teaching on personhood beginning at conception has emphasized the uniqueness of each and every fetus when we know now that identical twins do not separate until sometime from twelve to fifteen days after fertilization.[12] How does one unique human person become two human persons?

Even the practice of the church is inconsistent on this point, in that the church has refused grieving couples Christian burials for fetuses that miscarry. But if the fetus was a person for two, three, or four months, then why should it be denied either baptism or burial? It is not enough to say that it is dead, for Catholic hospitals routinely baptize stillborn children in the understanding that we cannot know the exact moment of death when the soul leaves the body. The reason we do not baptize and give Christian burial to miscarriages is tradition—for almost two millennia the church believed that in its early stages the fetus was not fully human, that ensoulment did not happen for anywhere from six weeks to over four months after conception. If the fetus were a person at fertilization, we should pour the water and say the words over the bellies of pregnant women—perhaps not only baptize, but also give the Anointing of the Sick—for like the elderly, the fetus is vulnerable. What has supported the present teaching on immediate personhood of the fetus has been the experience of medicine rolling back further and further the age of fetuses that can survive outside the mother. As the smallest babies to survive outside the womb became tinier and tinier, we became inclined to see tinier and tinier humans as full persons. It is still popularly imagined that science will continue to "save" fetuses earlier and earlier. But medicine has known for a couple of decades now that the rollbacks are largely done, and bioethics, in fact, has spent more time trying to set a limit on the size of fetuses we should even attempt to save. Why use the resources that could inoculate thousands of children against childhood diseases, or give prenatal care to hundreds of pregnant women, in order to "save" a child for weeks, months, or perhaps even a year or two of pain, repeated interventions, and severe disability, not to mention the helpless suffering to the child's family, if grossly premature death is still certain?

The Limitation of All Sexual Activity to Marriage

The teaching that all sexual acts, including arousal, should take place only within marriage has never been popularly accepted within Catholicism. The best indication of this is the illegitimacy rate in Christian Europe over the last fifteen centuries. Despite the fact that 10 to 15 percent of the population of Christian Europe was in convents and monasteries, mostly living celibately, the illegitimacy rates for Christian Europe are as high or higher than in many other non-Christian parts of the world.[13] Historian John Boswell in his book, *The Kindness of Strangers*,[14] wrote of child abandonment from the late Roman Empire to the Renaissance, and in *Sacrificed for Honor*[15] historian David Kertzer compared the child abandonment rates in early modern Italy to those in other parts of Europe. Using local birth, baptism, and foundling hospital records, they both report fluctuating rates of 20 percent to sometimes as high as 50 percent child abandonment rates—that is 20 percent to 50 percent of all babies born live were abandoned. Records indicate that roughly half of these babies were born out of wedlock. Church officials like to imagine that in their youth, and certainly in earlier times when the church and its teachings were more respected and obeyed, sex took place outside marriage only by exception. We have no living witnesses from former centuries to refute this, but certainly the historical records of the church itself tell a very different story.

When I was a teenager in the 1960s, I lived in a small town in Indiana of 2,000+ souls of Bavarian extraction, of whom only one person was non-Catholic. Other German Catholic rural towns surrounded ours. The only high school was owned by the parish. The sexual ethic of the time, recognized by all youth and most people who dealt with youth, was progressive in one sense. Only hand-holding and good-night kisses were allowed on dates until a couple was going steady, and then there was to be a very gradual progression toward "necking" or extended kissing. As engagement began to look likely, petting was introduced, first fully clothed and then progressing. The contraceptive pill was not yet available (Catholic doctors like my father, the town doctor, did not prescribe it during its first decade) and local pharmacists kept condoms behind the counter and did not sell to youth. Since the pharmacist knew everyone in town, and was related to half the town by blood or marriage, youth were not inclined to even ask about condoms. While some couples did cross the line into intercourse before marriage, the disgrace of those who had to get married restrained the majority from premarital intercourse. I do not particularly condone this sexual ethic; it had many problems, among them that girls were understood as the sexual gatekeepers while boys were encouraged to be proficient seducers, even at the risk of being "caught" by pregnancy. It did not conform to Catholic teaching, in that it allowed a great deal of sexual arousal, and completely ignored Catholic teaching on avoiding near occasions of sin. But it was progressive—it assumed that sexual expression should correspond to a deepening level of relational commitment, that one's partners in sex should never be simply means to individual pleasure, but ends in themselves. The means used to enforce this model of sexual behavior were simple—gossip and shotgun weddings. Such measures did not always treat individuals justly; many of the "guilty" escaped, and some of those punished were more sinned against than sinners, both male and female. But a minority of teens had intercourse while in high school. Moreover, the sexual discipline that developed among couples who dated and waited for years before marriage often helped them adjust to the sexual (and other!) frustrations that accompany the early years of parenthood—though it should be added that the female gatekeeper role sometimes was difficult to abandon after marriage, a fact which could and did sometimes damage a couple's capacity for shared sexual pleasure.

We have lost this sense of progression in sexual relationship. Some youth are attempting to restore some progression to sexual activity, but their process is somewhat shocking to older persons, who reserved oral sex for established relationships in search of experimentation. Today pressure for immediate sex among teens is so heavy that many young teens are engaging in fellatio as a way of postponing intercourse, avoiding pregnancy, and, they think, the danger of STDs.[16]

We all know the arguments in favor of divorce—people live longer, marriages are more mobile, thus moving couples away from sources of support such as extended family and friends, and there are infinitely more choices to be made in adult life today than in the past, offering more ways for spouses to grow apart. In short, marriages are more difficult to maintain today; spouses make more interpersonal demands on each other and are more emotionally dependent upon each other than in the recent past at the same time that they have less time for each other. Our economy demands that most wives enter waged labor, so that the domestic and childcare work that many wives used to do in the home on weekdays now must be shared in the evenings and on weekends.

Selection of spouses has become more difficult at the same time that it has become more important. Over the last thirty years, I have heard older women, including my mother-in-law and her sisters, as well as younger women in developing nations, protest the proclivity to divorce in late modern America. My mother-in-law was of the opinion that a good husband was one who had a steady job, brought his paycheck home, only got drunk on Friday or Saturday night, and only beat his wife when severely provoked. If a husband met those criteria, nothing else could be demanded or expected of him. She thought her own husband a model husband because he occasionally bathed the children or dried the dishes, seldom drank more than once a week, and never beat her.

Similarly, a group of Indian women at a Maryknoll conference twenty years ago decried American divorce. "What is so terrible if your husband is a jerk? So long as you have your children and your family network, just ignore him and live your life. Let him have other women, or gambling, or whatever. If you have to work, so be it. What do you need him for, once you have your children? You can still have a great life." They did not take to their marriages high expectations of personal intimacy or emotional love, needs that they satisfied with female family and friends, and they expected their primary relation to be with their children.

But today even in developing nations with cultures of arranged marriage, the trend is toward interpersonal marital relationships. Arranged marriage is not being abandoned; many Asian young people trust their parents' choices for them more than they trust their own choice, and they refuse to consider marrying without parental consent, as to be estranged from their families is for most still unthinkable. But they are increasingly demanding, especially those who are older and more educated, to meet the prospective spouse and to have a veto similar to the one their parents have. Though these communities do have far less divorce than we do, their divorce rate does not approach Western levels yet.

Europeans—Catholic, Protestant, and nonreligious alike—have largely accepted cohabitation as a prelude to marriage. Among Catholics in Europe, young couples—those under thirty—are often urged by parents and even pastors to cohabit when they want to marry, out of fear that divorce and remarriage would follow so young a marriage, and the spouses be thereby estranged from the church. Cohabitation is understood to preclude having children, often out of recognition that the partners are still in school or training and/or do not have sufficient income guaranteed to begin a family responsibly.

In the U.S. cohabitation is also common—in 2000 there were 5.5 million households with cohabiting adults[17]—but it seems to me that it is less accepted, and thus less regulated by universal custom, perhaps because the U.S. population is more diverse than most European nations. Most studies of U.S. cohabitation are not very useful. They do indicate that cohabitation in general does not lower the divorce rates in later marriage compared to those who do not cohabit. But most studies do not distinguish couples who share housing for a week or two from those who share a home, income, families, and vacations for a decade. Nor do many of them distinguish couples by age, though cohabiting couples of eighteen are much less likely to be headed toward marriage than cohabiting thirty-year-olds. Nor can the studies tell us whether, if cohabitation were not an option and all these cohabiting couples instead married, the divorce rate would rise or remain the same.

As the ecological need in most of the world to limit human population growth becomes more acute, education and training continues to extend longer and longer, and jobs that can support more than one person with basic dignity become still more scarce, youth find it necessary to wait longer and longer to begin families, and so cling together in cohabitation in the meantime. It does not seem to me that the church can reverse this trend, but it does seem to me that the church could and should influence this trend, distinguishing between casual sex in convenient cohabitation situations of the "let's live together and share expenses; it'll be cheaper and sex will be convenient" kind, and couples truly committed to each other who would like this relationship to develop into marriage. As a number of others have suggested, ritual—including public ritual preparation—is the traditional way to distinguish such differences.[18]

PART II. GENERAL AND THEOLOGICAL RESOURCES

Before turning to *theological* resources for a new moral discourse on sexuality, I need to briefly review scientific resources—what the sciences have learned about sexuality. We need to look to the sciences, both biological and social sciences, for data about human sexuality. Our theological perspective is critical for interpreting the meaning and value of the data, which science cannot do, but the data is necessary. Sometimes the very weight of the data can shift our theological perspective from one paradigm to another.

The nature vs. nurture arguments are largely over, with both sides having been right *and* wrong. There are biological aspects to sexual identity and behavior, and there are environmental aspects as well. Not only individual genes but chromosomal patterns, hormonal levels, brain patterns, and other biological aspects contribute to sexual identity and behavior, just as do relations with one's family, friends, religious community, and culture. Human sexuality is constructed, but individuals never get to be sole contractors in that construction. They in effect inherit partially-built structures. They can move pieces around and add to what is there, but they must deal with the pieces they inherit.

Not only is human sexuality constructed, but it is increasingly unclear that it is dimorphic.[19] There seems to be a great deal of plasticity in human sexuality, especially for women. Male sexuality seems somewhat more rigid. Men are much less likely than women to say that they fall in love with a person, not with a sex. Male homosexuals are less than half as likely as female homosexuals to have had significant heterosexual experience, as well as much more likely than women to use language of discovering, rather than choosing, homosexuality. In many aspects of sexual activity, the behaviors and explanations of men are much less varied and more predictable than those of women, though male sexual fantasies are much more varied, especially regarding numbers of partners. While women can reach orgasm from stimulation of virtually any part of their body under the right circumstances—some women even without physical stimulation at all, simply from a memory of sexual pleasure—most men's erogenous zones are pretty much limited to their genitals. The range of emotions expressed in men's sexual relationships is narrower, as is the range of emotions that they recognize in partners.[20]

There are a number of theories about why women's sexuality is so much more diffuse than men's, and most of them are environmental, though it is entirely possible that biology plays a role here as well. Many 1970–1980s studies of childrearing by parents and parent substitutes have found that girl babies are held more, talked to more—this being the supposed reason for girls' early verbal superiority. Boys are given more freedom of movement. They are put down on the floor earlier and for longer periods, taken outside more and left in a room by themselves earlier and more often. Boys are allowed to cry longer and more often than girls before they are picked up. Boys are played with more roughly from birth—held up higher, swung more roundly, held more with one arm. Perhaps the most interesting fact of all was that caretakers, including parents, were virtually oblivious of any differences in their treatment of male and female babies. And yet a simple test helped persuade many that perhaps they were acting stereotypically: carry a strange baby up to someone and urgently ask him or her to hold the baby for a moment while you run to the bathroom. Over 80 percent of people— more males than females—will ask the sex of the child before they will touch it. We do not know how to interact with a person until we know the sex of that person.

A logical question for most people is: where do homosexuals fit into this data? And the answer is that generally they don't, as homosexuals. Only a very few homosexuals—like their heterosexual counterparts—reject their sex/gender assignments. Homosexuality concerns not whether one desires to be male or female, masculine or feminine, but only what sex one is attracted to. The research on homosexuality is that again, lesbian sexuality is more diffuse and varied than gay sexuality; on the Kinsey spectrum between exclusive homosexuality and exclusive heterosexuality, men are more clustered near the poles than are women.[21] Bailey's twin and sibling research on homosexuality has, along with other supportive studies, demonstrated that there must be some genetic support for homosexuality at least as a predisposition. Bailey showed the likelihood of a homosexual twin having his/her twin also be homosexual is 50 percent, more than ten times the normal occurrence in the general population.[22] But there is clearly some environmental influence as well, since adopted siblings of homosexual twins had twice the likelihood of being gay/lesbian/bisexual as the general population.

Since the 1970s a number of studies and theories seeking to explain male/female differences have emerged. Perhaps best known is evolutionary (socio-biological) theory, which traces all male/female differences back to differing reproductive biologies prompting different reproductive strategies: males attempt to impregnate as many females as possible, and females attempt to ensure the best survival rates for their necessarily smaller number of offspring by attaching to a man to assist in material provision. Under this theory, homosexuality is interpreted as surviving in the evolutionary process because having adults without offspring of their own in the extended family group conferred an advantage on the rest of the extended family.

Yet most of the recent theories explaining differences have been environmental, rather than biological. Nancy Chodorow of UCLA observed in her *The Reproduction of Mothering* (1974)[23] that we have arranged society so that children before the age of two are in the almost exclusive care of females. She proposes that this fact, rather than any Freudian or neo-Freudian theories about normative sexuality, undergirds the sexual patterns we see in our society and many others. Toddlers face their first social task before the age of two—gender identity: differentiating sex and associating themselves with the correct one. Girls imitate their female caretakers, while boys are forced by the absence of males among caretakers to a strategy of separation from women and femaleness in general. While childhood gender identity is thus more anxiety-producing for boys, Chodorow points out that pubertal identity formation is more anxious for girls, who only then begin to separate from their primary caretaker (mother). Pubertal boys, on the other hand, have a head start in separating from the mother.

Building on Chodorow's work, Carole Gilligan's *In A Different Voice*[24] pointed out that boys' and girls' play differs, in that boys' play is much more competitive. Among girls, even when they play a game with winners and losers, if a dispute arises, the most common resolution is to abort the game and do something else in order to avoid having to take sides between the two disputants. Relationships come first, and cannot be allowed to be threatened by competition. Among boys, disputes over rules are as competitive as the games themselves, because, she says, boys have a stronger sense of individual identity at the same age, because they already began the process of separation from the primary caretaker. Gilligan sees this difference manifested in moral decision making in males and females: males tend to approach morality in terms of moral principles which are often absolute, and females in terms of protecting relationships—distributing goods and costs as evenly as possible so as to avoid suffering.

Dorothy Dinnerstein[25] weighed in with a parallel theory that both baby boys and baby girls long to return to the bliss they experienced in the womb and in their mother's arms before they were forced to understand her as a separate person not answerable to their will. Girls and boys both associate that bliss with the adult female body. Boys' most common path to regaining that infant bliss experienced in the female body is to possess and control a similar female body, while girls seek to recreate lost bliss with they themselves in the role of adult female longed for by the Other.

The newest addition to this set of theories for explaining the development of sexual differences is Eleanor Maccoby's *The Two Sexes*.[26] She distilled all the studies of interaction between young males and females, beginning in infancy. It seems that until the third year of life, neither boys nor girls show any sexual preference in playmates, but engage with the nearest child, or the child interested in the same activity. In the third year, however, girls and boys begin a separation that lasts until puberty. The separation is initiated by girls, but is then policed and enforced much more strongly by boys. Most of Maccoby's book elaborates the difference from, and ignorance of, the other sex that these years of separation create for both males and females. This difference, and general ignorance of the difference, disrupts male-female relationships at work, in sexual partnerships, and in shared parenting. Men and women must spend large parts of their adult lives learning, in one situation after another, that the other sex does not interpret the present situation as one's own sex is likely to, but in another way altogether, and thus will react in a very different way based on that different perception. Learning the ways of the other sex is an important aspect of maturity.

While Chororow, Dinnerstein, and Gilligan point to environmental sources of sexual differences in behavior and cognition, especially the assignment of young children to the exclusive care of females, Maccoby questions whether there might also be a biological source, since the segregation of the sexes beginning in the third year seems to be initiated by the toddlers themselves, and does not mirror any parallel adult behavior. While she admits the children may be responding to adult cues, it is not yet known what they might be.

Theological Resources

There are, I think, at least three different sets of theological resources associated with the Catholic tradition that are valuable in shifting to a new moral discourse about sex. The first set is particular theological resources that have been relevant in what we might call the first period of transition, which began with Vatican II. These resources have been sustaining pioneering individuals through that estrangement from, and even persecution by, the institutional church that has accompanied these pioneers in their search for a new moral discourse. These theological resources include historical Catholic teachings on probabilism, which recognizes a range of acceptable moral options in specific situations instead of only one, and conscience, which as St. Thomas Aquinas wrote, must be obeyed, even at the risk of excommunication, as well as the more recent theme of collegiality, which was so prominent in the speeches and documents of Vatican II but never implemented afterward. Much has been written on these; I will not repeat that here.

The second set of resources consists of myriad insights that arise from study of the history of the church, not merely the history of the institution, but the history of the people of God. Many times within that history, minority beliefs and practices later developed into official teaching and majority practice (Aquinas himself is a good example of this![27]). Though the dominant history of Catholicism on sexuality has been characterized by suspicion, repression, and even condemnation, it is possible to bring to the fore many minority teachings and traditions that can support a new moral discourse on issues as diverse as the ends of marriage, the role of sexual pleasure, methods of contraception, possibility of divorce, even the permissibility of early abortion. All reform movements need to justify themselves in terms of the past tradition. This is difficult for sexuality, given that Jesus himself only indirectly mentioned sex or sexuality and the tradition has not only preferred celibacy to marriage but also degraded women such that they have only recently been seen as capable of true partnerships with men. But it is not impossible; the task is greatly aided by the fact that, unlike esoteric teachings on the nature of the Trinity, or the Assumption of the Blessed Virgin, sexual morality is something that ordinary lay people experience. It is something about which (some of) their consciences speak.

A third set of resources comes from the mystical tradition of the church, and this is for a number of reasons. One important reason for traditional suspicion of sexuality in Roman Catholicism concerns the triumph of rationality in the Western church (though one hesitates to say that when the Catholic and Protestant traditions are compared!). That rationalism created distrust of any strong emotion, including distrust of popular religiosity for being imbued with passion (and irrational magic!). Mysticism was pushed to the periphery of church life for similar reasons, but also because mystics' insistence on direct personal communion with the divine rejected institutional mediation between persons and the divine.[28] Within the mystical tradition we find a useful sexual tradition emanating, interestingly enough, from persons who were almost exclusively celibate. But many of the mystics used very sexual language—even orgasmic language—to describe the relationship between the mystic soul and God.[29] This was especially true of female mystics, who often referred to Christ as their spouse, and of communion with him as pleasurable beyond endurance. Analogy must work in both directions or not at all. Today statements from the mystics about communion with the divine being unitive in a sexual sense—losing ones' embodied self in love of the other—can be joined to the experiential statements of many married Catholics who describe sexual communion in mystical terms so that the two statements reinforce one another.

Papal teaching has made some significant steps in the direction of new moral discourse on sexuality, though there are still some crucial missing elements preventing full reform. Since Pius XII there has been an increasing recognition of the growing equality between men and women based in modern education and labor function. While John Paul II refused to see a sufficient image of Christ in women to justify ordaining them, he did take a major step in his encyclical *Mulieris dignitatem*, in which he reversed almost two millennia of church teaching on the subjection of wives to husbands and thus provided a basis for sexual equality in the family.[30] What is perhaps more interesting, and just as useful for a new moral discourse, is the *way* that he discarded wifely subjection. He quoted the Biblical verse that says, "Wives, be subject to your husband as to the Lord, Husbands love your wives," and, calling upon the language of reciprocity in other nearby verses, reinterpreted this particular verse to mean that husbands and wives are to be *mutually subject* to each other. While this method is not indefensible, it is not at all traditional, and sets a radical precedent for dealing with gender in the Bible.

There is yet another area in which John Paul II made a significant contribution to a new moral discourse on sexuality, and that is in his discussions of marriage. He did not address sexuality directly—he did not, for example, caution couples that marital sex should be mutually pleasurable, and that if it isn't they should get counseling from an expert. But his personalist language for speaking about marriage replaced much of the contractual language that preceded it. He talked of marriage in terms of love, and assumed that this love precedes the vows, and is not created by and with the vows, as in earlier contractual models of marriage.[31] For all that he overstressed the need for every act of marital sex to be open to procreation, he also recognized that pleasurable sex bonds couples together, and that this is not merely an unexpected advantage accidentally produced by lustful couples' selfish indulgence, but rather such bonding is a product of the conjunction of an apt physical experience and the heightened interpersonal and intimacy needs that modern couples have which must be met if marital relationships are to survive. One of the principal reasons for John Paul's popularity around the world was this personalism, his acceptance of many dimensions of the modern individual psyche. His was not a new moral discourse on sexuality, but he contributed some of the elements that can be built upon.

Finally, I would suggest that at the same time that we discover greater and greater complexities in sexuality and sexual relationships, and find that sexual relationships are more and more central to meeting individual interpersonal needs, that human sexuality seems less and less core material for human personhood. It is one dimension of diversity, and only one. Perhaps the greatest service that the church could do to support families is to take the pressure off marriages. We should stress the need for maintaining extended families; too often today distance makes strangers out of adult siblings, and denies their children the support of extended family networks. But we also need to support the need for husbands and wives to have interpersonal relationships *outside* their marriages, especially the need for close friendships. Sometimes these can be friendships with other couples; often it will mean individual friendships. Overreliance on sexual relationship to provide intimacy puts great burdens on marriage. Close friendships can serve to support marriage by being other sources for reflex knowledge of the self, other sources for advice and comfort, and other places to blow off steam. With age, the importance of such friendships becomes clearer and clearer. It is the only way that many older adults survive the loss of a beloved spouse. All of us, given the anonymity of our society and the mobility that removes us from prior sources of intimacy, need to resist the temptation to invest ourselves only in a sexual partner, and cultivate friendships that support that partnership.

ONE OF THESE DAYS . . .

One of these days, the hierarchy of the Catholic Church is going to consult its laity about where God is present in their sexual lives, and decide to abandon its anti-sexual tradition. But the longer it takes until that day, the smaller will be the remnant of the laity that is still around to celebrate the change. For while it is true that these sexuality issues are not the primary issues of the new majority of Catholics in developing nations, these issues are becoming more and more central to those populations as well. It is not abstinence, but artificial contraception and (illegal and dangerous) abortion, which have taken fertility rates in Catholic Latin America from six children per woman forty years ago to three children per woman today. The socioeconomic trends that caused this shift are not abating. Nor is sexual abstinence likely to be more than one piece of any "solution" to the devastation of AIDS in Africa. Reproduction must be managed in an ecologically sustainable way, and there is no compelling reason why human society should have to surrender the pleasure, self-affirmation, and intimate bonding possibilities in sex in order to achieve sustainable rates of human reproduction.

NOTES

1. Just think of the couples who have been told in the confessional they were in mortal sin for using contraception, the professors and priests who have been silenced, fired, or otherwise disciplined for dissent around sexual matters, or for signing the *New York Times* ad calling for Catholic dialogue on abortion, not to mention the millions of couples who have gone through Catholic marriage preparation courses that taught them about joint checking accounts, natural family planning, and biblical verses on marriage, but never told them that sex must be fully consensual and should always be mutually pleasurable, that it could not only express but also deepen love, and could offer spouses not only release or comfort, but stimulation, self-esteem, and myriad other interpersonal goods.

2. Paul VI, *Humanae vitae*, par. 1; Charles Curran writes: "Vatican II and *Humanae vitae* were the two events that have significantly shaped and influenced Catholic moral theology in the last few decades." (Charles E. Curran, *History and Contemporary Issues: Studies in Moral Theology* [New York: Continuum, 1996], 128). Curran may be referring principally to (majority) dissenting moral theologians among those shaped by *Humanae vitae*, but the statement is equally true of the magisterium itself. Defense of *Humanae vitae* became one of the principal, perhaps the principal, criteria for orthodoxy.

3. Charles A. Gallagher, George A. Maloney, Mary F. Rousseau, and Paul F. Wilczak, *Embodied in Love: Sacramental Spirituality and Sexual Intimacy* (New York: Crossroad, 1986).

4. See Gudorf, *Catholic Social Teaching on Liberation Themes* (Washington, D.C.: University Press of America, 1980), 261, citing Benedict XV, *Natalis trecentesimi, Acta*

Apostolicae Sedis (hereafter cites as *AAS*) 10 (1918): 57; Pius XI, *Casti connubi, AAS* 22 (1930): 549–50; Pius XII, "Allocution to the International Association for the Protection of the Girl," in *Papal Teachings: Women in the Modern World* (Boston: Daughters of St. Paul, 1959), 178–79; John XXIII, *Convenuti a Roma, AAS* 53 (1961): 611. Paul VI was very clear on this same point: "Dear sons and daughters, We wish also to put you on guard against some deviations which affect the contemporary movement for the advancement of women. Equalization of rights must not be allowed to degenerate into an egalitarian and impersonal elimination of differences. The egalitarianism blindly sought by our materialistic society has but little care for the specific good of persons; contrary to appearances, it is unconcerned with what is suitable or unsuitable for women. There is then, a danger of unduly masculinizing women or else simply depersonalizing them." ("Janary 31, 1976 speech to the Study Commission on Women," *The Pope Speaks* 21 (1976): 165. John Paul II was similarly clear; see John Paul II, *Letter to Women* (Washington, D.C.: U.S. Catholic Conference, 1995), #7, and *Mulieris dignitatem* (Washington, D.C.: U.S. Catholic Conference, 1988), #10.

5. See Rosemary R. Ruether, "Virginal Feminism in the Fathers of the Church," in *Religion and Sexism,* ed. Rosemary R. Ruether, 158–60 (New York: Simon and Schuster, 1974).

6. Thomas Laquer, "Orgasm, Generation, and the Politics of Reproductive Biology," in *The Making of the Modern Body,* ed. Catherine Gallagher and Thomas Laquer, (Berkeley: University of California, 1987), 35.

7. For an extended treatment of this argument, see Gudorf, *Catholic Social Teaching,* Chapter 5, or in a slightly briefer but more recent version, "Probing the Politics of Difference: What's Wrong With An All-Male Priesthood?" *Journal of Religious Ethics* 27, no. 3 (Fall 1999): 377–406.

8. See Gudorf, *Catholic Social Teaching,* chapter 5, for an overview of papal teachings through Paul VI.

9. See Christine E. Gudorf, "Encountering the Other: The Modern Papacy on Women," *Social Compass: International Review of Sociology of Religion* 36, no. 3 (September 1989): 295–310.

10. For more information, see any college sexuality textbook. Most recently I have used Tina S. Miracle, Andrew W. Miracle, and Roy F. Baumeister, *Human Sexuality* (Upper Saddle River, NJ: Prentice-Hall, 2003), but also recommend Robert Crooks and Karla Baur, *Our Sexuality* (Belmont, CA: Wadsworth, 2005).

11. Susan L. McCammon, David Knox, and Caroline Schacht, *Choices in Sexuality,* Second ed., (Cincinnati: Atomic Dog Publishing, 2004), 125, 127, 155–61, 221.

12. Betsy Hawkins Chernof, www.gen.umn.edu/faculty_staff/jensen/1135/example_student_projects/Sum2000/Twins/twins.html.

13. S. Ryan Johansson, "The Moral Imperatives of Christian Marriage: Their Biological, Economic and Demographic Implications in Changing Historical Contexts," in *One Hundred Years of Catholic Social Teaching,* ed. John Coleman, S.J., 135–54 (Maryknoll, NY: Orbis Books, 1991).

14. John Boswell, *The Kindness of Strangers: The Abandonment of Children in Western Europe from Late Antiquity to the Renaissance* (New York: Vintage, 1988).

15. David Kertzer, *Sacrificed for Honor: Italian Infant Abandonment and the Politics of Reproductive Control* (Boston: Beacon, 1993).

16. Bonnie Halpern-Felsher wrote of her study of 580 young teens at two large California high schools in the April 2004 issue of *Pediatrics*. She found that one in five fourteen-year-olds intended to try oral sex in the next six months, and one in eight had already tried it.

17. Miracle, et al., *Human Sexuality*, 275.

18. See Rosemary Ruether, *Christianity and the Making of the Modern Family: Ruling Ideologies, Diverse Realities* (Boston: Beacon, 2000), 214–15, on covenant ceremonies.

19. See my "The Erosion of Sexual Dimorphism: Challenges to Religion and Religious Ethics," *Journal of the Academy of Religion* 69, no.4 (2001): 863–91.

20. Miracle, et al., *Human Sexuality*, 293–319, 92, 325–28, 349, 356–58.

21. Miracle, et al., *Human Sexuality*, 328.

22. Michael Bailey and Richard Pillard, "Are Some People Born Gay?" *New York Times*, December 15, 1991; Bailey and Pillard et al., "Heritable Factors Influence Sexual Orientation in Women," *Archives of Gender Psychiatry* 40 (1993): 217–33.

23. Nancy Chodorow, *The Reproduction of Mothering* (Berkeley: University of California Press, 1974).

24. Carol Gilligan, *In A Different Voice: Psychological Theory and Women's Development* (Cambridge: Harvard University Press, 1980).

25. Dorothy Dinnerstein, *The Mermaid and the Minotaur: Sexual Arrangements and Human Malaise* (New York: Harper and Row, 1976).

26. Eleanor A. Maccoby, *The Two Sexes: Growing Up Apart, Coming Together* (Cambridge, MA: Belknap/Harvard University Press, 1998).

27. Fergus Kerr, "Thomas Aquinas," in *The Medieval Theologians: An Introduction to Theology in the Medieval Period*, ed. G. R. Evans, 206–8 (Oxford: Blackwell, 2001).

28. Emilie Zum Brunn and Georgette Epiney-Burgard, *Women Mystics in Medieval Europe*, trans. Sheila Hughes (St. Paul, MN: Paragon House, 1989), xxiv.

29. This sexual language seems to have begun with Cistercian influence on Hildegard and the Beguines, based on Bernard's *Sermons on the Song of Songs* (Brun and Epiney-Burgard, *Women Mystics*, xxv).

30. John Paul II, *Mulieris dignitatem*, AAS 79 (1988): #18.

31. See Pius XI, *Casti connubi*, AAS 22 (1930): #6.

A Pastoral Response to Christine Gudorf, "A New Moral Discourse on Sexuality"

Harold D. Horell

I begin this pastoral response by thanking Christine Gudorf for her courage in calling for a new moral discourse on sexuality within the church. For years there has been, as Richard McCormick once noted, a "chill factor" in moral theology. The institutional church has often actively discouraged critically reflective scholarship in moral theology, and this has had a chilling effect on the field.[1] Because of her writings on sexual ethics, Gudorf is among those theologians whose work has been criticized by representatives of the institutional church and whose livelihood has been threatened. Yet, Gudorf has never given in or given up. On the one hand, she has never quit raising critically reflective questions. On the other hand, she has continued to be involved actively in the church and has remained in dialogue with the resources of Christian traditions and official church teachings.

The church as a whole owes Christine Gudorf a debt of gratitude for her work in sexual ethics. Her work has enabled us to recognize ways in which our sexual teaching is based on an inadequate understanding of sexuality. She has also helped us to see why some of our sexual teachings no longer resonate with the life experiences of a majority of Catholics, and she has offered constructive proposals for how we can re-envision these teachings so that they can be life-giving and life-sustaining guides for people today.

GUDORF'S SIGNIFICANT CONTRIBUTIONS

First, Gudorf's work helps the church to recognize and respond to the challenges to our sexual teachings posed by contemporary research in the biological and social sciences. In discussing personhood and conception, sex/gender identity, homosexuality, cohabitation, and other issues, Gudorf shows how we need to incorporate an awareness of contemporary scientific research into our theological reflections if we are to present credible positions about human sexuality and sexual issues. (At various times in the past the church has lost credibility because we ignored or even tried to suppress new scientific research. For example, because we as a church clung to outdated Aristotelian scientific views and refused to accept the mounting evidence in favor of a Copernican paradigm for science, we persecuted Galileo Galilei and, in the process, lost credibility among many of the people of that time.) While it can be difficult to admit that some current church teachings concerning sexuality have been invalidated by the findings of scientific research, Gudorf has done the church a great service by calling us to assess the extent to which our sexual teachings are based on inaccurate or outdated data and need to be revised.

Second, Gudorf's analysis of church sexual teaching demonstrates the value of adopting a practical or pastoral focus that is informed by collegial discussions. More fully, throughout her reflections Gudorf draws insight from historical, sociological, and scientific research. However, her analysis always has a practical/pastoral focus and is guided by insights from her participation in collegial discussions about human sexuality. (In the introduction to her chapter, Gudorf points out that the framework for understanding human sexuality that she presents "has, for the most part, been worked out over the last forty years through *discussions among* perhaps *a few hundred theologians*, both clerical and lay, *and many thousands of lay Catholics.*")[2] Overall, Gudorf is attentive to the life experiences of the people of the church. She is sensitive to how people experience God in their lives, especially their sexuality. And, as she builds upon insights from practical experience, she offers clear and sensible guides for evaluating expressions of human sexuality. For example, Gudorf's words have the ring of practical truth when she notes, "What works against the believability of all sexual sins as grave is that it is simply impossible to understand masturbation or contraception, much less an unintentional sexually arousing thought, as able to cut one off from God in the same way that mass murder, violent rape, human torture and mutilation, or any number of other horrible acts of violence do."[3]

In her conclusion Gudorf comments, "One of these days, the hierarchy of the Catholic Church is going to consult its laity about where God is present in their sexual lives."[4] Gudorf's work outlines some of the issues that would need to be addressed in a consultative discussion by the institutional church with the members of the church about sexuality. Moreover, it shows how honest discussions about sexuality can lead to greater pastoral insight that can become the foundation for a renewed theology of human sexuality.

GUDORF'S ANALYSIS RAISES
MANY IMPORTANT QUESTIONS

There are two areas in particular in which I think further reflection could lead us to even greater insight about human sexuality. First, in her discussion of "the centrality of sex/gender for personhood" and "sexual dimorphism and complementarity," Gudorf notes that characteristics often associated with maleness and femaleness actually name traits accessible to all, and she indicates that we should strive to move beyond our reliance on male/female traits. In reviewing Gudorf's analysis I suggest we ask: To what extent have understandings of "maleness" and "femaleness" been socially useful constructs that support the personal and social flourishing of human life? Would it really be beneficial to give up all understandings of maleness and femaleness?

Based on my pastoral and life experiences, I think that understandings of "maleness" and "femaleness" can continue to be useful guides in many situations. For instance, inviting a couple preparing for marriage to think about "maleness" and "femaleness" can help them to reflect upon the biological differences in male and female sexual energies and qualities they want to embody in their relationship with one another. Similarly, fathers and mothers can sometimes be led to deepen their relationships with their children by reflecting on how the dynamic energies of "maleness" and "femaleness" can be embodied in father-and-son, father-and-daughter, mother-and-son, and mother-and-daughter relationships. And, attending to the nuances of "male spirituality" can help us to understand why some men do not get involved in parish life, and it can provide a foundation for pastoral outreach to men.

However, Gudorf's analysis heightens our awareness of the injustices of using sex/gender roles to support sexism or discriminate against homosexual persons and couples. She also makes us aware of the need for greater openness and adaptability in defining sex/gender roles when she points out that "biologists today tell us that there are six indicators of biological sex, and that for many millions of people these indicators do not line up in any simple dimorphic pattern."[5] Moreover, as Cecero notes, we need to be aware of the difficulties that can develop because of gender role rigidity.[6] When gender roles are too narrowly or statically defined, or female and male qualities are too sharply contrasted or divided, a variety of personal and social problems can arise. Still, when "maleness" and "femaleness" are seen as useful yet limited categories for helping us to make sense of our lives and world, they can retain a social value.

Second, Gudorf argues that we need to abandon the teaching that personhood is present from conception. She bases her claims on recent scientific research that shows that "there is no 'moment' of conception" and that conception is a process that is not complete until sometime between twelve and twenty-four hours after intercourse. Gudorf also notes that traditional understandings of personhood as beginning at conception are challenged by research showing "that identical twins do not separate until twelve to fifteen days after fertilization."[7] Gudorf, however, does not mention that abandoning church teaching about personhood and conception makes the church's prohibition of abortion more difficult to sustain. Specifically, once we recognize that conception is not complete until up to twenty-four hours after intercourse and that a uniquely identifiable person may not be present until fifteen days after fertilization, we can no longer base opposition to abortion on the claim that there is a fetus who is a unique person with a right to life from the "moment" of conception onward. Moreover, once we take the recent research on conception and personhood into account, we need to admit that men and women of good will may disagree about the morality or immorality of abortion.

Still, even when recent research on conception and personhood is taken into account, I think a strong case can be made that the practice of abortion is morally problematic. Stated briefly, it can be argued that moral awareness and ethical reflection are based on a sensitivity to all life, especially the life of human persons. This also includes a sensitivity to the life and flourishing of human communities and a concern for the natural environment as a living system. A general or unconditional acceptance of abortion is morally problematic because it fails to respect the life energy that is in the process of formation during conception, developing into a person or persons in the early developmental period after conception, and is a living but dependent person during most of the stages of pregnancy. Socially, a general or unconditional acceptance of abortion is morally problematic because it contributes to a lack of respect for life and dulling of sensitivity to life that is, and perhaps always has been, a major social problem.

FURTHER REFLECTION AND DISCUSSION NEEDED

My comments on gender identity and abortion, as well as all of Gudorf's provocative analysis, raise more questions than they answer. Generally, we need more forums within the church today where we can discuss sex, sexuality, and sexual issues. Gudorf's work can serve as a useful starting point for such discussions.

NOTES

1. Richard McCormick, *The Critical Calling: Reflections on Moral Dilemmas since Vatican II* (Washington, D.C.: Georgetown University Press, 1989), 71–107.

2. Gudorf, "A New Moral Discourse on Sexuality," in this volume, 51 (emphasis added).

3. Ibid., 56.

4. Ibid., 67.

5. Ibid., 55.

6. Cecero, "Toward Christian Sexual Maturity," in this volume, 37.

7. Gudorf, "A New Moral Discourse on Sexuality," in this volume, 56.

5

Sexuality and Relationships in Ministry

Sidney Callahan

What are we going to pass on to future generations when it comes to Christian sexuality and morality? Many riches exist in our Catholic sexual tradition but these goods have been obscured and undeveloped. The struggle is now joined to develop a new integrated and coherent view of sexuality that is true to the Gospel. On the birth of a new millennium it is vital for the church to respond to new issues presented by scientific and social knowledge.

Unfortunately, the horror and shame of the sexual abuse crisis can turn many Catholics off the whole subject of sexuality. Many of the faithful have given up on efforts to connect human sexuality with Christian discipleship. They may be critical of the secular world's view of sex, which can be judged as promoting a promiscuous trivialization of sexuality that endangers men, women, marriages, families, adolescents, children, and the unborn—but what else is there? What does the church have to offer?

Quite a lot, actually. Our ever-reforming church gives us good and heartening news about sexuality, without jettisoning the realism and prudence of the tradition. There is good news to be reclaimed, bad news to be banished, and cautionary considerations to be taken into account. Let's start with the good news.

THE GOOD NEWS

Christians affirm that human sexuality is God's good creation and it matters. We *are* our bodies. The body-mind unity insisted upon by modern science is not news for Christians.[1] Believers in the resurrection of the body know that human beings are not ethereal souls floating through this life. Human beings are embodied creations that will live forever corporeally transformed in joy. No disdain or disregard for the flesh can be accepted by those who believe God becomes fully human in the Incarnation.

Whatever we Christian disciples do, "in word or work," we do for the glory of God. And human sexuality, with all of its multifaceted complexity, is definitely included in our movements toward God. Minute by minute we are cocreating our eternal selves through all of our thoughts, fantasies, emotions and bodily actions. As Pope John Paul II teaches, there exists a language of the body which humans employ in their sexual activity.[2] The morality of sexuality is not separate from the growth toward a converted heart, upright character, and mature virtue.[3]

At long last Christians are getting over the old dualistic suspicions of sexuality. In part, this older view grew up from ancient disdain for the body which was corruptible, animalistic, emotional, and irrational, and thus to be repressed and controlled. Women were included in this disdain and judged to be unclean and inferior. Bodily emissions were polluting, especially the blood of menstruation and childbirth—as were lapses of emotional control.[4]

The Christian good news about sexuality began when Jesus was born of woman and became fully human. God validates embodied life. Jesus proceeded to preach and witness against many things, including the purity taboos that declared any of God's children unclean. Christ had women as friends and measured his disciples' charity by their physical serving, healing, and meeting of others' bodily needs. Jesus ate and drank with all, and cured the blind and the deaf by prayer and mud mixed with his saliva.

Today, embodied sexuality and pleasure is being rehabilitated and appreciated.[5] We can now appreciate the goodness of involuntary responses. It was the involuntary and seemingly uncontrollable nature of emotional and sexual responses that worried St. Augustine and led him (along with his modern followers) to think of sexuality as shameful. Having a new understanding of the way the brain and body work, we can be reassured by how adaptive some of our involuntary responses can be. Think of the immune system or perceptual processes. Moreover, the best things of life, such as creativity and new ideas, just arrive from God as good gifts. Love, pleasure, and joy are not achievements of the will.

The involuntary pleasures of sexuality and the ecstasies of orgasm can now be seen as good; they are not little deaths but little births and surprise presents from God. Once you affirm that God lovingly gives GodSelf to the world in Christ, with nothing held back, you validate ecstasy. Total, complete, physical self-giving acts of love imitate God. The high joys and pleasure of loving sexuality can be seen as a preview of the graced communion of heaven. Traditional images of the kingdom as the marriage of the Lamb and a joyful wedding feast affirm this truth.

One of the best things about the good news of human sexual intercourse is that while it takes place within an ongoing conversation, it includes more than words can tell. Love and mutual assent are marked by touch, gesture, and shared emotions, sometimes of a comic nature.[6] Sex can be seen as a form of high play and celebration. Like all communal play, sexuality demands mutual courtesy and tactful care for the others in the game. Before diving into deep waters or losing one's self in the dance, the mutual consent must be assessed as appropriate. Once immersed in the exhilarating swim or in the self-forgetful flow of altered consciousness, there springs up a mutual delight that heals life's wounds and waters the deserts of duty. Past fears and hurts from bodily rejection can be overcome.

Married people have experienced the truth that unity and love are recreated and nourished by sexual intercourse. Today theologians see ongoing marital acts of lovemaking as a way of recalling and reaffirming the couple's consent and commitment to their marriage.[7] In an intimate loving marital friendship, two become one and create a community. Just as the celebration of the Eucharist recalls and reinstitutes our essential Christian relationship of communion, so does sexual lovemaking.

The mystery of Christ being one with the whole church and simultaneously living within each individual is also reproduced in marital union. Two individuals give to each other, create a united life, and yet increase and grow as individuals within the relationship. Losing the self in giving is a way of gaining one's self, as found in the absorbed psychological states called "flow." This surprise is another of God's win-win games. The staying power of marital commitment gives a solid ground with enough space and time to get your act together and learn to love and be loved.

Another truth in the Christian tradition of sexuality is that children are wondrous gifts. The miracle of birth begins the good and creative life of the world anew. Babies are like the fire in the hearth, focusing and magnifying the bonds of love in the couple, and in the grandparents. In this sense the procreative and unitive ends of sex work together.[8] But it is also true that the procreative end can be fulfilled in a psychosexual generativity, as well as through biological offspring.[9] Sexuality flourishes when it is fruitfully enlarged by giving to others.

Evolutionary thinkers emphasize anew the centrality of reproduction in sexuality. Sex is nature's way to spur evolution onward by ensuring new generations that can survive through the extended parental caretaking that big-brained animals like Homo sapiens require. The sexual pair bonding strengthens mutual parenting and also produces kinship ties. Families formed through mating provide care for the sick and old, as well as for survival of the young.

Happily, Christian requirements for human flourishing go beyond a reductive biological focus on survival of the species. Humans possess free will and the self-reflective ability to make promises and stick to them.[10] Chastity, continence, and sexual fidelity are possible for humankind and work for the well being of the group. Keeping commitments strengthens trust and security within a community.

Religiously vowed celibates for the sake of God's kingdom also help the flourishing human groups. They increase the trust and religious resources of a community. Those who dedicate their love and sexual energy to the praise and service of God and neighbor bear fruit for the whole community's life. Vowed celibacy is a witness to the power of the unseen reality of God's Spirit. The Kingdom of God is real; the kingdom is coming and has begun.

In an earlier day dedicated religious celibacy was considered superior to marriage as the main way to holiness. But no more justifications exist for the second-class status of marriage, now that the underlying prejudices against the body and women have been overcome and officially corrected. Theologians now know that it was a mistake to think of God as another being in the universe who might compete for love with that of a spouse.[11] A God of infinite love is the ground of all being, and exists where love is.

But sometimes whiffs of prejudice against marital love and sexuality as a less committed state than the religious life still waft about. When a theologian speaks of "mere genitality," the phrase is tinged with the bias and purity taboos of old. No one who attempts to live a sexual relationship of love and genital generosity is going to use an adjective like "mere." Sometimes too, in the effort to offset past prejudices, defenders of sexuality seem to deny the specific focused power and programmed development of human sexuality by blurring sex with all forms of embodiment. I think reality is better served by seeing human bodily life as consisting of far more than sexual capacities and powers. All embodied energy is not sexual, as a pansexual theorist like Freud might have it. A mother nursing her child is engaging in an act of embodiment but not of sexuality; an aged sick person being fed is partaking in an embodied relationship but not a sexual one.

Finally, another distinct gift of the Christian sexual tradition, often ignored in practice, has been the assertion of moral equality between men and women in their sexual moral obligations and marital rights. This demand for equality in a monogamous marriage was a revolutionary move. Christians freed women and men from subordinating their sexuality to the family lineage, the state's need for manpower, or the market's demands for pleasure. The vocation of dedicated female virginity was particularly important in giving women's bodies and lives intrinsic dignity. Women flocked to Christianity in response.[12]

The requirement of free mutual consent of the individuals in contracting a marriage also attacked the family and the state's power over sexuality. Of course, we are so used to ideals of autonomy, freedom, and equality between the sexes that we hardly notice this positive Christian sexual tradition—until we confront cultures where women are controlled and oppressed. And with the concern for women's condition we are forced to face the dark side of human sexuality.

CAUTIONS IN THE CHRISTIAN TRADITION OF SEXUALITY TO BE TAKEN SERIOUSLY

Since sexuality is a good and central to embodied human life, it follows that sexuality can be distorted and misused. Realistically it has to be admitted that all powers and goods can be abused. Religion, family, the gift of language, reason, and inventive technology can be used for evil ends. The human sexual condition includes sexual abuse, sexual torture, and sexual exploitation of the vulnerable by the strong. In the same way, selfish aggression, greed, domination, and war have always afflicted and exploited humankind. Evils also feed upon each other. AIDS ravages the undeveloped world just as the sexual traffic in women and children takes advantage of a society's sexism and poverty. War and imprisonment breed rape and sexual torture.

The Christian tradition has been realistic about the fact that greed and sexual desire can distort human thought and behavior. Human beings are subject to temptations for gratifications at the expense of others. The drive for pleasure and power has always produced influences that can affect the will, blind the conscience, or induce self-deception. Christians have always asserted that there is some inner division in human beings that must be integrated. Ascetics striving for holiness have taken vows of poverty, obedience, and sexual abstinence.

Sexually active persons today who seek to reconnect their sexuality with Christian discipleship will have to be prudent and develop new and appropriate examinations of conscience.[13] To be innocent as a dove, a modern Christian has to be shrewder than a serpent. If sexuality is a fundamental language of the body I must ask whether I am speaking the truth, or even the whole truth? Language is a useful analogy for thinking about the ethics of sexuality. Do I mean what I say and do what I mean? Have I indulged in willful ignorance about the effect of my sexual behavior for others? As always, the practice of justice, care, courage, and responsibility is required to achieve sexual virtue. Developing character and good-heartedness is a process of conversion.

Deploring past prejudices and failings of the church toward sexuality doesn't justify ignoring the present pitfalls in a culture that trivializes, markets, and exploits sexuality. Sexual dangers may have been overemphasized in past ascetic traditions that disdained sexual embodiment and ecstasy, but then earlier Christians were dealing with Caligula-style decadence, sexual exploitation of slaves, women's inequality, and all the cruel horrors of the Roman Empire followed by barbarian invasions. Today only the naïve would deny the widespread harm arising from spousal and child sexual abuse, STDs, abortion, prostitution, rape, and other sexual evils. Yet there is still hope for a better future.

MOVING TO A BALANCED FUTURE

A living tradition responds to the Holy Spirit and evolves. The authoritative sources for development in the church are Scripture, church teachings, reason, liturgical prayer, and human experience. Certainly, human experiences of the dark side of sexuality have shaped past vigilance and suspicions of sexuality. Central moral teachings have evolved everywhere to regulate sexuality because of the natural consequences inherent in group life of immoral behavior. Adultery and selfish sexual exploitation engender hate, distrust, and social chaos. Prostitution soils the spirit, lust degrades, promiscuity debases emotions, breeds disease, and increases abortion.

Christians need to integrate the positive goodness of sexuality into our teaching and pastoral practice. The positive experiences of Christian disciples trying to be responsive to the Spirit in active sexual lives have not yet become fully articulated or accessible. Unfortunately, the way the church is currently organized leaves little opportunity for hierarchical celibate leaders to listen to the experience of lay Christians. The sense of the married faithful has been more or less silenced.

Another ironic condition that suppresses the good news of Christian experiences of sexuality is tactful courteousness. Mature persons do not wish to publicize their intimate sexual experiences of joy and love. The vulgarity of current tell-all media displays makes this point. Have these poor people no sense of privacy, family loyalty, or the boundaries of self-respecting behavior?

Thus, the bad news is publicized and the church hears little of the good news. For example, a point I have never heard mentioned anywhere before, even by me, is the parental hope that one's adult children have turned out to be good lovers, and tender, playful sexual partners. This particular vindication of one's embodied legacy and childrearing must remain hidden, since otherwise the privacy appropriate to families would be violated. But sexual development and marriage preparation will continue in and out of the church and the Spirit blows where it will. Truth has a way of dispelling falsity while love casts out fear. Peers can help peers, as various marriage and sexual education programs have found.

Perhaps too, those working out their sexual morality in new and uncertain sexual situations have the most to give to other seekers. After fifty years I know how to be a faithfully married spouse and I think I understand how one can live a vowed celibate and holy religious life. But what will discipleship mean for the single or young career women desiring marriage, or a divorced father, or a young gay person? Are there new forms of moral cohabitation evolving among those delaying marriage in changed social conditions? I don't know. It seems difficult to make the transition from experimentation to commitment. And it must be even more of a challenge to search for love while you remain committed to promise keeping. But I belong to a learning church and I am willing to listen and learn.

Surely the witness, character, and experience of those in the present community of Christians are going to be decisive in the church's achievement of sexual balance. A final grace note that should be sounded here in conclusion is that there also exist resources in the creative imagination. Art allows us to have vicarious human experience. Scripture gives light to God's core truths, and novels, poetry, music, and movies provide complementary sources of insight. The Spirit leads us gradually but surely in every dimension of life. The educated heart has learned to laugh, playfully rejoice in sexual gratitude, *and* stand steadfast in the Truth.

NOTES

1. Lisa Cahill, *Sex, Gender & Christian Ethics* (Cambridge: Cambridge University Press, 1996).

2. Pope John Paul II in numerous writings that can be found on the Vatican website www.vatican.va; see also Mary Shivanandan, *Crossing The Threshold Of Love: A New Vision of Marriage in the Light of John Paul II's Anthropology* (Washington, D.C.: The Catholic University of America Press, 1999).

3. John S. Grabowski, *Sex and Virtue: An Introduction to Sexual Ethics* (Washington, D.C.: The Catholic University of America Press, 2003).

4. Peter Brown, *Body and Society: Men, Women and Sexual Renunciation in Early Christianity* (New York: Columbia University Press, 1988).

5. Christine E. Gudorf, *Body, Sex, and Pleasure: Reconstructing Christian Sexual Ethics* (Cleveland, OH: The Pilgrim Press, 1994).

6. Richard R. Gaillardetz, *A Daring Promise: A Spirituality of Christian Marriage* (New York: Crossroad, 2002).

7. Grabowski, "Intercourse as Anamnesis: Theological Developments," in *Sex and Virtue,* 43–48.

8. James P. Hannigan, "Unitive and Procreative Meaning: The Inseparable Link," in *Sexual Diversity and Catholicism: Toward the Development of Moral Theology,* ed. Patricia Beattie Jung, with Joseph Andrew Coray, 22–38 (Collegeville, MN: The Liturgical Press, 2001).

9. Margaret Monahan Hogan, *Marriage as a Relationship* (Milwaukee, WI: Marquette University Press, 2002).

10. Margaret A. Farley, *Just Love: Sexual Ethics and Social Change* (New York: Continuum, 1997).

11. Karl Rahner, "Love," in *The Practice of Faith: A Handbook of Contemporary Spirituality,* (New York: Crossroad, 1986), 117–42.

12. Rodney Stark, *The Rise of Christianity: A Sociologist Reconsiders History* (Princeton: Princeton University Press, 1996).

13. Kevin T. Kelly, *New Directions in Sexual Ethics* (London: Geoffrey Chapman, 1998).

A Pastoral Response to Sidney Callahan, "Sexuality and Relationships in Ministry"

Kieran Scott

I am honored and feel privileged to have the opportunity to respond to Sidney Callahan. Dr. Callahan has been a lucid voice, one of the most responsible voices and one of the richest, reformist, and centrist voices in nearly all things Roman Catholic in our lifetime. Her gifts and charism shine forth in her presentation.

I will briefly raise a few points that I see as signs of grace, and offer a short commentary that is a logical extension of her proposals.

To begin, Dr. Callahan's diagnosis of the disordered forms of sexuality in the ecclesia (and beyond) seems accurate and credible to me. I also agree that some of our present teachings on sex and gender are contributing to the current disarray. As Dr. Callahan notes elsewhere, the last thing we need is a "reaffirmation of rigid teachings which are seriously flawed morally and theologically."[1] This only weakens the church's moral authority, and places her pastoral ministers in endless dilemmas or on a collision course with church officials.

On the other hand, for Sidney Callahan, diagnosis is insufficient. There must be a cure for the disorder/disease. She finds it deep at the center of the tradition's life. She reclaims and reshapes our Catholic sacramental vision, but also inserts a healthy dose of the Protestant (critical) principle. Callahan is concerned with authentic traditioning. She asks: What wisdom are we Roman Catholics going to pass on to the next generation on sexual morality? Since Vatican II, theological infighting and controversies have tended to obscure many of the riches that lie in the bosom of the tradition. We do have good news to proclaim on sexuality.

83

Callahan's first move is affirmation: we believe in the goodness of sexual embodiment, the goodness of the joys and pleasure of loving sexually, the goodness of committed love, and the goodness of gender equality. Children are wondrous gifts and vowed celibacy can be a witness to the unseen reality of God's Spirit. A healthy Christian sexuality does not attack or deny what has already been redeemed. There can be no distain or disregard for the flesh for those who believe in the Incarnation.

On the other hand, Callahan warns against sexual naiveté. Sexuality can be distorted and misused. The drive for pleasure and power can affect the will, blind the conscience, or induce self-deception. The evidence is widespread: spousal and child sexual abuse, STDs, prostitution, rape, and human sexual trafficking, etc. These sexual evils cannot be ignored. Callahan's second move is a firm resistance and negation: saying NO to sexual abuse in its multiple forms; NO to the trivializing, marketing, and exploitation of sexuality in church and society. Sex matters for Sidney Caliahan.[2] She knows it can be a divine or demonic force.

For the third step, Callahan takes us beyond this negativity. There is a need to reconnect our sexuality to Christian discipleship. This calls for prudence and development of new and appropriate examinations of conscience. Do I mean what I say and do what I mean sexually? "As always," Professor Callahan notes, "the practice of justice, care, courage, and responsibility is required to achieve sexual virtue."

What might be some logical pastoral extensions of Dr. Callahan's project? In the broadest terms, it could be stated simply: if one wishes to transform sexuality and relationships in ministry, transform the political design of the organization. Roman Catholicism has an organizational problem. Its current design is semi-authoritarian, a caste structure, and an Exhibit A in sexist pattern. Each of these "isms" erects barriers to mutual sexual relations at every level in our ministerial lives. They are wounds on the Body of Christ.[3] They are lifetraps in the ecclesia—crippling it as a sacramental sexual community.

In the briefest of terms, I would suggest a threefold educational strategy and response. I will frame it in the form of three questions:

1. Do we need a new framework to understand our current crisis?
2. Do we need a new language to understand ourselves?
3. Do we need new structures to organize our common life in ways that facilitate the collaboration of men and women in ministry?

In our current ecclesial context, the questions, I believe, are the correct ones. The answers have profound pastoral implications for the whole religious body.

A NEW FRAMEWORK FOR UNDERSTANDING

The crisis in the Roman Catholic Church in the last four years is the most dramatic example of how questions about power/authority and sexual morality have become intertwined over the past several decades. Together they threaten the integrity of the church. You cannot separate the crisis of authority from the crisis of lack of legitimation of official church teaching on an array of sexual matters. They are inextricably tied together. In the Roman Catholic Church, Charles Curran writes, "Whenever sexuality and authority meet, a volatile situation is bound to result."[4] Issues of ecclesiology inevitably arise: questions of patterns of power; questions of the source of authority; questions of legitimate dissent.

There is a need for critical understanding of the institutional form in which we are immersed. The patriarchal form of the Roman Catholic Church and its teachings on sexuality cannot be denied. Its exclusion of women from any kind of significant decision-making role still prevails. As Sidney Callahan mournfully notes, "The way the church is currently organized leaves little opportunity for hierarchical celibate leaders to listen to the experience of lay Christians. The sense of the married faithful has been more or less silenced." The problem should not be personalized, individualized, or trivialized. The problem is the institution's inherent sexism, its pervasive clericalism, its heterosexism, and its imperial religious claims. This is at the heart of the matter and at the root of our problems.

A NEW LANGUAGE FOR UNDERSTANDING OURSELVES

One cannot change an institution while accepting uncritically its terms of self-description. Naming is power. And how we name and categorize ourselves shapes how we deal with problems.

For example, it is Roman Catholic practice to describe a parish by the number of families. This is misleading. Why? This language and (description) eliminates the other—all people who do not fit its family category. Not everyone lives in the sexual form we call family. It is not the only sexual game in town.[5] Does our parish language reflect the great number of widows, divorced people, single persons, and gay and lesbian persons in our midst? Do many of our programs exclude them by self-definition? There may be a need, at times, for some of these groups to have their own parish organizations. But our overall aim should be communities that cut across these divisions in liturgical settings, catechetical settings, outreach settings, and settings of hospitality.

A parish or local church is a sexual community.[6] It should be a place to open up communication and interplay between the familial and non-familial forms of life. This would be profoundly enriching and educational. But we cannot get there from here. We need a language for discussion to more adequately name the variety of sexual forms in our midst. We need a more inclusive language to understand who, in fact, we are. Two strategies are needed here: first to engage in linguistic resistance to the current exclusive familial category, and second, to offer an inclusive counterdiscourse to the prevailing one.

This will be a slow but seminal process. We all experienced this phenomenon in the reshaping of our everyday sexist language some forty years ago. With this reshaping came a corresponding reconstruction of consciousness and conduct. A similar linguistic conversion is called for that acknowledges the variety of sexual forms in the Body of Christ. Language is action. The employment of an inclusive pastoral language that is representative of the whole community would give witness to what we profess and sing: all are welcome; all are welcome; all are welcome in this place.

NEW STRUCTURES

If we are to live our vocation as an inclusive sexual community of hospitality, new structures are inevitable. Our task is to imagine them so that we might bring them into existence. If we are to get at the heart of the matter, we need to be concrete about what these might look like, and, at the same time, note the shortcomings with which we currently have to work. The way we organize our common sexual life together ought to reflect our religious values—namely, love, justice, and table fellowship. Sidney Callahan declares, "Surely the witness, character, and experience of those in the present community of Christians are going to be decisive in the church's achievement of sexual balance." Creative recourses are available to aid us in imagining such a grace-filled sexual life together. And, once again, some of the richest sources are deep within our own tradition. Revelation is one of those resources.

Revelation is a set of relations in which the divine is revealed.[7] It is a present, personal, living interaction. It is a kind of relation: receptive listening and deep responding. It is a mode of relating that is redemptive, healing, and salvific. In other words, redesigning our lives together, with a sense of mutuality and reciprocity, allows us to practice revelation. It enables the Spirit of God to be present in all our really real sexual relations. It is the mission of the church to practice this revelation. However, our current church institution needs new forms, new structures, new policies, and new teachings in order to facilitate these revelatory experiences in the lives of its people.

NOTES

1. Sidney Callahan, "Stunted Teaching on Sex Has Role in Church's Crisis," *National Catholic Reporter*, March 21, 2003, 12.

2. Sidney Callahan, "Sex Matters," *National Catholic Reporter*, March 19, 2004, 10–11.

3. Eugene Cullen Kennedy, "Healing the Wound: The Sacraments and Human Sexuality," *National Catholic Reporter*, October 3, 2003, 13–16.

4. Charles E. Curran, "Roman Catholic Sexual Ethics: A Dissenting View," in *Sexual Ethics and the Church: A Christian Century Symposium*, introduction and conclusion by James B. Nelson (Chicago: The Christian Century, 1989), 51.

5. Gabriel Moran, "Family and Community: The Way We Are: Communal Forms and Church Response," in *Parish Religious Education*, ed. Maria Harris, 25–40 (Mahwah, NJ: Paulist Press, 1978).

6. James Nelson, "The Church as Sexual Community," in *Embodiment* (Minneapolis, MN: Augsburg, 1978), 236–71.

7. Gabriel Moran, *Both Sides: The Story of Revelation* (Mahwah, NJ: Paulist, 2002).

II

SPECIFIC ISSUES

6

Engaging the Struggle: John Paul II on Personhood and Sexuality

Jennifer Bader

INTRODUCTION

In the years before his death, John Paul II became a force to be reckoned with in what he himself called the "great and fundamental contest for the essence of man."[1] Since his election to the papacy in 1979, Karol Wojtyla/ John Paul II's moral philosophy, philosophical anthropology, and theological reflections, including reflections on human sexuality, have had an undeniable effect on Catholic theology, especially in the areas of anthropology and ethics. We hear not only of his defining influence on a particular school of theology that transcends national boundaries, but also of the efforts of this school to popularize his theology of the human person in parishes, Catholic schools, and university Newman clubs.[2] Indeed, the pope who succeeded him, while a theologian in his own right, embraces key points in John Paul II's theology of human sexuality, as is evident from the document on the collaboration of women and men in the church promulgated by the Congregation of the Doctrine of the Faith in 2004.[3] For example, the document criticizes forms of feminist thought that define gender as both culturally constructed and disengaged from sex, which most feminist theologians define as the biological fact of being male or female.

What is at stake here is our understanding of what it means to be human and, thus, what it means to be sexual beings. Indeed, John Paul II recognized these stakes and focused much of his papal writings on issues of the relationship between human personhood and sexual difference. Ultimately, in a Christian context, what is at stake is the ability and claim of both women and men to be in the person of Christ—and to speak and act as such. While many feminist theologians have also recognized these high stakes, the places, voices, and experiences of women in particular have yet to hold a secure place of authority in the church and its theological tradition. John Paul II himself recognized the sin of sexism in the church and made significant strides to overcome it. The fact that it still exists in church structure, theology, and teaching is a sad witness to the insidiousness of sexism.

With these stakes in mind, this chapter will examine Karol Wojtyla/John Paul II's understandings of personhood, the body, and sexual difference for potential contributions and limitations toward a holistic understanding of human sexuality. By holistic, I mean an understanding of human sexuality that considers the human being from a perspective that flows from the creation in the *imago Dei* as a human person, a self, and a beloved of God, in which all parts and elements are considered *good*, and all are integrated into one's personal being, from which flows one's unique and unrepeatable identity and vocation. Such an understanding avoids historically, psychologically, and spiritually harmful dualistic hierarchies, such as body/soul, rational/affective, and male/female. Only such an anthropology can be consistent with the dignity of the human person, which arises from a unique relationship to God and is expressed in Genesis 1:17 as the *imago Dei*. In fact, this standard of the *imago Dei* is one shared by John Paul II himself.

In this chapter, I focus not on constructing a theology of human sexuality, or even a complete critique of Karol Wojtyla/John Paul II's thought on the subject, but rather on exploring selected salient themes in his writings for strengths and limits of his thought toward that end. First, I will briefly discuss features and themes of his anthropology that form the philosophical and theological foundations of his theology of human sexuality, especially sexual difference. These include his philosophical method, his treatment of the unity of the human person and human experience, the relationship between person and body, and pre- and post-lapsarian anthropologies. Then I will dive more deeply into his theology of sexual difference itself. After each of the above analyses, I will offer a critical summary of its strengths and limits for a holistic understanding of human sexuality as defined above.

FOUNDATIONS

Philosophical Influences and Method

Karol Wojtyla/John Paul II was convinced that he was engaged in a cosmic battle for the soul of humankind. Originally, he waged this crusade in the politically charged environment immediately during and following World War II, wherein the world did battle with Nazism, and then afterward, when the ideology of communism became pervasive in Poland. He writes:

> Ours is an age of violent controversy concerning man, the essential meaning of his existence, and, consequently, the nature and value of this being. It is not the first time that Christian philosophy has been confronted by materialist doctrine. But it is the first time that materialism has mustered such a wide variety of resources and expressed itself in so many different ways as it now does in Poland in the political climate spawned by a dialectical Marxism that seeks to capture men's minds . . . The discussion about man's role in the world over the past twenty years in Poland clearly shows what the heart of the matter is: It is not just a question of cosmology and natural philosophy; it is a question of philosophical anthropology and ethics—it is the great and fundamental contest for the essence of man.[4]

It is within this historical context that Karol Wojtyla developed his unique synthesis of Schelerian phenomenology and Thomistic scholasticism.[5] From Thomas Aquinas, he takes his understanding of objective moral values and how such values contribute to or detract from the good of the human person. From Max Scheler, Wojtyla takes his phenomenological treatment of human experience. Scholar Michael Novak asserts that utilizing Scheler's phenomenological method is Wojtyla's way of being holistic. "Phenomenology is a sustained effort to bring back into philosophy everyday things, concrete wholes, the basic experiences of life as they come to us." Phenomenology rescues these things from the empiricists, who reduce them to sense data, and the idealists, who "break them up into ideal categories, and forms."[6] Nevertheless, the value of Max Scheler's work for Wojtyla lies in describing the experience of personal and therefore ethical realities.[7] Jaroslaw Kupczak asserts, "Wojtyla emphasizes that Scheler was right in asserting that the method needed for ethics is the phenomenological method, because it grasps the entire content of human experience, including its ethical dimension."[8]

For example, Wojtyla/John Paul II insists that human knowledge is gained in lived experience rather than through a fictional, disembodied "pure" reason. This insistence on human experience as holistic is especially obvious when he speaks of the human being's experience and intuition of self as person and subject, as well as in his treatment of affectivity and relationality. His emphasis on relationality and affectivity is also highlighted when he speaks of interpersonal relationships, participation, and *communio personarum*. The philosopher Wojtyla discusses this communion of persons as the communion formed when persons enter into I-Thou relationships, in which each relates to the other through self-giving and with the respect due to another person, another "I." In fact, John Paul II points out that the human being individually as well as humanity collectively becomes the image of God precisely in this communion of persons. In his discussion of this *communio*, Wojtyla/John Paul II never loses sight of the fact that it is impossible to give oneself to or accept another person fully without really *caring* about the other.[9]

Wojtyla/John Paul II's integration of his dual influences lends itself to a decidedly holistic understanding of the human person and therefore human sexuality. In insisting on an anthropology that relies on both metaphysics and phenomenology, Wojtyla integrates essence and existence, being and experience, into his understanding of what it means to be human. One of his greatest strengths is his view of *knowing* as experiential and intuitive rather than solely rational (which he gets from both Thomas and Scheler). Moreover, this understanding of knowledge as tied to human experience offers possibilities toward an integrated and holistic understanding of both sexual experience and sexual morality. This is most evident in his treatment of intuition, affectivity, and relationality, essential components to such a holistic understanding.

The Unity of the Human Person in Action

Wojtyla/John Paul II's chosen philosophical and theological task is to insist upon the *unity* of the human person.[10] He thus maintains that human experience is an organic whole, which contains both intellectual and sensual content due to the "dual structure" of the human person.[11] His philosophical starting point is his consideration of the *whole person* in the process of acting. Wojtyla recalls that in Aristotle's thought the unity of the human person was manifested especially in "the human act" (*actus humanus*). "The view that man is a psychosomatic unity presupposes the concept of the 'person' who manifests himself first of all in action." This is because in action, "the whole psychosomatic complexity develops into the specific person-action unity."[12] In other words, action unifies the intellectual and sensual content of human experience.

Wojtyla's insistence that the dual structure of the human person is unified in action is strength for a holistic understanding of human sexuality, especially in its ethical dimension as this pertains to human acts. At the same time, one must point out that Wojtyla accepts the idea of a dual structure—the intellectual content of the psyche and the sensual content of the body—that needs to be unified in the first place. In the interest of a holistic anthropology, including but not limited to an understanding of human sexuality, one must question this idea of dual structure. Indeed, the more we learn scientifically about the human being, the more we discover that the psyche, too, has a biological basis, as do thoughts, emotions, and experiences of well-being. As I will discuss in more depth later, Wojtyla's initial acceptance of the paradigm of a dual structure to the human person ultimately will lead to a hierarchical ordering[13] of person and body in his pre-papal philosophy as well as to ambiguity regarding the relationship between person and body in his later papal works. Indeed, this acknowledgement of duality between intellectual and sensual content belies an acceptance of the very Cartesian compartmentalization of the human that Wojtyla/John Paul II is fighting.

Person and Body in the Pre-Papal Writings

The philosopher Wojtyla articulates the relationship between the person and the body thus: "The dynamic transcendence of the person—spiritual by its very nature—finds in the human body the territory and the means of expression." The body belongs to and is subordinate to the person as the "territory and means of the manifestation of the soul, of the specific dynamism of its spiritual nature, and of freedom in its dynamic relation to truth." Wojtyla is careful to assert that the human being *is* not the body, but rather only *has* it, and speaks of the body as a "compliant tool." Moreover, as the means of expression of the person, the body plays an important role in human action for Wojtyla. "The ability to objectify the body and to employ it in acting is an important factor of the personal freedom of man."[14]

In these pre-papal writings, Wojtyla fails to completely counteract the Cartesian division between body and soul/mind/consciousness. His use of terms such as "compliant tool" and "means of expression" betrays a lingering Cartesian perspective, even while he insists that these separate (and unequal!) parts are integrated into the unity that is the human person. As will be discussed later in this chapter, this hierarchical ordering of body and soul will have a limiting effect on John Paul II's ability to posit a holistic understanding of human sexuality.

Person and Body in the Papal Writings

John Paul II's papal writings represent a significant development in his understanding of the relationship between body and person. In his theological reflections on the creation stories in Genesis he explores the human being's first consciousness of the body.[15] In this self-consciousness, the human being discovers the complexity and unity of the human psychosomatic anthropological structure. For John Paul II, nakedness in the pre-lapsarian context "signifies the original good of God's vision." It is the state or situation in which the human being does not know a "rupture and opposition" between the spiritual and sensible within the person.[16]

Therefore, in John Paul II's reflections on Genesis, the psychosomatic unity of the person seems more intimate and integrated than it appears in his pre-papal, philosophical works. In the papal writings, John Paul II insists on the simultaneity of being a body and being a person. He identifies the body not as the *means* of the expression of the person, but the *expression* of the person itself. "Man is a subject *not only* because of his self-awareness and self-determination, but also on the basis of his own body. The structure of this body permits him to be the author of a truly human activity. In this activity *the body expresses the person*," and again, "the body reveals man." John Paul II refers to the "very core of anthropological reality, the name of which is 'body.'" Moreover, the body "expresses the person in his ontological and existential concreteness. . . . Therefore, the body expresses the personal human self."[17]

However, John Paul II's language in the papal writings is not unambiguous. The human being's likeness to God as a person is what enables one to "transcend" and "dominate" one's visibility, corporeality, sex, and nakedness.[18] For John Paul II, this ability to transcend and dominate the human body is the basis of humanity's dominion over the rest of creation, which is given by God to humanity in Genesis and which is linked with the *imago Dei* in the biblical text.

The language of *domination* rather than *integration* connotes a reference to Wojtyla's earlier assertion that the body is a "means" that must be dominated by the person, to whom it is subordinate. Nevertheless, the language in the papal writings represents a much more holistic perspective on the relationship between person and body than does his pre-papal work, wherein Wojtyla asserts that the person is "spiritual by its very nature" and that the body is the means and locale of the person's self-expression.

Pre- and Post-Lapsarian Anthropologies

Why this ambiguity in his writing? On the one hand there is the stark contrast between the pre-papal philosophical works, in which Wojtyla speaks of the body as a "compliant tool" in the service of the person, and his papal theological reflections, in which the body is "the core of anthropological reality." In the pre-papal writings, Wojtyla posits a distinctly hierarchical relationship between body and person; in the papal theological reflections, John Paul II *identifies* the body with the person. Yet, at certain places in the papal writings, one still detects an echo of this previous way of thinking which seems to exist in tension with his new, more holistic view of the person.

I suggest that this tension is due, first, to a methodological difference between philosophy and theology. Second, this tension is due to John Paul II's understanding of the fall. These are interrelated factors. In his philosophical writings, his starting point in reflecting on human personhood is human experience. In this phenomenological treatment of human experience, the philosopher Wojtyla cannot help but take note of the *experience* of internal division that is common to most actual human persons. In his theological writings, on the other hand, his understanding of the human person is informed by revelation and grace. In other words, John Paul II, in theologically reflecting on Genesis, can discern the "original goodness of God's intention"—that is, the human created as a beautifully integrated whole, fully alive and in grace. Therefore, he concludes, any existing and experienced divisions within the person must be a result of the fall. For John Paul II, the fall of humanity has a direct and radical effect on the reality of the holistic integration of the human person.

A brief exploration of John Paul II's understanding of the *imago Dei* and the fall supports this view.[19] In his treatment of humanity before the fall, the dominant category in John Paul II's anthropology is the *imago Dei*. The most important and perhaps definitive aspect of the *imago Dei* for John Paul II is the reality that the *imago Dei* expresses a *relationship* between God and humanity. John Paul II states that this relationship is "manifested" by the expression found in Genesis: "God created humankind in his image; in the image of God he created them" (Genesis 1:27a, NRSV). The most defining characteristic of this relationship is the aspect of gift. John Paul II asserts that the divine act of creation is at the same time an act of giving. "The reality of the gift and the act of giving . . . [are] the content constituting the mystery of creation."[20] Creation as an act of giving in turn implies a relationship between the Giver and the receiver of the gift—that is, God and humanity, respectively. The gift itself is the "existential content contained in the truth of the 'image of God.'"[21] This existential content is none other than human identity, or "the whole truth about man," a phrase commonly used by John Paul II. For John Paul II, everything that is said about humanity, all philosophical and theological anthropology, must be seen in the context of this covenant of creation between God and humanity.

In contrast to the holistic picture of humanity *as created*, John Paul II asserts that, after the fall, humanity had a "different composition of the interior forces of man himself," that is, "almost another body/soul relationship, and other inner proportion between sensitivity, spirituality, and affectivity, that is, another degree of interior sensitiveness to the gifts of the Holy Spirit." After the fall, humanity lost what belonged to it in the fullness of the image of God. Specifically, before the fall,

> the human body bore in itself, in the mystery of creation, an unquestionable sign of the image of God. It also constituted the specific source of the certainty of that image, present in the whole human being. . . . The words "I was afraid, because I was naked, and I hid myself" (Gn 3:10), witness to a radical change in this relationship [between the body and the *imago Dei*]. In a way, man loses the original certainty of the image of God, expressed in his body. He also loses to some extent the sense of his right to participate in the perception of the world, which he enjoyed in the mystery of creation. This right had its foundation in man's

inner self, in the fact that he himself participated in the divine vision of the world
and of his own humanity.

Thus, the fall, for John Paul II, precipitates a "constitutive break within the
human person . . . which is almost a rupture of man's original spiritual and
somatic unity."[22] Original sin obscures the vision of the truth, of reality, of
the world as created and humanity's place in it, our vision of the image of
the divine within ourselves, and finally our trust in our own spiritual and
physical perception of these things.

For John Paul II, after the fall the body ceases to draw "upon the power
of the spirit, which raised [the human being] to the level of the image of
God." Rather, after the fall the body contains within it a "center of resistance to the spirit." This yields a "fundamental disquiet in all human existence," in which there exists a contradiction between intentions and actions. This disquiet is due to the fact that after body/soul unity is ruptured,
bodily desires are often a threat to the "structure of self-control and self-
mastery, through which the human person is formed . . . the structure of
self-mastery, essential for the person, is shaken to the very foundations in
him."[23]

John Paul II's sharply drawn contrast between the pre- and post-lapsarian
states both exemplifies and explains the ambiguity in his thought about the
psychosomatic unity of the human person. His theological reflection on
Genesis enables him to discern the way God created humanity to be, while
both his understanding of the fall and his phenomenological method allow
him to posit distinctly unholistic divisions within the person. His understanding of the fall allows him to posit these divisions ontologically; his
phenomenological method enables him to do so existentially.

Because John Paul II paints such a stark contrast between pre- and post-
lapsarian humanity, one could be led to believe that, while he asserts that
humanity was created as an integrated whole, in humanity's current post-
lapsarian state there is such division within the person that such a holistic
anthropology is no longer valid. However, John Paul II is quite explicit that
such a bleak picture of current human existence rests on a chronological understanding of "before" and "after" the fall. On the contrary, he insists, the
state of original innocence (or integration) and the state of original sin (or
division) exist simultaneously in human life and even within the human
self. We are *simul iustus et pecator*.

One of John Paul II's strongest contributions to a holistic understanding
of human sexuality is his understanding of our creation in the *imago Dei* as
a covenantal relationship between God and humanity. John Paul II understands human sexuality to be an expression of the self-giving relationality
that is essential to both divine and human personhood. Moreover, his understanding of this relationality as, at its best, covenantal contributes to his

understanding of marriage as a *communio personarum*, a communion of persons, which he posits as a primary expression of the *imago Dei* within humanity.

On the other hand, one of the most limiting factors for John Paul II's contribution to a holistic understanding of human sexuality is the positing of an *ontological* division within humanity as a result of the fall. Even if the original goodness of God's vision, that is, the holistic unity of the human person, exists alongside this division, the existence of the division itself means that, ontologically, humanity is divided against itself. The psychosomatic unity of the person is broken, and therefore, we cannot trust our bodies, our desires, emotions, or intuition, as these may be distorted and not give us reliable knowledge of what is true and good. While John Paul II gives us a detailed and comprehensive picture of the holistic unity that *is* the human person, this holistic anthropology cannot apply to us, except to provide ambiguity and tension with the post-lapsarian anthropology that describes us *now*.

One needs only to look around at the state of the world and most human persons themselves in order to see that there is, in existential fact, disorder, and to acknowledge that sometimes our desires and emotions and even thought processes lead us into choices and situations that are obviously contrary to God's good intentions for us. We are indeed *simul iustus et pecator*. It is not Wojtyla's phenomenological insight with which I take issue, but rather his claim that the cause of this experienced division was that the fall precipitated some kind of an ontological change, a division within the very structure of human being, such that a completely different—and not very holistic—relationship between body and soul describes and is applicable to us now. Specifically, his assertion of a body/soul break within the person, his subsequent designation of the body as the "center of resistance" to the spirit, and his location of disordered desire in the body denigrate the body and its desires such that sexual desire and therefore sexuality in general become something to be treated with suspicion, and, thus, carefully controlled—and limited in their expression to very precise circumstances (i.e., heterosexual marriage).[24]

THEOLOGY OF SEXUAL DIFFERENCE

Sexual Difference and the Body-Person

Having laid the foundation for his theology of human sexuality in his discussions of the relationship between person and body, John Paul II proceeds to develop a theology of human sexuality, and especially sexual difference, based on the principle that the body expresses the person.

In his analysis of the second creation account, John Paul II notes that

> corporeality and sexuality are not completely identified. In its normal consti-
> tution, the human body bears within it the signs of sex and is male or female
> by its nature. However, the fact that man is a "body" belongs to the structure
> of the personal subject more deeply than the fact that in his somatic constitu-
> tion he is also male and female.

In fact, John Paul II notes that in the Genesis text, *'adam*—the human being—
precedes *'ish* and *'issah*—man and woman.[25] He takes this as symbolic of the
fact that common humanity precedes—is prior to—sexual differentiation.

This would imply that a theology of the body should begin with the
shared embodiedness of all human beings, rather than sexual difference. In
fact, even after sexual differentiation,

> somatic homogeneity, in spite of the difference in constitution bound up with
> the sexual difference, is so evident that the man, on waking up from the genetic
> sleep, expresses it at once, when he says: "This at last is bone of my bones and
> flesh of my flesh. . . ." In this way the man manifests for the first time joy and
> even exaltation, for which he had no reason before, owing to the lack of a be-
> ing like himself. Joy in the other human being, in the second "self," dominates
> the words spoken by the man on seeing the woman.

Thus, in his theology of the body, John Paul II begins from the commonality of humanness—humanity. "In his solitude, man opens up to a being
akin to himself. . . . This opening is no less decisive for the person of man;
in fact, it is perhaps even more decisive than the distinction [of man from
other animals]."[26]

However, with the introduction of the communion of persons, constituted by sexual differentiation in the creation of male and female, John Paul
II notes that "the theology of the body . . . becomes, in a way, also the theology of sex, or rather the theology of masculinity and femininity."[27] The
communio personarum between the man and the woman constitutes the
imago Dei because it has a nuptial quality that mirrors the nuptial quality of
the covenant between God and humanity.[28] "Man and woman constitute
two different ways of the human 'being a body' in the unity of that image."
Masculinity and femininity are "two different 'incarnations,' that is . . . two
ways of 'being a body' of the same human being created 'in the image of
God.'"[29] Moreover, woman and man are "two complementary dimensions
of self-consciousness and self-determination and, at the same time, two
complementary ways of being conscious of the meaning of the body."[30] For
John Paul II, the creation of humanity was not complete until the human
being was sexually differentiated. "The complete and definitive creation of
'man' . . . is expressed in giving life to that *communio personarum* that man
and woman form."[31]

Here again, John Paul II returns to the *imago Dei* as his anthropological standard.

> Man became the "image and likeness" of God not only through his own humanity, but also through the communion of persons which man and woman form right from the beginning. . . . Man becomes the image of God not so much in the moment of solitude as in the moment of communion. Right "from the beginning," he is not only an image in which the solitude of a person who rules the world is reflected, but also, and essentially, an image of an inscrutable divine communion of persons.

In this way, John Paul II insists that humanity's ultimate dignity lies in heterosexuality—in the union and complementarity of the sexes. The human being "became the image and likeness of God not only through his own humanity, but also through the communion of persons which man and woman form right from the beginning."[32]

Indeed, for John Paul II, this unity of male and female "constitutes the deepest theological aspect of all that can be said about man." Thus, the understanding of the meaning of one's own body through the *communio personarum*, that is, the gift of woman and man to each other, is the nuptial meaning of the body. The nuptial meaning of the body is "the fundamental element of existence in the world."[33] The body is a sacrament of the person, and the sexual union between male and female body-persons is a sacrament of the original *communio personarum* through which Adam and Eve became conscious of themselves and each other as body-persons.[34] "Right from the beginning, that unity which is realized through the body indicates not only the 'body' but also the 'incarnate' communion of persons—*communio personarum*—and calls for this communion."[35]

Thus for John Paul II, sexual difference is a "constituent part of the person," not just "an attribute of the person."[36] Using Aristotle's (and Aquinas's) terminology here, sexual difference is essential to human personhood; a human person would not be a human person without being male or female. John Paul II takes this a step further and asserts such a close relationship between body and person that masculinity or femininity dictates the purpose and vocation of the person.[37] This is especially apparent in *Mulieris Dignitatem*, wherein John Paul II explicates and defines the "dignity and vocation" of all women as virgin and/or mother, based simply on the fact that they are women.[38] In combating the Cartesian dualism that sees the body as external to the person, John Paul II goes to the other extreme, arguing that "sex decides not only the somatic individuality of man, but defines at the same time his personal identity and concreteness."[39]

This close association between masculinity/femininity and personhood leads John Paul II to address the "pastoral problem" of the dignity of women in a particular way. For example, addressing a national congress at the Italian Feminine Center in January 2004, the pope declared, "The dignity of woman is intimately related to the love she receives because of her femininity and also because of the love that she gives in turn."[40] Paraphrasing John Paul II, *Zenit* reported that, at the same conference, the pope stated that "in an age when women participate more in areas of public life, it is important that they have a keen awareness of their fundamental vocation: to fulfill themselves through love." Then, quoting the pope, "It is important that woman keep alive the awareness of this fundamental vocation. . . . She fulfills herself only by giving love, with her singular 'genius' that assures sensitivity for all human beings in all circumstances." Again, the pope exhorted women to live their mission fully, "expressing the feminine 'genius' that characterizes you."[41]

By way of summary and critique, the crux of what is most holistic in John Paul II's sexual anthropology is his statement that the body expresses the person. The importance of this statement in his theology of sexual difference cannot be overestimated because it implies that "biology is destiny" in the sense that one's body expresses who one is and who one is created to be. It is a deceptively simple next step to assert, as the pope does, that if biology is destiny, then one's maleness or femaleness determines in large part the dignity and vocation, and therefore identity, of oneself as a human person. In fact, it would seem that this deceptive simplicity accounts for the traditional feminist rejection of the idea that "biology is destiny."

Moreover, John Paul II reasons, there is something the "same" about the dignity, vocation, and identity of all women on the one hand and all men on the other.[42] That is, all women have a common way of being a person, which he calls femininity, and all men have a common way of being a person, which he calls masculinity. Thus femininity and masculinity have essential and unchanging content. What is that content? One needs only to look to the biblical bridal imagery that describes Israel's relationship to God in the Hebrew scriptures and the church's relationship to Christ in the New Testament to arrive at John Paul II's sacred archetypes of femininity and masculinity, exemplified perfectly in human history by Mary and her Son, respectively.[43]

In asserting that there are masculine and feminine human persons, John Paul II avoids the soteriological problem that arises when one postulates two human natures.[44] In other words, it is important to note that he is not implying here that there are two human natures, one feminine and the other masculine; rather, John Paul II asserts that masculinity and femininity describe two distinct and distinctive ways of being a person.

However, he does not follow through on the implications of this move from the level of nature to the level of person. In moving masculinity and femininity to the realm of "person," he maintains rigid archetypes that belie the *uniqueness* of personal characteristics as opposed to the *shared* elements of human nature. In other words, in order to truly and really move sexual difference from an essential component of nature to an essential component of personhood, one must reject rigid archetypes and allow the uniqueness of each individual person to affect the very *content*—not just the way it is expressed—of what it means to be a man or a woman.

A closer look at the human body itself calls into question these unchanging, sacred archetypes. As Christine Gudorf points out in her chapter earlier in this book, science tells us that the human body varies from person to person, even in the physical markers of maleness and femaleness. While most (although by no means all) people consider themselves male or female depending on which genitalia they possess—and whether or not they can contribute a sperm or an egg to the process of human reproduction—the scientific, bodily reality of sex is much more complex and involves chromosomes, hormones, brain structure and chemistry, and the like, that vary from person to person.[45] In fact, hormonally, there seems to be more of a *spectrum* than a *dichotomous division* in which a given individual falls into one of the two categories "male" and "female" and is identical with other individuals in the same category.[46] Moreover, some (albeit few) people do not clearly possess one set of genitalia over another or (as is more common) cannot contribute an egg or sperm to natural human reproduction due to infertility. Are these human persons not men or women?

One major limitation of John Paul II's insistence that all people fit into two sexual categories is that all people do not actually fit into two sexual categories. It is insulting to the reality and complexity of each human being to consider only genitalia as an indicator of sexual difference, thus reducing physical sex to genitalia and ignoring other markers of sexual difference in one's reading of a unique body-person. The reality of persons is that sexuality—including physical sex and sexual orientation and the interaction of biological and environmental factors—is much more complex than the strictly dimorphic model allows. Most real people do not fit into the binary, sacred archetypes of masculinity and femininity to which John Paul II adheres. Physical sex manifests uniquely in every person, even if the vast majority of humans are either *mostly* male or *mostly* female.[47] The reality of variance and change through evolution, across the lifecycle, and from organism to organism suggests that one's precise "sex" or sexual makeup is unique to oneself. Given this scientific knowledge, any theology of sexual difference should be a theology of sexual differences.

In light of the biological and sexual uniqueness of each human person, applying John Paul II's own assertion that the body expresses the person, and therefore accepting that biology is destiny, means that each person's destiny—dignity, identity, and vocation—is unique. If the body truly expresses the person, then reading the person through the body involves allowing it to "speak" for itself—not reading the body according to preconceived and ultimately inaccurate archetypes (even though there's no such thing as an unfiltered, immediate interpretation). Moreover, reading the body according to preconceived archetypes contradicts the phenomenological method that John Paul II uses elsewhere to describe other experiences of personhood, such as affectivity. Rather, for John Paul II, the person, as male or female, is to be "integrated" into—or rather forced to conform to—an archetype of masculinity or femininity that has been arrived at by an interpretation of Genesis 1:27 through the lens of Ephesians 5. Ultimately, this kind of forcing to fit pre-established archetypes is a decidedly unholistic move in that it denies the complexity of actual human beings, and does so to their detriment. As feminist theologian Elizabeth Johnson puts it, "By boxing women's and men's identities into innate differences that are based on traditional stereotypes . . . a dualistic anthropology [emerges that] inevitably compromises the human and spiritual potential of both."[48]

In reading the human body through the lens of fixed, sacred archetypes of masculinity and femininity, John Paul II denies the relevance of scientific knowledge in his reading of the human body as the expression of the person. In *Theology of the Body*, John Paul II explicitly engages the relevance of the question of science. On the one hand, he admits that Genesis tells us little scientifically regarding the body. "From this point of view, in our study we are at a completely pre-scientific level. We know hardly anything about the interior structures and the regularities that reign in the human organism." On the other hand, while acknowledging his own ignorance, he dismisses the relevance of science as a source for theological reflection and therefore conclusions about the body. "Modern bio-physiology can supply a great deal of precise information about human sexuality. However, knowledge of the personal dignity of the human body and of sex must still be drawn from other sources."[49]

Another limitation of Wojtyla/John Paul II's anthropology is his ambivalence about whether embodiment or sexual difference is deeper anthropologically and therefore the proper starting point for theological reflection on the human person. Karol Wojtyla/John Paul II begins with the embodiment of the person and asserts that it is deeper than—and enjoys a certain priority over—sexual difference. This starting point seems to disappear, however, in his language about sexual difference being the deepest theological thing that can be said about the body and about humanity, and his assertion that the whole of humanity is made of sexual difference. In some places, he equates corporality with masculinity or femininity: "By means of his corporality, his masculinity and femininity, man becomes a visible sign of the economy of truth and love." In fact, John Paul II comes dangerously close to reducing all human embodiment to sexual difference. For example, this is obviously the case when he states that "the sacrament, as a visible sign, is constituted with man, as a body, by means of his visible masculinity and femininity."[50]

Whether one emphasizes commonality or difference in one's theology of the body matters for a holistic understanding of human sexuality. Elizabeth Johnson, in her discussion of John Paul II's theology of sexual difference, points out that starting with common embodiedness puts the fact that there are sexual differences among human beings in the perspective that there are many differences between human beings. Colleen Griffith argues further that emphasis on the common experience of bodiliness—its givenness, its materiality, the structure of human consciousness, the interdependence that it brings with it, the fact that we are sexual beings who have "sexuality"— allows us to appreciate that the very fact that we have differences is a common human characteristic. Distinctiveness becomes something we share in common.[51]

Given our common embodiedness, the question then arises: Are other aspects or components of embodiment—namely, walking upright and using our hands to create things, to write, or our vocal chords that allow us to express ourselves in words and music—not sacramental or equally so as sexual difference? Moreover, in the statement above, John Paul II limits the sacramentality of the body to *external* sex characteristics and, as Gudorf points out, ignores those that science tells us are there but are invisible to the naked eye. On the contrary, from the perspective of a holistic anthropology, the whole human body is sacramental, interior and exterior. The sacrament that is the whole body (including but not limited to sex) is much more complex than John Paul II is allowing; this is precisely where science becomes relevant in a holistic reading of a human body-person.

CONCLUSION: CONTRIBUTIONS AND LIMITATIONS FOR A HOLISTIC ANTHROPOLOGY

At the beginning of this chapter, I defined a holistic understanding of human sexuality as one that considers the human being from a perspective that flows from creation in the *imago Dei* as a human person, a self, and a beloved of God, in which all parts and elements are considered *good*, and all are integrated into one's personal being, from which flows one's unique and unrepeatable identity and vocation. The many nuances of John Paul II's work demand that it not be uncritically praised or simply dismissed on the basis of this definition.

A study of the foundational elements of Wojtyla/John Paul II's theology of the body yields three major limitations in terms of a holistic understanding of human sexuality: (1) an initial acceptance of a "dual structure"; (2) a treatment of the body as a "compliant tool"; and (3) the location of disordered desire in the body. A further study of his theology of sexual difference reveals an understanding of "body" that includes rigid archetypes of

"masculinity" and "femininity"—archetypes that have historically functioned as destructive stereotypes—as well as a lack of consideration for the
body in all its complexity (that is, including but not limited to the reproductive system). Moreover, in all of this, John Paul II dismisses the relevance of scientific knowledge, which at the very least provides descriptive
insight into sexual differences as well as other bodily realities.

In the "great and fundamental contest for the essence of man," Wo-
jtyla/John Paul II has much to contribute—and during his lifetime contributed significantly in various ways to the struggle for human rights
against "isms" such as Nazism, communism, nationalism—and sexism. Indeed, John Paul II was a tireless and uncompromising advocate for safe-
guarding the dignity of the human person. One wonders, however, if, in his
struggle against the "isms" of the world, he adopted a certain rigidity in the
application of his own lenses for viewing the human person. In the case of
human sexuality, his chosen lens was that of sacred archetypes of femininity and masculinity. Even more dangerously, he was closed to dialoging
with other lenses that might contribute to our understandings of human
sexuality, namely biological (and social) scientific lenses as well as those
that would come through a careful and critical listening to the experience
of contemporary, *simul iustus et pecator* human beings. This chapter, in keeping with the intent of this book, has the aim of bringing Wojtyla/John Paul
II's thought into precisely such a mutually critical dialogue, in the hopes
that his strengths will make a significant contribution to that conversation.

And what are these strengths? Karol Wojtyla/John Paul II's most promising contributions to a holistic understanding of human sexuality include
(1) his comprehensive understanding of the *imago Dei* as personal and
covenantal relationship; (2) his phenomenological understanding of intuition, affectivity, and relationality; and (3) his consequent insistence that
human experience is an integrated whole and as such is the source of
knowledge. Finally, his greatest strength is his insight that the body expresses the person, which should form the very foundation of such a holistic understanding of human sexuality.

NOTES

1. Karol Wojtyla, "From *The Controversy about Man*," in *Toward a Philosophy of
Praxis*, translated and edited by George Czuczka (New York: Crossroad, 1981), 12.
Throughout, I leave the quotations in the language in which I find them, while I myself use inclusive or gender-neutral language. While this may be jarring for the
reader, it is this very quality that speaks to the point of this chapter.

2. See Nireya Navarro, "Spreading the Pope's Message of Sexuality and a Willing
Spirit," *New York Times*, 7 June 2004, regarding Christopher West's work in various
pastoral contexts across the United States. Moreover, there are nine John Paul II in-

stitutes in Italy, Benin, Australia, Austria, Brazil, India, Mexico, Spain, and the United States.

3. Joseph Cardinal Ratzinger and Angelo Amato, SDB, "Letter to the Bishops of the Catholic Church on the Collaboration of Men and Women in the Church and in the World" (www.vatican.va/roman_curia/congregations/cfaith/documents/rc_con _cfaith_doc_20040731_collaboration_en.html; 31 May 2004).

4. Wojtyla, "From *The Controversy about Man*," 12.

5. In the introduction to *Acting Person*, Wojtyla asserts that he "owe[s] every-thing to the systems of metaphysics, of anthropology, and of Aristotelian-Thomistic ethics on the one hand, and to phenomenology, above all in Scheler's interpreta-tion, and through Scheler's critique also to Kant, on the other hand." Karol Wojtyla, *Acting Person*, translated by Andrzej Potocki and edited by Anna-Teresa Tymieniecka, *Analecta Husserliana* 10 (Boston: Reidel, 1979), xiv. Ironically, given Wojtyla's ac-knowledgment of his dual influences, there is a consensus among scholars familiar with Wojtyla's work that Tymieniecka's edition, which has the copyright in English, is flawed because it does not allow the reader to identify instances when the author is using Thomistic terms.

6. Novak, introduction to *Destined for Liberty: The Human Person in the Philoso-phy of Karol Wojtyla/John Paul II* (Washington, D.C.: The Catholic University of Amer-ica Press, 2000), xiii and ibid.

7. However, Wojtyla/John Paul II does not use the phenomenological method uncritically. In his philosophical dissertation on Scheler (*Evaluation of the Possibility of Constructing a Christian Ethic Based on the System of Max Scheler*), Wojtyla uses "the revealed sources of Christian ethics" as a criterion by which to judge Scheler's ade-quacy for Christian ethics. While acknowledging that Christian revelation is not de-pendent on or tied to any philosophical system, Wojtyla wanted to find out if he could speak of and interpret Christian revelation through the use of Schelerian phe-nomenology. Ultimately, he arrived at a negative answer because of Scheler's inabil-ity to determine the objective value of acts and because of his concept of person, which is not a substance but rather a unity of feelings and experiences. Wojtyla as-serted that these issues could only be treated in metaphysics, which explicitly deals with the objective order of the good, or of being (see Kupczak, *Destined for Liberty*, 23). Thus, Scheler's phenomenology could be only "accidentally" helpful to the Christian philosopher. See also Ronald Modras, "A Man of Contradictions? The Early Writings of Karol Wojtyla," in *The Church in Anguish: Has the Vatican Betrayed Vatican II?* edited by Hans Küng and Leonard Swidler (San Francisco: Harper and Row, 1987), 42.

8. Kupczak, *Destined for Liberty*, 22.

9. John Paul II, *Theology of the Body: Human Love in the Divine Plan* (Boston: Pauline Books and Media, 1997), 46 (November 14, 1979). For a fuller discussion of *communio personarum*, see John Paul II, *Mulieris Dignatatum* (Washington, D.C.: United States Catholic Conference, 1988), nos. 7ff.

10. Wojtyla himself states as much in *Acting Person*, viii.

11. See Wojtyla, "The Personal Structure of Self-Determination," in *Person and Community: Selected Essays*, translated by Theresa Sandok, O.S.M. and edited by An-drew N. Woznicki, volume 4 of *Catholic Thought from Lublin* (New York: Peter Lang, 1993), 188.

12. See Wojtyla, *Acting Person*, viii; ibid., 196; and ibid., 197.

13. This language of "hierarchical ordering" I take from my colleague Colleen Griffith. See, for example, "Human Bodiliness: Sameness as Starting Point," in *The Church Women Want: Catholic Women in Dialogue*, edited by Elizabeth A. Johnson (New York: Crossroad, 2002), 63.

14. Wojtyla, *Acting Person*, 205; ibid.; ibid., 206; and ibid.

15. See John Paul II, *Theology of the Body*, 38–39 (Oct. 24, 1979). See also John Paul II, *ibid.*, 52 (December 12, 1979), where John Paul II seems to be elaborating on his assertion in *Acting Person* that one's experience of one's body is synonymous with self-feeling (the Polish is *samo-poczucie*). This is Kupczak's translation (Kupczak, *Destined for Liberty*, 136) of *Osaba y Czyn*, 271 (in the English translation, *Acting Person*, 229).

16. See John Paul II, *Theology of the Body*, 40 (Oct. 31, 1979); ibid., 57 (Jan. 2, 1980); and see *ibid.*, 57 (Jan. 2, 1980).

17. See John Paul II, *Theology of the Body*, 61 (Jan. 9, 1980); ibid., 40 (Oct. 31, 1979; emphasis mine); ibid., 47 (November 14, 1979); ibid.; and ibid., 56 (Dec. 19, 1979).

18. See John Paul II, *Theology of the Body*, 76 (Feb. 20, 1980).

19. For a more in-depth discussion of John Paul II on the *imago Dei*, see my doctoral dissertation, *Personal Consciousness and Freedom in the Thought of Karl Rahner and Karol Wojtyla/John Paul II: A Comparison of Their Contributions to Theological Anthropology and Moral Theology* (University Microforms International, 2003), especially 134–43.

20. See John Paul II, *Theology of the Body*, 28 (Sept. 12, 1979) and 38 (Oct. 24, 1979); ibid., 59 (Jan. 2, 1980); and ibid., 66 (Jan. 16, 1980).

21. John Paul II, *Theology of the Body*, 59 (Jan. 2, 1980). See also *Dominum et Vivificantem* (May 18, 1986), no. 64.4, in *The Encyclicals of John Paul II* (Huntington: Our Sunday Visitor Press, 1996), 333. The original Latin text can be found in *AAS* 78 (1986): 809–900.

22. John Paul II, *Theology of the Body*, 73 (Feb. 13, 1980); see ibid., 112 (May 14, 1980); ibid., 113 (May 14, 1980); and ibid., 115 (May 28, 1980).

23. All references in this paragraph are to John Paul II, *Theology of the Body*, 115 (May 28, 1980).

24. Earlier in this volume, Christine Gudorf takes up this discussion in more detail. See Christine Gudorf, "New Moral Discourse," in this volume, 51–69.

25. John Paul II, *Theology of the Body*, 43 (November 7, 1979); and see *Mulieris Dignitatem*, nos. 5–7.

26. John Paul II, *Theology of the Body*, 46–47 (November 7, 1979); and ibid., 45 (November 14, 1979).

27. John Paul II, *Theology of the Body*, 47 (November 14, 1979).

28. For support for his assertion regarding the nuptial quality of the relationship between God and humanity, John Paul II cites the prophets in the Old Testament, in particular Hosea, Ezekiel and Deutero-Isaiah, and Ephesians 5 in the New Testament. See *Theology of the Body*, 357 (Jan. 12, 1983).

29. John Paul II, *Theology of the Body*, 58 (January 2, 1980); and ibid., 43 (November 7, 1979).

30. John Paul II, *Theology of the Body*, 48 (Nov. 21, 1979). It may be his analysis of sexual difference that prompts John Paul II to assert a more intimate and integral psychosomatic unity than is apparent in his pre-papal, philosophical works. It is unclear which logically comes first—his assertion that sexual difference is fundamental to the person in such a way that it defines the person *or* his shift from the body being the "territory and means of expression" of the spiritual person (Wojtyla) to the body being an integral part of the unity that is the spiritual-sensual person (John Paul II). Is he arguing on the basis of a newly developed understanding of body/soul unity that sexual difference is not something purely physical but rather determines the whole person? Or is he arguing from this idea of sexual difference as fundamental to the person to a concept of body/soul unity that can support that assertion?

31. John Paul II, *Theology of the Body*, 46 (November 14, 1979).

32. John Paul II, *Theology of the Body*, 46 (November 14, 1979); and ibid.

33. John Paul II, *Theology of the Body*, 47 (November 14, 1979); ibid., 58 (January 2, 1980); and ibid., 66 (January 16, 1980).

34. See *Theology of the Body*, 48 (November 14, 1979), wherein John Paul II states, "Masculinity and femininity express the dual aspect of man's somatic constitution . . . [and] . . . they indicate the new consciousness of one's own body. . . . Precisely this consciousness through which humanity is formed again as the communion of persons, seems to be the layer which in the narrative of the creation of man . . . is deeper than his somatic structure as male and female."

35. John Paul II, *Theology of the Body*, 47–48 (November 14, 1979).

36. John Paul II, *Theology of the Body*, 49 (Nov. 21, 1979).

37. See John Paul II, *Theology of the Body*, 79 (March 5, 1980). See also *Mulieris Dignitatem*, no. 10, where John Paul II discusses the "feminine originality" of woman as person; *Mulieris Dignitatem* 18 where he states that "motherhood is linked to the personal structure of the woman to the personal dimension of the gift"; and, finally *Mulieris Dignitatem*, no. 20, where he uses the terminology "feminine personality."

38. John Paul II, *Mulieris Dignitatem*, nos. 5, 17–22.

39. John Paul II, *Theology of the Body*, 79 (March 5, 1980). This is one of John Paul II's most controversial claims. Christine Gudorf critiques this claim in her chapter in this volume, "New Moral Discourse," 54ff. Philosophers, theologians, and feminist scholars in many fields continue to debate the relationship of sexual difference to the person. While John Paul II asserts that masculinity or femininity defines one's personal identity, scholars on the other extreme argue that the fact of sexual difference is simply a matter of physical characteristics and that any other difference between the sexes is socially constructed. A majority of scholars argue that reality lies somewhere in between. For such a perspective, as well as an early treatment of John Paul II on the subject, see, for example, Elizabeth A. Johnson, "The Incomprehensibility of God and the Image of God Male and Female," *Theological Studies* 45 (1984): 441–65.

40. John Paul II, speaking to the national congress organized by the Italian Feminine Center on Jan. 16, 2004, quoted in Zenit, the online Vatican newspaper (www.zenit.org/English, January 16, 2004) in an article titled "Women's Vocation

Tied to Love, Says John Paul II: Believes Their Genius Assures a Sensitivity for All People."

41. Zenit, "Women's Vocation"; and ibid.

42. While in the apostolic letter *Mulieris Dignatatem* John Paul II defines and explicates at length the dignity and vocation of women, there is no comparable definition or explication of men in his work (although he treats the issue poetically in his early plays). On the one hand, one could argue that it is the role and equality of women that is at stake in the church and in the world, and so John Paul II is responding to the pastoral need to address those issues. On the other hand, as a (however well-intentioned) man defining the dignity and vocation of women, he is perpetuating the very problem he is trying to address, namely sexism.

43. See especially *Mulieris Dignitatem*, no 23.

44. The soteriological problem is the following: If what Christ assumed is redeemed, and Christ assumed a male human nature, then how are women redeemed? For a fuller discussion of this question in relation to women in the history of Christian thought, see Rosemary Radford Ruether, *Women and Redemption: A Theological History* (Minneapolis: Fortress Press, 1998).

45. In the writing of this chapter, I originally called upon the presentation Christine Gudorf gave to the Women's Constructive Theology group at the Catholic Theological Society of America in 2004 (Christine Gudorf, "Sex, Gender and Science in Catholic Ethics," unpublished presentation, CTSA, 2004). Her critique of John Paul II's lack of engagement with science was a key point of insight for me in the development of this chapter, and she was generous to share an unpublished copy of her presentation with me.

46. See Gudorf, "New Moral Discourse," in this volume, 55ff.

47. Again, see Gudorf, "New Moral Discourse," in this volume, 55ff.

48. Elizabeth Johnson, "Imaging God, Embodying Christ: Women as a Sign of the Times," in *The Church Women Want*, 54.

49. John Paul II, *Theology of the Body*, 88 (April 2, 1980); and ibid., 89 (April 2, 1980).

50. John Paul II, *Theology of the Body*, 76 (February 20, 1980); and ibid.

51. Griffith, "Human Bodiliness," in *The Church Women Want*, 65.

7

A Disembodied "Theology of the Body": John Paul II on Love, Sex, and Pleasure*

Luke Timothy Johnson

Papal teaching on human sexuality has received some positive reviews recently. A number of these have appeared in the journal *First Things*. In "Contraception: A Symposium,"[1] Archbishop Charles J. Chaput, O.F.M. Cap., declares that Pope Paul VI has a lock on the title of prophet because, in *Humanae Vitae*, he was right. In the same issue, Janet E. Smith thinks that people who regard the papacy's condemnation of contraception to be based on the "artificial" methods employed simply have not acquainted themselves with the richness of papal teaching. In particular, she says, "those who appreciate precise and profound philosophical reasoning should read Karol Wojtyla's *Love and Responsibility*," while offering a strong recommendation also for "the extensive deliberations of Pope John Paul II." Even more recently, Jennifer J. Popiel states that "unlike many women, I find the church's doctrinal statements on contraception and reproduction to be clear and compelling," and argues that Natural Family Planning is fully compatible with feminism, since "only when we control our bodies will we truly control our lives."[2]

George Weigel joins this chorus of praise in his biography of John Paul II, *Witness to Hope*.[3] Under the heading, "A New Galileo Crisis," Weigel traces the pope's systematic response to the "pastoral and catechetical failure" of *Humanae Vitae* in a series of 130 fifteen-minute conferences at papal audiences beginning on September 5, 1979 and concluding on November 28, 1984. The conferences were grouped into four clusters: "The Original Unity of Man and Woman," "Blessed Are the Pure of Heart," "The

---

*This chapter originally appeared in *Commonweal* 128, no. 2 (January 26, 2001): 11–17; © 2006 Commonweal Foundation, reprinted with permission.

Theology of Marriage and Celibacy," and "Reflections on *Humanae Vitae.*" These talks were brought together under the title *Theology of the Body: Human Love in the Divine Plan.*[4]

Weigel himself considers John Paul II's work to be a "theological time bomb" that may take almost a century to appreciate fully, or even assimilate. It "may prove to be the decisive moment in exorcising the Manichaean demon and its deprecation of human sexuality from Catholic moral theology," because the pope takes "embodiedness" so seriously. Weigel considers these conferences to have "ramifications for all of theology," and wonders why so few contemporary theologians have taken up the challenge posed by the pope. He is surprised as well that so few priests preach these themes and only a "microscopic" portion of Catholics seem even aware of this great accomplishment, which he considers to be "a critical moment not only in Catholic theology, but in the history of modern thought." Weigel provides three possible reasons for this neglect: the density of the pope's material, the media's preoccupation with controversy rather than substance, and the fact that John Paul II is himself a figure of controversy. It will take time to appreciate him and his magnificent contribution.

Is Weigel right? Have the rest of us missed out on a theological advance of singular importance? Can the claims made for the pope's *Theology of the Body* be sustained under examination? Recently, I devoted considerable time (and as much consciousness as I could muster) to reading through the 423 pages of the collected conferences, and I have reached a conclusion far different from Weigel's. For all its length, earnestness, and good intentions, John Paul II's work, far from being a breakthrough for modern thought, represents a mode of theology that has little to say to ordinary people because it shows so little awareness of ordinary life.

I want to make clear that I am here responding to the theological adequacy of papal teaching. I do not dispute the fact that, in some respects, papal positions can legitimately be called prophetic. Certainly John Paul II's call for a "culture of life" in the name of the gospel, against the complex "conspiracy of death" so pervasive in the contemporary world, deserves respect. Likewise, the pope's attention to the "person" and to "continence" stands as prophetic in a time of sexualized identity and rationalized permissiveness. It is small wonder that those worried about moral confusion in sexual matters would want to accept all the papal teachings, since some of them are incontestably correct.

But I want to ask whether we ought to make some distinctions even where the pope does not, whether while approving some of his positions we can also challenge others. Weigel is correct in noting that these conferences are dense and difficult to read—what must they have been like to hear? But Weigel fails to note how mind-numbingly repetitious they are. He does not seem to notice that the pope only asserts and never demonstrates, and that he minimizes the flat internal contradictions among the conferences. For example, on October 1, 1980, the pope declares that a husband cannot be guilty of "lust in his heart" for his wife, but a week later, in the conference of October 8, he states confidently that even husbands can sin in this fashion. But beyond such relatively minor deficiencies (how many theological writings are not dense, repetitive, and inconsistent?), the pope's *Theology of the Body* is fundamentally inadequate to the question it takes up. It is inadequate not in the obvious way that all theology is necessarily inadequate to its subject, and therefore should exhibit intellectual modesty, but in the sense that it simply does not engage what most ought to be engaged in a theology of the body. Because of its theological insufficiency, the pope's teaching does not adequately respond to the anxieties of those who seek a Christian understanding of the body and of human sexuality, and practical guidance for life as sexually active adults.

If the pope had only made casual or passing comments on the subject in a homily, then a critical response would be unfair. But everything suggests that John Paul II intended these conferences to be read as a "theology of the body" in the fullest sense of the term "theology." The pope uses academic terms like phenomenology and hermeneutics, refers to contemporary thinkers, provides copious notes, and in the very commitment to the subject over a period of 5 years in 130 conferences, indicates that he wants his comments to be given serious attention. It is perhaps appropriate to offer a number of observations concerning things that someone far removed from the corridors of doctrinal declaration, but not unschooled theologically, and certainly not disembodied, might want to see yet does not find in John Paul II's discourses.

PRELIMINARY OBSERVATIONS

A starting place is the title itself, which, while perhaps not chosen by the author, legitimately derives from his frequent reference to a "theology of the body" and his constant focus on "human love in the divine plan." Surely, though, an adequate theology of the body must encompass far more than human love, even if that were comprehensively treated! The pope cites 1 Corinthians 6:18 approvingly: "Flee fornication. Every sin a person commits is apart from the body. But the one who fornicates sins in his own body." But Paul's rhetorical emphasis cannot be taken as sober description. Do not the sins of gluttony and drunkenness and sloth have as much to do with the body as fornication, and are not all the forms of avarice also dispositions of the body? Reducing a theology of the body to a consideration of sexuality falsifies the topic from the beginning. Of course, an adequate theological phenomenology of the body as the primordial mystery/symbol of human freedom and bondage must include every aspect of sexuality. But it must also embrace all the other ways in which human embodiedness both enables and limits human freedom through disposition of material possessions, through relationships to the environment, through artistic creativity, and through suffering—both sinful and sanctifying. The pope's title provides the first example of the way in which a grander—or, to use his word, "vast"—conceptual framework serves to camouflage a distressingly narrow view of things.

The pope's subtitle is "Human Love in the Divine Plan," but no real sense of human love as actually experienced emerges in these reflections. The topic of human love in all its dimensions has been wonderfully explored in the world's literature, but none of its grandeur or giddiness appears in these talks, which remain at a level of abstraction far removed from novels and newspapers with their stories of people like us (though not so attractive). John Paul II thinks of himself as doing "phenomenology," but seems never to look at actual human experience. Instead, he dwells on the nuances of words in biblical narratives and declarations, while fantasizing an ethereal and all-encompassing mode of mutual self-donation between man and woman that lacks any of the messy, clumsy, awkward, charming, casual, and, yes, silly aspects of love in the flesh. Carnality, it is good to remember, is at least as much a matter of humor as of solemnity. In the pope's formulations, human sexuality is observed by telescope from a distant planet. Solemn pronouncements are made on the basis of textual exegesis rather than living experience. The effect is something like that of a sunset painted by the unsighted.

The objection may be made: Isn't it proper to base theology in Scripture, and isn't John Paul II correct to have devoted himself so sedulously to the analysis of biblical texts, rather than the slippery and shoddy stuff of experience? It depends on how seriously one takes the Catholic tradition concerning the work of God's Holy Spirit in the world. If we believe—and I think we have this right—that revelation is not exclusively biblical but occurs in the continuing experience of God in the structures of human freedom,[5] then an occasional glance toward human experience as actually lived may be appropriate, even for the magisterium.

As for the pope's way of reading Scripture, the grade is mixed. Certainly he is careful with the texts. Nor does he misrepresent those aspects of the text he discusses in any major way—although he leaves the impression that Matthew's "blessed are the pure of heart" (5:8) refers to chastity, when in fact he knows very well that the beatitude does not have that restricted sense. Even more questionable are the ways John Paul II selects and extrapolates from specific texts without sufficient grounding or explanation. First, he scarcely treats all the biblical evidence pertinent to the subject. His discourses center on a handful of admittedly important passages, with obligatory nods at other texts that might have rewarded far closer analysis, such as the Song of Songs (three conferences) and the Book of Tobit (one). Other important texts are given scant or no attention. A far richer understanding of Paul would have resulted, for example, from a more sustained and robust reading of 1 Corinthians 7, which truly does reveal the mutuality and reciprocity—and complexity—of married love.

Second, John Paul II does not deal with some of the difficulties presented by the texts he does select. For instance, he manages to use Matthew 19:3–9, on the question of marriage's indissolubility, without ever adverting to the clause allowing divorce on the grounds of porneia (sexual immorality) in both Matthew 5:32 and 19:9. What does that exceptive clause suggest about the distance between the ideal "in the beginning" evoked by Jesus, and the hard realities of actual marriages faced by the Matthean (and every subsequent) church?

Third, for all of his philosophical sophistication, John Paul II seems unaware of the dangers of deriving ontological conclusions from selected ancient narrative texts. He inveighs against the "hermeneutics of suspicion," but the remedy is not an uncritical reading that moves directly from the ancient story to an essential human condition. He focuses on the Yahwist creation account in Genesis 2, because that is the account cited by Jesus in his dispute with the Pharisees concerning divorce (Matt. 19:5), and, I suspect, because its narrative texture—not to mention its human feel—allows for the sort of phenomenological reflection he enjoys. But as the pope certainly understands, this creation account must also be joined to that in Genesis 1 if an adequate appreciation of what Jesus meant by "from the beginning" (Matt. 19:8) is to be gained. If Genesis 1—which has God creating humans in God's image as male and female—had been employed more vigorously, certain emphases would be better balanced. John Paul II wants, for example, to have the term "man" mean both male and female. But the Genesis 2 account pushes him virtually to equate "man" with "male," with the unhappy result that males experience both the original solitude the pope wants to make distinctively human as well as the dominion over creation expressed by the naming of animals. Females inevitably appear as "helpers" and as complementary to the already rather complete humanity found in the male. Small wonder that in virtually none of his further reflections on sexuality do women appear as moral agents: men can have lust in the hearts but not women; men can struggle with concupiscence but apparently women do not; men can exploit their wives sexually but women can't exploit their husbands sexually.

Such tight focus on male and female in the biblical account also leaves out all the interesting ways in which human sexuality refuses to be contained within those standard gender designations, not only biologically, but also psychologically and spiritually. What appears in the guise of description serves prescription: human love and sexuality can appear in only one approved form, with every other way of being either sexual or loving left out altogether. Is it not important at least to acknowledge that a significant portion of humans—even if we take a ludicrously low percentage, at least tens of millions—are homosexual? Are they left outside God's plan if they are not part of the biblical story? Would not an adequate phenomenology of human sexuality, so concerned with "persons," after all, rather than statistics, take with great seriousness this part of the human family, who are also called to be loving, and in many fashions to create and foster the work and joy of creation?

Even within this normative framework, out of all the things that might be taken up and discussed within married love and the vocation of parenting, John Paul II's conferences finally come down to a concentration on "the transmission of life." By the time he reaches his explicit discussion of *Humanae Vitae*, it is difficult to avoid the conclusion that every earlier textual choice and phenomenological reflection has been geared to a defense of Paul VI's encyclical. However, there is virtually nothing in this defense that is strengthened by the conferences preceding it.

WHAT THE POPE LEAVES OUT

John Paul II is certainly to be appreciated for trying to place the knotty and disputed questions concerning procreation into a more comprehensive theology of the body. But there are a number of things lacking in these conferences and in the various declarations of the pope's apologists. I will simply list some obvious ones without development.

Most important, I would like to see a greater intellectual modesty, not only concerning the "facts" of revelation but also with the "facts" of human embodiedness. In everything having to do with the body, we are in the realm of what Gabriel Marcel calls mystery. The body does not present a series of problems that we can solve by detached analysis. The body rather is a mystery in two significant ways. First, we don't understand everything about the body, particularly our own body. The means by which we reveal ourselves to others and lovingly unite with others is not unambiguous. The body reveals itself to thought but also conceals itself from our minds. Second, we cannot detach ourselves from our bodies as though they were simply what we "have" rather than also what we "are." We are deeply implicated and cannot distance ourselves from the body without self-distortion. Our bodies are not only to be schooled by our minds and wills; they also instruct and discipline us in often humbling ways. Should not a genuine "theology of the body" begin with a posture of receptive attention to and learning from our bodies? Human bodies are part of God's image and the means through which absolutely everything we can learn about God must come to us.

In this regard, I find much of contemporary talk about "controlling our bodies" exactly contrary to such humility, whether such language derives from technocrats seeking to engineer reproductive processes or from naturalists who seek the same control through continence. I am not suggesting that a lack of continence or temperance is a desirable goal. But self-control is not the entire point of sexual love; celibacy is not the goal of marriage! And it may help to remember, in all this talk of controlling the body, that Dante assigned a deeper place in hell to the cold and the cruel than to the lustful. It can be argued, especially from the evidence of this century, that more evil has been visited upon us by various Stalins of sexless self-control than by the (quickly exhausted) epicures of the erotic. Recognition of the ways in which we suffer, rather than steer, our bodies is a beginning of wisdom.

Along these lines, I would welcome from the pope some appreciation for the goodness of sexual pleasure—any bodily pleasure, come to think of it! Pleasure is, after all, also God's gift. A sadly neglected text is 1 Timothy 6:17, where God supplies us all things richly for our enjoyment. Sexual passion, in papal teaching, appears mainly as an obstacle to authentic love. Many of us have experienced sexual passion as both humbling and liberating, a way in which our bodies know quicker and better than our minds, choose better and faster than our reluctant wills, even get us to where God apparently wants us in a way our minds never could. Along the same lines, papal teaching might find a good word to say about the sweetness of sexual love —also, I think, God's gift. Amid all the talk of self-donation and mutuality, we should also remember, "plus, it feels good." Come to think of it, why not devote some meditation to the astonishing triumph of sexual fidelity in marriage? Faithfulness, when it is genuine, is the result of a delicate and attentive creativity between partners, and not simply the automatic product of "self-control." In short, a more adequate theology of the body would at least acknowledge the positive ways in which the body gifts us by "controlling" us.

As with pleasure, so with pain. A theology of the body ought to recognize the ways in which human sexual existence is difficult: how arduous and ambiguous a process it is for any of us to become mature sexually; how unstable and shifting are our patterns of sexual identity; how unpredictable and vagrant are our desire and craving, as well as our revulsion and resistance; how little support there is for covenanted love in our world; how much the stresses of life together—and apart—bear upon our sexual expression. John Paul II and his apologists seem to think that concupiscence is our biggest challenge. How many of us would welcome a dose of concupiscence, when the grinding realities of sickness and need have drained the body of all its sap and sweetness, just as a reminder of being sentient! I would welcome the honest acknowledgment that for many who are married the pleasure and comfort of sexual love are most needed precisely when least available, not because of fertility rhythms, but because of sickness and anxiety and separation and loss. For that matter, a theology of the body ought to speak not only of an "original solitude" that is supposedly cured by marriage, but also of the "continuing solitude" of those both married and single, whose vocation is not celibacy yet whose erotic desires find, for these and many other reasons, no legitimate or sanctified expression, and, in these papal conferences, neither recognition nor concern.

The pope does not examine these and many other aspects of the body and of "human love in the divine plan." Instead, the theology of the body is reduced to sexuality, and sexuality to "the transmission of life." The descent to biologism is unavoidable. What is needed is a more generous appreciation of the way sexual energy pervades our interpersonal relations and creativity—including the life of prayer!—and a fuller understanding of covenanted love as life-giving and sustaining in multiple modes of parenting, community building, and world enhancement.

REVISITING *HUMANAE VITAE*

John Paul II's conferences and the recent articles I have quoted have meant to defend the correctness of *Humanae Vitae*, but paradoxically they remind readers with any historical memory how flawed that instrument was, and how badly it is in need of a fundamental revisiting. George Weigel calls it a "pastoral and catechetical failure," as though the encyclical's deficiencies were merely those of tone or effective communication. John Paul II's biblical reflections, in fact, appear as nothing less than a major effort to ground *Humanae Vitae* in something more than natural law; an implicit recognition of the argumentative inadequacy of Paul VI's encyclical. As my earlier comments indicate, I would judge his success as slight. It would be a weary business to take up the entire encyclical again, but it is important at least to note five major deficiencies that require a genuinely theological response rather than enthusiastic or reluctant apology.

In these comments, I will speak of "artificial birth control" only in terms of using a condom, diaphragm, or other mechanical device, mainly because I have considerable unease concerning chemical interventions and their implications for women's long-term health.

First, the encyclical represents a reversion to an act-centered morality, ignoring the important maturation of moral theology in the period leading up to and following Vatican II, which emphasized a person's fundamental dispositions as more defining of moral character than isolated acts. I am far from suggesting that specific acts are not morally significant. But specific acts must also be placed within the context of a person's character as revealed in consistent patterns of response. The difference is critical when the encyclical and John Paul II insist that it is not enough for married couples to be open to new life; rather, every act of intercourse must also be open, so that the use of a contraceptive in any single act in effect cancels the entire disposition of openness. But this is simply nonsense. I do not cancel my commitment to breathing when I hold my breath for a moment or when I go under anesthesia. Likewise, there is an important distinction to be maintained between basic moral dispositions and single actions. The woman who kills in self-defense (or in defense of her children) does not become a murderer. The focus on each act of intercourse rather than on the overall dispositions of married couples is morally distorting.

Second, the arguments of Paul VI and John Paul II sacrifice logic to moral brinkmanship. When Paul VI equated artificial birth control and abortion, he not only defied science but also provoked the opposite result of the one he intended. He wanted to elevate the moral seriousness of birth control but ended by trivializing the moral horror of abortion. Similarly, from one side of the mouth, John Paul II recognizes two ends of sexual love, unitive intimacy and procreation. But from the other side of his mouth he declares that if procreation is blocked, not only that end has been canceled but also the unitive end as well. He has thereby, despite his protestations to the contrary, simply reduced the two ends to one. This can be shown clearly by applying the logic in reverse, by insisting that sexual intercourse that is not a manifestation of intimacy or unity also cancels the procreative end of the act.

Third, the position of the popes and their apologists continues to reveal the pervasive sexism that becomes ever more obvious within official Catholicism. I have touched above on the way John Paul II's reading of Scripture tends to reduce the moral agency of women within the marriage covenant and sexual relationships. This becomes glaringly obvious in the argument that artificial birth control is wrong because it tends to "instrumentalize" women for men's pleasure by making the woman a passive object of passion rather than a partner in mutuality. Yet the argument makes more experiential sense in reverse. Few things sound more objectifying than the arguments of the natural family planners, whose focus remains tightly fixed on biological processes rather than on emotional and spiritual communication through the body. The view that "openness to life" is served with moral integrity by avoiding intercourse during fertile periods (arguably times of greatest female pleasure in making love) and is not served (and becomes morally reprehensible) by the mutual agreement to use a condom or diaphragm, would be laughable if it did not have such tragic consequences. And what could be more objectifying of women than speaking as though birth control were something that only served male concupiscence? How about women's moral agency in the realm of sexual relations? Don't all of us living in the real world of bodies know that women have plenty of reasons of their own to be relieved of worries about pregnancy for a time and to be freed for sexual enjoyment purely for the sake of intimacy and even celebration?

Fourth, the absolute prohibition of artificial birth control becomes increasingly scandalous in the face of massive medical realities. One might want to make an argument that distributing condoms to teenagers as a part of sex education is mistaken, but that argument, I think, has to do with misgivings concerning sex education—and a general culture of permissiveness—as a whole. But what about couples who can no longer have sexual relations because one of them has innocently been infected by HIV, and not to use a condom means also to infect the other with a potentially lethal virus? When does "openness to life" in every act become a cover for "death-dealing"? Given the fact that, in Africa, AIDS affects tens of millions of men, women, and children (very many of them Christian), is the refusal to allow the use of condoms (leaving aside other medical interventions and the changing of sexual mores) coming dangerously close to assisting in genocide? These are matters demanding the most careful consideration by the church, and the deepest compassion. It is difficult to avoid the sense that the failed logic supposedly marshaled in the defense of life is having just the opposite result. If the political enslavement of millions of Asians and Europeans led the papacy to combat the Soviet system in the name of compassion, and if the enslavement and murder of millions of Jews led the papacy to renounce the anti-Semitism of the Christian tradition in the name of compassion, should not compassion also lead at the very least to an examination of logic, when millions of Africans are enslaved and killed by a sexual pandemic?

Fifth, and finally, shouldn't *Humanae Vitae* be revisited rather than simply defended for the same reasons that it was a "pastoral and catechetical" failure the first time around? It failed to convince most of its readers not least because its readers knew that Paul VI spoke in the face of the recommendations of his own birth-control commission. The encyclical was, as Weigel calls it, a "new Galileo crisis," not simply because it pitted papal authority against science, but also because the papacy was wrong both substantively and formally. It generated an unprecedented crisis for papal authority precisely because it was authority exercised not only apart from but also in opposition to the process of discernment. Sad to say, John Paul's theology of the body, for all its attention to Scripture, reveals the same deep disinterest in the ways the experience of married people, and especially women (guided by the Holy Spirit, as we devoutly pray) might inform theology and the decision-making process of the church. If papal teaching showed signs of attentiveness to such experience, and a willingness to learn from God's work in the world as well as God's word in the tradition, its pronouncements would be received with greater enthusiasm. A theology of the body ought at least to have feet that touch the ground.

Since God is the Living One who continuously presses upon us at every moment of creation, calling us to obedience and inviting us to a painful yet joyous quest of wisdom, theology must be inductive rather than deductive. Our reading of Scripture not only shapes our perceptions of the world, but is in turn shaped by our experiences of God in the fabric of our human freedom and in the cosmic play of God's freedom. Theology that takes the self-disclosure of God in human experience with the same seriousness as it does God's revelation in Scripture does not turn its back on tradition but recognizes that tradition must constantly be renewed by the powerful leading of the Spirit if it is not to become a form of falsehood. Theology so understood is a demanding and delicate conversation that, like sexual love itself, requires patience as well as passion. If we are to reach a better theology of human love and sexuality, then we must, in all humility, be willing to learn from the bodies and the stories of those whose response to God and to God's world involves sexual love. That, at least, is a starting point.

NOTES

1. Charles J. Chaput, O.F.M., Cap, "Contraception: A Symposium," *First Things* (December, 1988).

2. Janet Popiel, "Necessary Connections? Catholicism, Feminism, and Contraception," *America* (November 27, 1999).

3. George Weigel, *Witness to Hope* (New York: Cliff Street Books, 1999).

4. *Theology of the Body: Human Love in the Divine Plan* (Boston: Pauline Books and Media, 1997).

5. See *Dei Verbum: Dogmatic Constitution on Divine Revelation*, Solemnly Promulgated by His Holiness Pope Paul VI, November 18, 1965, in *Vatican Council II: A Completely Revised Translation in Inclusive Language*, ed. Austin Flannery, O.P., (Northport, NY: Costello Publishing Company, 1988), 2:8.

8

Graceful Pleasures: Why Sex Is Good for Your Marriage*

Christine Gudorf

The debate over contraception that emerged in the U.S. Catholic Church in the 1960s convinced many lay Catholics that clerics who controlled the decision-making process in the church had a very different approach to sexuality than married couples.

Within the papal commission appointed by John XXIII to study conception, for example, married couples were appalled when the moderator, a cleric, opened one session with the question: "Is the sexual act necessary for couples?" They were even more appalled when it became clear that for many of the clerics, this was a serious question.

In the decades since the sixties, we have learned that there are priests and bishops who understand sex as central to the meaning and function of marriage as well as married couples who understand sex as both sinful and peripheral to marriage. Yet many married couples are examining their experiences of sex and finding that much of their emerging appreciation of sex and its role in marriage runs contrary to the dominant treatment of sex in Christian tradition.

Beginning with the Fathers of the Church, the dominant Christian perspective has been anti-sexual. The most positive traditional treatment of sex posited that sex was good because it produced children; helped alleviate temptation to sin (nonmarital sex); and, according to St. Augustine, functioned as a symbol of the unity between Christ and the Church.

*This chapter originally appeared as "Why Sex Is Good For Your Marriage" in *U.S. Catholic* 57 (November 1992): 6–13. Copyright 1992 *U.S. Catholic*. Reproduced by permission from the November 1992 issue of *U.S. Catholic*. Subscriptions: $22/year from 205 West Monroe, Chicago, IL 60606; call 1-800-328-6515 for subscription information or visit www .uscatholic.org/.

On the other hand, virtually all early Christian writers agreed that the problem with sex was that it was so pleasurable that it overrode reason, weakened the resolution of the will, and led persons into sin. Some of the Fathers believed that there had been no sex at all until Adam and Eve sinned. Then God tacked on genitals as they left the garden so that humanity might survive the loss of its immortality.

Even the view that prevailed, shared by Augustine and St. Thomas Aquinas among others, is not much better: Adam and Eve had genitalia (which they might or might not have used, depending on how long they lived in the garden); but before sin, sex was "perfect"—that is, without physical pleasure. It was a reproductive act governed solely by the will, not the emotions, and was performed like a farmer sows seed, with deliberation, not ecstasy.

Augustine asserted that even marital sex for purposes of procreation was venially sinful because it was so impossible to experience it without pleasure.

Such attitudes are not without modern adherents. Some couples still cultivate the sexual abstinence they were taught to practice during Lent and Advent—understanding abstinence as both virtuous in itself and necessary for good prayer or other spiritual feats. And many Christian couples who appreciate sex feel that what should be valued is the companionship, comfort, and intimate bonding that can arise in sex and not the physical pleasure of sex, which seems somehow not Christian.

WAS IS IT GOOD FOR YOU?

I want to develop a very different position on sex in marriage. Marriage is a vocation, a distinctive spiritual path, a way of living out one's faith. The relational goods—as distinct from the reproductive goods—that emerge from sex in marriage are, without exception, dependent upon sex being pleasurable.

While pregnancy can result from painful or abusive sex, sex that is not pleasurable does not create intimacy, does not prompt companionship, does not spur bonding. The more pleasurable the sex—the more deeply satisfying it is—the more it sows the seeds for other goods in the marital relationship.

Sex—good, frequent, mutually pleasurable—is as vitally important to the vocation of marriage as reception of the Eucharist is to membership in the church community. One of the tasks of the church should be to help make marital sex more pleasurable.

This will shock many. It will threaten many married persons who have learned to survive in marriage without the support of a nurturing sexual relationship. Many of these people have come to accept the traditional understanding of sex as morally suspect because their own experience of sex has been less than mutually pleasurable.

They are not alone. For various reasons, close to half of all couples experience less than optimal sex in marriage. Ten percent of women have total lifelong anorgasmia (the failure to reach orgasm) and an additional 20 percent are usually anorgasmic in intercourse. More than 10 percent of men experience erection difficulties (impotence), and about 20 percent report premature ejaculation—though some professional estimates of the incidence of regular premature ejaculation run as high as 50 percent.

Twenty percent of women report pain in intercourse, a great deal of it due to insufficient vaginal lubrication, which is itself most often the result of insufficient stimulation. (Only 40 percent of women can become sufficiently aroused from intercourse itself to reach orgasm. Direct or indirect stimulation of the clitoris, which is much more densely endowed with nerve-endings than is the vagina, is necessary for most women to reach orgasm.)

About 13 percent of men and 27 percent of women report a lack of sexual desire in marriage, which can be either a long-term result of these physical problems or a result of problems in the relationship such as alcoholism, physical abuse, fear, dislike, resentment, or disputes over such things as money and children. For most couples, if sex has normally been pleasurable both physically and emotionally, desire will not be a problem.

In the presence of such sexual problems in marriage or when, because of illness, accident, or extreme age, a sexual relationship ceases, some married couples have constructed nonsexual relationships. (Often such recourse is not necessary for the impossibility of penile/vaginal intercourse does not, despite popular opinion to the contrary, rule out other forms of sexual sharing.)

These nonsexual relationships can be good and healthy. They can meet individual needs for companionship and giving and receiving love and can be sources of grace. But even so, they are not essentially marriages but intense friendships. This does not mean they are inferior to marriages, only different from, and therefore should not be suggested as nonsexual alternatives to sexual marriages.

Sexual loving is central to marriage. The friendship and commitment of marriage is conveyed in sexual form. Without the sexual exchange of love and grace, the relationship is not marital.

The church needs to confirm the importance of pleasurable sex for the vocation of marriage. Such a shift is only one part of a much larger shift away from the traditional—but very unbiblical—separation between our spiritual and material lives.

Contemporary theology is in the process of eliminating the traditional dividing line between the material and the spiritual and asserting that in human experience we learn that the spiritual is not separate from but rather one integral part of the natural world. We can experience the presence of God when we view a beautiful sunset; we can feel trust in God and others from the experience of physical, sexual love; and we can feel the goodness of God and of God's creation when we experience the joy of bringing new life into the world.

When people fall in love with each other, they want to spend more time with each other. The reason for this desire is that being with the loved one makes one feel more real, more alive, more loving, more at peace with one-self. These are spiritual qualities, qualities for which all humans hunger. All love puts us in touch with ultimate reality—the divine presence—for which we have an innate hunger and thirst.

But love is not something abstract. It is a relationship with a real person, which usually means, a flesh and blood material person. We can only know of, relate to, and love ultimate reality—God—through interacting with persons and things in the material world. All of our sources for knowledge of God—from the Bible to contemporary experience—reflect human experience of God, which occurs in a specific material history, mediated by the senses of the human person.

For many persons, the experience of orgasm in loving marriage is the clearest experience of the divine they have ever known. In this orgasmic experience, we feel known to the depth of our souls, loved by one from whom we have no secrets, and freed to risk ourselves, let go our very consciousness, and become totally vulnerable to the loved one. Is there a better way to describe the optimal relationship with God?

In my own marriage I was very clear that sex had for me an intensely religious dimension, which for a while made my husband somewhat uncomfortable. He came to agree that sex in our marriage functioned to bestow grace on us as individuals and as a household; but it took some time before he no longer feared to find Jesus, the pope, or a Marian apparition sharing our bed.

In restructuring Christian attitudes toward the material world and toward sexuality in particular, Catholic theologians call upon some very positive and useful parts of our tradition that can be helpful in overcoming more repressive understandings of sexuality. Perhaps the Catholic tradition that is most useful in this overall shift is the church's insistence on the sacramentality of marriage.

FULL OF GRACE

To say that marriage is a sacrament means that marriage bestows grace on the spouses. Grace has not always been explained well within the church. It is true that grace is not something that we can easily touch, or see, or taste.

Grace is not easily measured. But grace *can* be experienced. We cannot only learn to "feel" the presence or absence of grace in ourselves, but sometimes we can even recognize the presence of grace in others. Though we must be careful not to enforce judgments based on our limited intuitions, at times we may be convinced that we have been blessed by the presence of a truly graced person.

Grace is a power that gives us strength to love, resist sin, and act courageously in the face of suffering. Grace is not only present at extraordinary times. We are called to pursue grace as the ongoing presence of God in our lives, as that which allows us to make virtue a habit. It is grace in marriage that helps us to exert ourselves to solve problems, to share our lives, to sacrifice for the other, and to grow both as individuals and in our relationship.

If grace is recognized, accepted, and used, the ability of spouses to understand each other, to share themselves, and to support each other in times of trouble and suffering all grow. It is this grace-conveying sacramental quality that older couples refer to when they say that their love grew stronger as their marriages aged.

The church also understands that sexuality is central to this particular sacrament. Sexual intercourse is the primary symbol of sacramental marriage, just as washing with water is the primary symbol of baptism. Sacramental symbols signify what the sacrament means. These symbols are more than arbitrarily chosen signs. The physical reality of a symbol conveys something of what the symbol represents.

The symbol of sexual intercourse and in particular its culmination, orgasm, is not merely one physical reality associated with marriage. Instead, it embodies in a real way the entire meaning of marriage. Sacramental marriage is about love and bonding between spouses; and sexual intercourse is an important way of creating, nurturing, and multiplying that love and bonding.

Crucial to the effectiveness of sexual intercourse as the sacramental symbol of marriage is the pleasure that it involves. If sexual intercourse were not pleasurable, it would not work as the symbol of marriage. All human persons seek to maximize pleasure and minimize pain. Our search for pleasure, for satisfaction, is what drives our hunger for food, for friendship, for love, for beauty, for security, for God. The pleasure of sexual intercourse, and in particular the ecstatic communion of orgasm, functions as a reward.

Orgasmic pleasure is our reward for allowing ourselves to be open and vulnerable to the spouse, for trusting that the spouse will respect and cherish our person (our body as well as our feelings and dignity), for letting down the mask or guard behind which we usually shield ourselves from others. If we are to achieve orgasm in sex, we must even let go, to some extent, of self-consciousness and control. We become no longer conscious of how we appear to the other, we have no control over what we are doing and saying. We have surrendered to the other who has surrendered to us, and the mutual reward is ecstasy.

Wait, some may say. People who aren't married, people who don't even know or like each other, can share sex and even orgasm. True. But in sex without love and commitment the sex is not a fully functioning symbol. In those circumstances the baring of one's body, the offering of the pleasures of one's body, symbolize something less than the opening and offering of one's entire self to the other. What comes back to us as reward is almost always proportional to what we extended as gift. Sex without love and commitment can be pleasurable physically, if we only seek physical pleasure. But it cannot offer the same degree of reward, of pleasure, as if we had risked our very selves in self-disclosure.

Only by risking our whole selves do we receive the whole of the other as a gift. We are each enhanced by the love of the other. Our deepest human needs are not for purely physical pleasure—or for the momentary release of tension and stress that orgasm brings—but for a linked physical and emotional intimacy, for bonding. If we enter a sexual relationship seeking only physical pleasure and offering only physical pleasure to the other, we can achieve physical pleasure, but not the pleasure of satisfying our deeper needs.

There is entirely too much romanticization of love and sex in our culture. I would not want to add to it. Even in marriage, even in loving marriage, sex does not always function ideally. Spouses can use sex for physical pleasure alone without the offer of their bodies symbolizing their whole selves. They may be feeling anger, resentment, or fear of disclosure, despite their desire for sex with their spouse. These spouses, too, will get out of sex what they put into it. If both spouses offer only the use of their body, the pleasure they receive will be similarly limited.

DON'T GO TO BED ANGRY

Some couples mistakenly believe that sex resolves anger, resentment, fear, or other obstacles to intimacy. Sometimes sex is used to replace expressions of sorrow and contrition, as if it obliterates problems and divisions. There are, in fact, situations in which sex can resolve small distances within the relationship if these are only due to the irritations of everyday life.

If I come home from work and snap at my husband because I am tired from working late and getting stuck in traffic, initiating sex can be one way to say "I'm sorry" and smooth our ruffled feathers. It is, however, dangerous to get into a habit of avoiding verbal apologies through recourse to sex.

But if there is some very real problem within our relationship that has undermined feelings of love and trust, then sex alone cannot make that problem disappear. Going through the motions of sex, without having first gone through the struggle to understand, disclose, and compromise around differences is sex without symbolic meaning. Once couples know what marital sex can be, when they have experienced the reward that follows mutual self-giving in sex, they can only be disappointed by anything less and often feel cheated by the experience, as if something holy had been profaned.

Even lovemaking that has been passionately and satisfyingly pleasurable may leave spouses feeling emptied rather than filled if they brought to it expectations for re-establishing emotional bonding and psychic oneness that were not satisfied. The physical release of orgasm in marital sex can sometimes feel less satisfying than masturbatory orgasm precisely because the integrity of marital sex—its sacredness—which is instinctively understood in terms of mutual self-giving, has been undermined by the failure to lower emotional and psychic barriers by the use of the other as an object.

If we choose to make marital sex truly symbolic of our marital love, then marital sex becomes a school for love. It teaches us that we bare our full selves, not only our bodies but our feelings, desires, fears, and commitments and offer ourselves to the loved spouse who loves us, that we are rewarded not only by physical pleasure but with intimacy that offers us closeness, communion, stimulation, and companionship. As we learn that giving ourselves fully in sex is rewarding, we feel encouraged to give ourselves fully to the spouse in other nongenital ways as well because we trust that these other gifts—of time, effort, confidences—will also be returned multiplied.

Giving of ourselves in a loving marriage becomes habitual, something we do not need to consider, but something we just do. In a grace-filled marriage, we move from feelings of love and commitment to giving of ourselves in sex, to giving ourselves to the spouse in all the other areas that make up our shared life, to giving of our time, effort, love, and trust to others, such as friends, children, neighbors, and our wider communities. Grounded in marital love, we can risk loving others even before they have loved us. Sex is the concrete physical symbol of this process.

The sexual desire created by marital sex is a source of tremendous energy in marriage—loving energy that overflows on others. This fact is obvious to children whose parents do not hide their sexual attraction for each other. Before my own sons were adolescents, they had learned that when either my husband or I was tense and irritable, the best way to make the home atmosphere more warm and comfortable was for one or all of them to approach one of us and suggest that he or I entice the irritable one into a "little nap," the euphemism we had given them for our retreat to our bedroom.

Good marital sex creates more sexual desire, which is also a kind of energy. The popular understanding that sexual desire draws us to sexual activity, which then exhausts desire, is only partially true. Sexual desire does draw us to sexual intercourse, but it is also re-created and nourished by sexual intercourse.

Many married couples are amazed to discover this fact and view it as an aberration, as evidence of some strange wantonness in their characters. They expect that a pleasurable lovemaking session will satisfy sexual desire, which will need to build again over time. They are often shocked to discover that a prolonged lovemaking session produces a greater need to touch one another, be near one another, and be sexually aware of the other—not only for the first moments of the resolution phase following orgasm but for hours and even days afterward. We want to cuddle up to the spouse in sleep—sleeping like spoons, as Giles Milhaven calls it. We want to prolong the intimacy that loving sex creates; we want to stay close to the person who gave us such deep pleasure.

Often such behavior is attributed to newlyweds, who, whether or not they have waited until marriage for sex, are assumed to have stored up immense quantities of hitherto unsatisfied sexual desire that can for the first time be freely indulged. But such behavior is not limited to newlyweds. It is part of the symbolism of sexual intercourse within sacramental marriage. It is how sex *creates* the love it signifies.

The church has always taught that the ability to engage in sexual intercourse, and not the ability to reproduce, is an essential requirement for marriage. Women who had never menstruated, women past menopause, and men sterile due to accidents or disease were allowed marriage. But impotent men, men who could not achieve penile erection, were not marriageable. A true marriage has always required consummation (sexual intercourse). Still today, the failure, for whatever reason, to consummate a marriage is grounds for annulment—the declaration by the church that no real marriage ever existed, regardless of the existence of a marriage ceremony.

The church has always emphasized the need for mutual sexual self-giving in marriage. The language for self-giving often contained negative concepts like obligation and debt, rather than mutual pleasure, but there was recognition that spousal bonding involved sex that was not only for the purpose of reproduction.

WIVES, PAUL WAS WRONG

Another reason why the sexual bond between spouses was not fully understood or valued in the church's past tradition was the hierarchical model of the dominant husband and subordinate wife assumed by the broader society and by the church.

Such a power imbalance makes open communication difficult. Men and women were understood to be mutually bound: husbands to command,

and wives to obey. This is a far cry from loving the other for his or her own sake. Such a bond invites dependency more than trust. Yet it is trust, not dependency, that is required if we are to open ourselves to intimacy with another. We trust because we love, not because other persons have obligations to us or us to them.

When power is unequally divided between a dominant and a subordinate partner, love is never truly voluntary. It is always based on an obligation of some kind: the obligation to render that which the other demands or to render that for which the other is dependent upon us.

The assumption of dominant/subordinate relations is especially inappropriate in the area of marital sex. In general, the most satisfying sex presupposes equality because equality in sex allows each of us to have the broadest range of sexual experiences within the relationship. The couple that feels that men should initiate and control sex will have a narrower sexual repertoire.

The husband in such a couple will never be free to be a receptive partner who is touched and stroked and lays back feeling himself carried from arousal to orgasm without responsibility or planning. The wife in such a couple will never have the freedom to touch, stroke, and control the pace and force of the lovemaking as she wills and learn her own ability to arouse her spouse, successfully control the experience, and carry them both to orgasmic communion. Over a lifetime they will miss the many lovemaking sessions that she could have and would have initiated, either by letting him know that she was interested or by taking the initiative and arousing him to a willingness to sexual play. Even couples who still adhere to traditional sex roles in other areas of their lives are less likely to preserve those limiting roles in the marital bed once they realize the alternatives—for to do so can be boring.

Sex is not only about passion; it can and should be varied and be at different times playful, companionable, and experimental. Sex can be silent and vigorous, or relaxed and interspersed with conversation. To keep levels of sexual interest and energy high, sex needs to be all these and more. Such variety requires that both partners can communicate their desires freely.

In our society, influenced as it has been by notions of men as active and women as passive, men frequently have been trained to take too much responsibility for sex. But now that society is more aware of women's equality and right to sexual pleasure, the understanding of sex as men's responsibility makes men anxious about their sexual performance (a frequent cause of erectile problems), since they feel responsible not only for their own pleasure but for women's also. This social pressure for men to accept all responsibility for sex can also contribute to anorgasmia in women because taking an active role in sex is, for women, very closely related to achieving orgasm.

WE DESIRE SEX SYMBOLS

One of the greatest challenges in the church today is to better implement an understanding of the symbolic centrality of sex to marriage. There has probably never been a culture so influenced by and hungry for symbolism and the meaning and values it conveys, which is, at the same time, so disdainful of symbols and so ready to abandon all the symbols inherited from the past.

We are only beginning to see that contemporary blindness to symbols and their meanings leaves us open to be manipulated by the symbols we refuse to consciously recognize. For example, when a person takes seriously the would-be lover who offers a brief, pleasurable sexual exchange, that person—and possibly the would-be lover as well—is really dealing with two messages. One message is the overt offer of a casual sexual exchange, and the other is sex's unspoken symbolic message that offers a great deal more than momentary pleasure. That symbolic message offers the possibility of two souls touching and bonding, of finding a home in another, of joy that is more than bodily well being, as important as that is.

The dual messages are confusing. To which is the person to respond? It is no wonder that so many persons are left wounded by sexual affairs.

Sex and sexual pleasure are so important to marriage that every care should be taken to prepare persons to be good lovers of their spouses. The sacramental status of marriage dictates that a great deal of the responsibility for such preparation should fall on the church. Unfortunately, virtually none of the church's marriage preparation programs deals adequately with sexuality. In fact, the level of sexual education that engaged couples bring to marriage preparation is so low that it would be impossible for the church to deal adequately with the subject before marriage, no matter what resources were available. It is just not possible to cram into even the most extensive programs all the sexual information that has been excluded from people for most of their lives.

One basic step in improving marriage preparation in the future, then, is for the church to support comprehensive sexual education programs in both public and parochial schools. When the Kinsey Institute tested thousands of U.S. citizens—adults of all educational levels—in October 1989, it found that only 20 percent could answer twelve of eighteen questions concerning basic sexual information, such as how women get pregnant, how AIDS can be contracted, who needs breast/testicular self-exams, and normal penis size.

But alongside great ignorance about sexuality in U.S. society is also tremendous curiosity that is both healthy and hopeful. I continue to be encouraged that my students complain because their comprehensive social science textbook on sexuality is hard to hold on to—their roommates, friends, parents, grandparents, and older siblings repeatedly borrow the book.

People tease about interest in sex, as if all interest is prurient. But we should want our children, our friends, and our own spouses to seek help in becoming the best sexual lovers of their partners that they can be. And that means learning about how bodies work and about gender differences, sexual techniques, and sexual communication.

GO ASK YOUR FATHER

Even if marriage preparation did not have to face massive sexual ignorance, there would still be other problems with the sexuality component of marriage preparation. The legacy of sexual repression in our churches and society has failed to produce many people who are comfortable teaching about sexuality.

In the past, marriage preparation in the church was usually left to priests. Priests have had as little sexual education as lay people but have, unlike most lay people, usually had no personal experiences of marital sex upon which to draw. Most of them, like lay people, emerged from families in which parents did not talk about sexual activity or about their own sexual relationships.

In addition, especially in earlier decades of this century, many priests left their families for the seminary at very young ages before they were very conscious of parental sexual relationships. Such priests often tended to understand their parent's marriages, and therefore their general model for marriage, as more or less nonsexual and as revolving around children. This has traditionally been a severe problem for clerical marriage preparation and counseling.

In recent years, more and more parishes have involved married couples in preparing the engaged for marriage. This trend is excellent, but for most of these married couples, what they know of marital sex has been learned almost exclusively in the privacy of their own marriage beds. They have done very well if they have learned to feel comfortable discussing their sexual activity with each other. We live in a culture in which few friends and relatives discuss marital sex, especially not sexual technique or the role of sex in marriage.

Consequently, most married couples involved in preparing engaged couples for marriage are unlikely to feel comfortable giving any instruction or advice around lovemaking because they feel that their own base of personal experience is too narrow to be useful to others.

Minimal training for mentoring couples in marriage preparation programs should involve teaching couples to use sexual vocabulary comfortably in groups, characterize and disclose their own sexual experiences and learning processes to others, and especially describe how sex has functioned in their marriages as a source of grace. This does not mean that we discard all our notions about sexual behavior as private. For example, I tell many stories about sexuality in the classroom. A large number of them come from my own experience. But not all of them do because my sexual experience is limited to my twenty-three-year marriage. I respect anonymity, of course, and occasionally change details that might narrow the identity of the subjects.

For years, my husband was somewhat uneasy whenever he was likely to meet my students for fear they were privy to the secrets of our marital bed. Then we began to do marriage preparation together, and he too started using stories from our marriage, some of them about sex, when he sensed delicate issues needed to be discussed. The teacher in him knew instinctively that the most effective way to convey information was not to lecture in the abstract but to tell a story. In telling some of our stories, he began to understand that the telling is not like a camera filming each physical gesture and response as they happen but is rather a telling from hindsight, which focuses on what was created and learned, shared, and communicated.

Parents, too, must be able to talk to their children about sex in marriage, and that means that husbands and wives must first learn to communicate with each other about sex in their marriages. The fact that two-thirds of married women and almost a third of married men in the U.S. regularly fake orgasms says very clearly that the level of honest communication about sex in marriage is not high.

In working with married couples, my husband and I have often seen the simplest sexual issues become major problems. One young couple, who we suspected had a problem just by the physical distance between them, when asked if they had any problems about sex, answered no. But when asked whether their sex was, then, completely satisfying, they both immediately answered "No!" As it turned out, she felt that he was interested in sex but not in her because he would sometimes barely get in the front door before he was removing her clothes and would sometimes initiate sex in bed after ignoring her all evening to watch TV. On the other hand, he felt unloved because of her frequent disinterest in and rejection of sex, which he attributed to frigidity and understood as common among women.

When asked whether she felt she was frigid, she said no, that she had often enjoyed sex during their two years together but only when he first spent some time with her talking, sharing some task, or holding her while they watched TV. When asked, he said maybe that was true; he remembered her being very interested and responsive a couple of months before when they returned from a wedding at which they had danced together a great deal.

Two weeks later they returned to see us, glowing, holding hands, and marveling over the improvement in their sex life. They had made some simple changes: (1) they arranged to go out twice a month for an evening; (2) they set aside one hour each night after their son was asleep to spend together and decided to limit the number of times per week they used it to watch TV together; and (3) they agreed to share more of their feelings about sex. It took no special expertise to resolve their problem. They did it entirely by themselves once they heard each other state the situation.

Many troubled marriages could be helped without professional counsel if couples could learn to communicate with each other, especially about marital sex, where lack of communication seems to be so profound that the smallest problems can become lethal for the relationship.

Within good marital sexual communication, some basic guidelines that should be explicitly agreed upon are that sex should be mutually pleasurable and that when sex is not mutually pleasurable, both partners share responsibility for making and keeping sex pleasurable. No one, no matter how much he or she loves the spouse, is a mind reader. Acting pleasured without feeling it can set up very risky situations in which one spouse has no idea the other is not pleasured; and the unpleasured spouse often becomes dissatisfied with his or her lack of pleasure and resentful of the other's unconcern about it—despite the fact that lack of pleasure was not communicated to the other.

Other kinds of communication about sex are also appropriate and necessary within marriage. Anniversaries are great times for couples to review the changes in their marriage. Some good friends of mine once observed in an anniversary discussion of their marriage that in the last year or two their pattern of sexual initiation had changed and that he, rather than she, was now much more likely to suggest or initiate sex. The husband had been worried that this indicated dwindling interest on her part. But for her, the trend was extremely positive. She interpreted it to mean that for the first time in their marriage, he was as highly interested in sex (and his spouse) as she.

With some reflection, they placed this shift in their sexual relationship within the context of their overall relationship. They realized that, like many marriages, theirs had initially been somewhat male-controlled. During those years, the wife had taken the initiative in sex in part because that was, for this couple, the least controversial area in which she could exercise power without threatening her husband.

During the middle age of the marriage, the wife began to share more in the everyday decisions and future planning for the marriage. In response to the wife's increased role in decision making, the husband began to take more initiative in sex. Once they recognized the pattern, they both felt very comfortable with the changes because neither one of them wanted total control or responsibility for their sexual relationship or for other areas of their relationship.

MOM AND DAD? NO WAY!

If couples can learn to talk about their sexual relationships with each other, then they can learn to talk about it with their children. What children need more than anything else from their parents concerning sex is a sense of how sexual relationships function. Children want to know that their parents are loving, affectionate, and physically appreciative of each other.

I will never forget my pleasure at hearing my father's Christmas toast to my mother at a family dinner when I was a young girl (even though I only dimly understood the vocabulary): "To Lucie, and her multiple orgasms!" Only many years later did I realize how extremely rare this kind of openness and appreciativeness about sex was. But for me it reinforced the everyday evidence of my parents' marital intimacy: they touched each other frequently with affection; they liked to spend time together; and when they emerged from their bedroom with their arms wrapped around each other, they were invariably warmer and more affectionate with us and more likely to suggest a game, a drive, or sharing a bowl of popcorn in front of the TV.

For all these reasons, increased attention should be given in both the church and society to strengthening the role of sex in marriage by removing the ignorance of sexuality, the lack of communication skills, and the lack of theological appreciation for sexuality and sexual communion, all of which put marriage at risk.

9

The Gift of Celibacy*

Evelyn Eaton Whitehead and James D. Whitehead

Christian faith proclaims its deepest truth in paradoxes. Like the grain of wheat, we must die in order to find life. We meet Christ in the unlikely guise of the sick and the imprisoned and the stranger. Celibacy is another of our faith's paradoxes. As Christians we know that we can love one another well apart from sexual sharing; we recognize that, even without offspring, we can live fruitful and generous lives. But in a culture such as ours, obsessed with sex as performance, this paradox provokes surprise and disbelief.

Celibacy is a durable mystery. From early on, some who follow Christ have chosen a path that excludes marriage and family. Over centuries of Christian history and across a wide range of cultural contexts, many people have experienced committed celibacy as a grace. This lifestyle has nurtured Christians in their personal journeys of faith. In addition, celibacy has borne fruit in generous service to the world as celibate women and men served in the formal ministry of the church.

A consideration of the lifestyle of vowed celibacy is essential in any discussion of Catholics and sexuality. As we turn to that consideration, let us offer an initial clarification. Although we—the authors—are married, the reality of committed celibacy is significant to us, personally and professionally. Our ministry puts us in touch with the convictions and concerns of many religious and priests; our friends who are vowed celibates share with us the wisdom of their own experience. So it is as interested and sympathetic companions that we observe the ongoing conversation about the meaning of celibacy for the church today.

---

*This chapter originally appeared in Evelyn Eaton Whitehead and James D. Whitehead, *Wisdom of the Body: Making Sense of Our Sexuality,* 2001. Reprinted with permission of The Crossroad Publishing Company; permission conveyed through Copyright Clearance Center, Inc.

In reevaluating the meaning of sexuality, the community of faith comes to reexamine the lifestyle of celibacy. In the process, some earlier understandings of celibacy have come under question. These images and expectations no longer provide celibate Christians with a compelling explanation of their own lives. They no longer provide the basis for a genuine appreciation of celibacy in the larger community of faith. Catholics today struggle to come to a renewed vision of celibacy as an authentic Christian way of life.

The vitality of the gift of celibacy has been repeatedly proven in its ability to take on new meaning, to be persuasive in many different historical and cultural settings. The challenge now is not to do away with celibacy but to find what meaning this gift holds for the future. Like other parts of Christian faith, celibacy will survive by being purified. Our goal in this chapter is to examine where we are, as a community of faith, in the conversation about the purpose and practice of celibacy today.

THE WHY OF CELIBACY

The why of celibacy raises questions of meaning and motive. What is the religious significance of the lifestyle of celibacy? Why do some Christians commit themselves to this way of following Jesus? Among Catholics in the 1940s and 1950s, the religious meaning of celibacy was clear. The church recommended this special way of life to those who would follow the path of perfection. Celibacy, or consecrated chastity, was understood to be one of the *evangelical counsels*. It was evangelical because it was rooted in the gospel. It was a counsel or advice that Jesus issues to his followers. To the rich young man who inquired about holiness, Jesus replied: "If you would be perfect . . . leave all and follow me." In Catholic spirituality, the vowed life of poverty, chastity, and obedience came to be seen as the principal way in which the gospel call to perfection could be followed. Most Christians would seek God by the ordinary way of life and work in the world; consecrated celibacy was an option for those who would seek the "better way."

But why was the choice of celibacy a "better way"? In the piety that had come to prevail in Catholic life, virginity was seen as preferable to marriage. Both Mary and Jesus were virgins. Moreover, the choice of celibacy helped one avoid the snares of sexual engagement and the entanglements of human love. Many Christians had been taught that sex was inevitably involved in sin and that human love was a distraction from a wholehearted devotion to God. True, these suspicions were seldom stated so baldly, and our best theology constantly battled against these aberrations. But many of us who grew up Catholic were influenced by these powerful, even if unorthodox, sentiments.

The problem with linking the religious significance of celibacy to these convictions is, of course, that they are heretical. That is not what Christians believe. Some religious traditions *have* judged sex to be evil; Manichaeism tempted the early Christians in this way. Christians, however, have consistently, even if not always successfully, insisted that sex—like all that God has created—is good.

Christians also dispute that the love of God is in competition with human love. In truth, some early proponents of an enforced celibacy for the clergy argued that the demands of marriage and family would distract the minister from his constant occupation with God. These advocates of celibacy were profoundly suspicious of the compatibility of the sacred and the sexual. But the best and most enduring conviction of Christians is that the love of God and the love of neighbor are essentially linked. In the love that others show us, we come to know the love of God. And only by loving other people is our love of God purified and matured.

The renewal of Catholic life generated by the Second Vatican Council brought with it a rethinking of the meaning of celibacy. The council's reaffirmation of the spirituality of marriage challenged earlier understandings of celibacy as the "better way" or "higher calling." Church historians showed that the lifestyle of vowed celibacy has emerged gradually, its meaning and purpose understood differently at different times in Christian tradition. Earlier explanations of celibacy no longer seemed adequate. Even when they were not in error, they could no longer persuade.

Over the past forty years, the vocabulary of the evangelical counsels has undergone profound purification. Vowed religious do not live in poverty as much as they do in simplicity. Their shared responsibility in community life is better understood as mutual accountability than as obedience to a quasiparental authority. And the chastity to which they aspire is not meant to deliver them from the dangerous demands of friendship, affection, and charity that other Christians face.

The spirituality of a "higher calling" drove a wedge in the community of faith, creating different classes of Christians. Recently this understanding has fallen into disuse. More and more celibates find that such a spirituality neither reflects their religious experience nor energizes their continuing commitment. An interpretation of celibacy as a "higher calling" does not serve the rest of us either, since it no longer reveals to the larger community of faith the religious significance that celibacy can hold.

This leaves the Catholic community at a loss. Our understanding of celibacy is moving away from the image of the evangelical counsel, but as yet no well-developed or widely accepted interpretation of celibacy replaces this image. Such a new consensus is sure to emerge, but only as we listen to the living tradition of consecrated celibacy as it takes shape in our own time. In the meantime, we are all at a disadvantage. Here, as in so many other areas of sexuality, we sense that we know more than we are able to say. Our religious vocabulary has not kept pace with our religious experience. Fortunately, the images used today in the discussion of celibacy hint at an emerging theology.

We will examine three of these images that are used most often in theology and by celibate Catholics. In each image, we will point out the positive understanding of celibacy as well as some of its limitations. The images we will consider are celibacy as a charism, as a choice, and as a call.

CELIBACY AS A CHARISM

The image of celibacy as a charism is often part of current discussion. Sometimes the term is simply a rhetorical flourish, but often it has more substance. The intent here, as in the understanding of celibacy as an evangelical counsel, is to root the lifestyle of consecrated celibacy in the gospel. This is a fruitful direction for the discussion, since every Christian lifestyle finds its source and significance in the witness of Jesus the Christ. The understanding of celibacy as a charism will surely be strengthened if it can be shown to bear the marks of the other gospel charisms.

Recent biblical scholarship helps clarify the meaning of charism. St. Paul reported the charisms that enlivened the church in Corinth: preaching, healing, prophecy, administration. These vital activities in the early Christian communities had three essential characteristics. They were, first, *personal abilities*. Charisms are specific strengths, identifiable talents, activities that a particular member of the community does well.

Second, these abilities are experienced as *gifts*. A follower of Jesus who finds herself capable in these ways is drawn to acknowledge that more than just herself is involved. She readily admits, "This is something that I do well, but I am not the sole or even the principal author of this talent. I experience myself as gifted and I am grateful." These gifts, Paul reminds us, come from the Spirit (1 Corinthians 12:11). They are not the result of administrative decision or official largesse. Instead they are discovered throughout the community, due to the generosity of God's Spirit.

Third, genuine charisms serve a *distinctive purpose*. These talents are not for private satisfaction or personal aggrandizement, but for the building up of the body of Christ. A charism is a gift that is meant to be given away. Acknowledged in gratitude, it is exercised in generosity. Charisms reside *in* particular people but exist *for* the community of faith.

If the image of charism is to serve as the basis for a more adequate appreciation of the religious significance of celibacy, then celibacy must be shown to meet these scriptural criteria. While celibacy is not listed among the charisms that Paul cites explicitly, that in itself is not the critical issue.

Catholics are not biblical fundamentalists; our appreciation of God's action in human history is not limited to proof texts. But if the powerful scriptural category of charism is to be used to explore the meaning of celibacy in our own time, the lifestyle of consecrated celibacy will have to display the three characteristics of a charism. We will have to show how this way of living is rooted in personal ability, how it is experienced as a gift, and how it serves the larger needs and hopes of the community of faith. Many of us are confident that celibacy—at least in a purified form—can show these characteristics. But the Christian community needs to expand this discussion and make it available in a compelling way.

CELIBACY AS A CHOICE

Another image figures significantly in current theology and spirituality: celibacy as a *choice*. Here the discussion is especially sensitive to the negative attitudes toward sex that so easily creep into a piety of celibacy. Historically, this piety had often urged Catholics to choose celibacy for negative reasons: to avoid the temptations of sex and the demands of a family. But, as Catholic theologians insist today, only if sex is evil, only if marriage is a "lesser way," is it praiseworthy to choose celibacy for these negative motives. The choice of celibacy must be a decision not *against*, but *for* something. The person must choose not just to avoid, but to engage. As with every Christian choice, the motivating force of this decision must be love for something. Christians make the decision to be celibate for the sake of the kingdom of God.

In some discussions, celibacy is chosen for the sake of the eschatological kingdom, the reign of God at the end of history. Celibates live among us as witnesses to the end-time, "where there will be neither marriage nor giving in marriage." This perspective, which acknowledges the goodness of sex and significance of married love, reminds us that these are only limited and partial realties. At its best, human love reveals God's love for us. But the immediacy of sex and the complexity of our relationships often blind us to the larger transcendent presence of God who is love. The lifestyle of committed celibacy is chosen for the sake of the kingdom. The committed celibate serves humankind as a sign of contradiction, forcing us to confront the deeper issues of human existence and meaning that are so easily masked in our culture's obsession with sex.

This argument is not persuasive with everyone, but it has a powerful influence on many whose ministry brings them into contact with persons whose lives have been devastated by our culture's sexual compulsions. To know strong, mature, caring celibates is a liberating experience for those who have been sexually abused, for young people caught in prostitution, for people grown sated with sex and yet cynical of any other source of personal worth. The eschatological or symbolic value of celibacy in our sex-crazed culture is an area that deserves much more thought. But a theology of celibacy that focuses on its witness value also remains accountable to the importance questions: Who is looking and what do they see?

The credibility of the Catholic Church in the area of sexuality is not unquestioned. Recent statements and actions make many persons of good will suspicious of what religious officials have to say on these issues. We must acknowledge that not many people today are looking to Catholic celibates for guidance and revelation concerning their sexuality. And some who do look to celibates do not see their lives as signs of love or generosity or joy. This theological interpretation of celibacy will become more credible as it confronts the practical question of what persons of good will see when they come in contact with the lives of religious celibates. Some suspect that many celibates are not faithful to their vows or that most are faithful only under duress and would marry if given that option. These perceptions undermine the persuasiveness of religious celibacy.

Another understanding of celibacy for the sake of the kingdom carries weight today. Participating in the mission of Jesus, some Christians are drawn into demanding work in potentially dangerous circumstances. They choose to share their life with the poor, care for the critically ill, work for social justice in the midst of politically repressive regimes. Devoting one's life to these efforts is often all-consuming; it can be perilous as well. Here the choice for celibacy may be part of a larger sense of vocation. A person reflects on the importance of his calling:

> Weighing the circumstances that surround my own life's work, I realize that wholehearted devotion to this mission will make it impossible—or at least difficult—for me to honor the practical and emotional commitments of marriage and family life. So, aware of the demands and dangers associated with my vocation, I've decided not to marry.

Celibacy is chosen not "for itself" but "for the sake of the kingdom."

This can be a compelling argument for committed celibacy. Some tasks in our time make these demands; some roles require such courage; some responsibilities ask for this kind of generous response. We have only to recall the patient heroism of the four women pastoral workers murdered in San Salvador or the witness of the others who risk imprisonment and disgrace by speaking out for justice in the face of repression.

But we must acknowledge that most of us involved in the mission of Jesus are not engaged in this kind of difficult and dangerous work. Most persons who are celibate today are in fact involved in work that does not, on the face of it, exclude the commitments of marriage and family life. The experience of other Christian denominations shows us that effective religious leadership does not always require a celibate clergy. Protestant missionaries, usually married and often with families, have a long history of generous service in remote and dangerous settings. Within the Catholic community, more and more married persons are found in roles of pastoral ministry and religious leadership once available only to celibates. Catholics who are celibate, single, and married work side by side in ministry these days—doing similar work with similar results of success and failure. In this closer collaboration, many celibates recognize that in the lives of their lay colleagues the commitments of marriage and family life often do more to support effective ministry than to distract from it.

Another understanding of celibacy as a choice must be mentioned here. At issue is the linking of celibacy with priesthood. Scriptural studies have made clear that celibacy was not an essential element of Christian leadership in the New Testament: Simon Peter and others of Jesus' closest followers were clearly married; in the Pastoral Epistles bishops are described as married men (1 Timothy 3:2; 3:12; Titus 3:6). The study of Catholic history, however, shows the gradual development of the celibate priesthood: in the fourth century, married priests were exhorted to abstain from sexual intercourse; gradually, fewer and fewer bishops and priests married; then in the twelfth century, celibacy was made mandatory for priesthood in the Latin Rite. Because of this biblical and historical evidence, most theologians have concluded that celibacy is not a necessary part of the ministry of priesthood. Rather, celibacy is a religious discipline required by the Roman Catholic Church.

Compulsory celibacy is part of Catholic priesthood today. To be ordained, a candidate for priesthood must accept the requirements of celibacy. Seminarians know this from the outset; over the course of training, they are made aware of the practical and spiritual requirements of the celibate way of life. Therefore, it is said, celibacy is a free choice by those who are ordained.

Among many diocesan priests and seminarians, however, this discussion of celibacy as a choice rings hollow. Their experience is not that celibacy is a choice open to them in the Spirit. Rather, it is a formal requirement demanded of them if they are to move forward toward ordination. For many, the choice they have made is for the ministry of community and liturgical leadership to which they know themselves to be called. In order to be allowed to exercise that ministry, they have accepted the stipulation that goes with it—that they will not marry. Many diocesan priests do not, in fact, experience celibacy as a personal charism or a vocational choice. They experience it neither as a gift of the Spirit nor as a personal strength. They would choose to marry if it were possible. Since marriage is not an option at this time, these priests strive courageously to live in a way that is faithful to their public declaration of celibacy, even though their own spiritual gifts and personal temperament do not offer much support for this lifestyle.

CELIBACY AS A CALL

We have been exploring the images that are part of the discussion of celibacy today. For many people, the most important image is celibacy as a call. The strength of this understanding of celibacy is its close connection with spirituality: celibacy is experienced as an integral part of one's personal journey of faith. This can be the experience of the young adult who feels drawn into a deepening relationship with the person of Jesus. Through prayer and discernment, often assisted by a spiritual director or other religious guide, she comes to recognize that her own spiritual journey includes remaining celibate. For her, celibacy is part of God's call. Here the decision for celibacy is rooted in an openness to God's mysterious action in one's own life.

For another person, the decision for celibacy is part of a call to live in religious community. He feels drawn to share life with this religious congregation. Their vision and values, their mission and spirit, the work they do, the way they live together appeal very strongly to him. After a period of reflection and evaluation, he comes to the conviction that this way of life can be for him a way to God. His commitment to celibacy is made as part of a larger commitment to share life with this particular religious group. Here again, celibacy is seen as part of one's personal journey of faith. The decision to remain celibate is made because it is seen as part of God's call *for this person* rather than because celibacy is objectively a higher or more holy way of life.

The mature witness of celibate persons in mid-life and beyond offers us another rich experience of celibacy as a personal call. This experience is an especially significant source of renewed appreciation of the meaning of celibacy today. These people have lived the celibate life for many years. Their experience bridges the gap between the earlier understanding of celibacy as the "higher calling" and the current confusion over the validity of the life choice of celibacy. Such mature members of the community of faith bring both candor and confidence to the discussion.

In moments of reflection, the mid-life religious muses:

> The reasons that brought me to religious life are not the reasons that see me through today. My understanding of myself, my sexuality, what celibacy means, what it demands—all these have changed significantly. I am aware of the mixed motives that were part of my earliest decision for celibacy: generosity and fear, guilt and idealism, openness to God and susceptibility to social pressure. However, this hodgepodge of motives does not mean I made the wrong choice. I am aware that all important life choices combine a range of motives. But I also recognize that I have been able to face some of the shadows, to purify some of the compulsions that made my earlier decisions less than free. The convictions that hold me in this lifestyle today are in many ways

different from the beliefs I held twenty years ago. But I remain celibate, or better, I continue to choose celibacy because it fits. As a celibate, I have grown and deepened and learned to love. The celibate life, with its joy and sorrow, has given me much of what is best in myself. This is the way I have been led: this has been the path of my own journey with God.

Mature celibates like this testify most convincingly to the adequacy of the celibate commitment today. The church in the United States is blessed with thousands of such mature religious and priests whose lives attest to the contemporary significance of celibacy. This is a rich source of information to bring more explicitly into the larger ecclesial discussion of celibacy. Such lives serve not as justifications of a questionable theology of the "higher way," but as witness to the power and purpose of celibacy as one of the trustworthy ways in which the Christian journey may be followed in faith.

TWO CHALLENGES

Christians continue to acknowledge that celibacy is an authentic way to live our religious faith. In the community of faith today we recognize how fruitful this paradoxical lifestyle can be. However, two special challenges for the survival of celibacy arise from our shared history.

The first challenge we face is to unyoke the gift of celibacy from biases against sexuality. Celibacy first flowered in a milieu hostile to sexuality and the body. Virginity was judged to be the most genuine way to live the faith. Marriage was a poor second best—a concession to nature and a sure distraction from Christian virtue.

Because sexual activity was portrayed as unavoidably stained by selfishness and compulsion, many Christians were attracted to the choice for a celibate life. As the bias against sex is healed, the negative motive for celibacy is removed. Increasingly, Christians choose a celibate life, not to avoid the threat of sexuality but because consecrated celibacy fits their temperament, vocation, and spirituality. This lifestyle allows them to love generously and well.

The second choice we face is to disengage the lifestyle of celibacy from the ministry of priesthood. Many Catholics remain unaware that the links between celibacy and priesthood were forged only gradually, in a historical process that began many years after the life of Jesus. In the fourth century, when the pastoral discipline of celibacy was first applied to priests who were not also monks, many priests and bishops were actually married. Not until almost eight hundred years later, in the Second Lateran Council of 1139, did the requirement of priestly celibacy become part of official church law.

Historical research shows that the growing conviction that priests ought not to marry was strongly influenced by negative attitudes toward sexuality that dominated the Mediterranean world. These attitudes no longer prevail. Only slowly and painfully are we returning today to a more biblical-based confidence in the compatibility of sexuality and spirituality.

The time has come for Catholics to disengage the choice for celibacy from the community service of the priestly ministry. Both celibacy and the priesthood will survive this separation. The ministry of the priesthood will profit by the influx of generous and gifted married persons, and celibacy will be appreciated as the special gift it is meant to be. This paradoxical grace will be a more convincing witness in those Christians who freely and courageously choose to follow the Lord in this way.

REFLECTIVE EXERCISE

Consider your own experience of committed celibacy. First, take a moment to recall a celibate person who has influenced you—a teacher or a pastor, perhaps a member of your own family or a close friend. What do you find most attractive or admirable about this person? In what ways has this person been influential in your life? What is the chief conviction about celibacy that your draw from this person's life?

Next, broaden the focus of your reflection by responding to these questions. What contribution does the Christian vision of celibacy make to you personally? As you see it, what does the lifestyle of consecrated celibacy make to the community of faith? To the larger human community?

Finally, are there any concerns you have about the vision and lifestyle of celibacy in the Catholic community today?

ADDITIONAL RESOURCES

The work of theologian Sandra Schneiders continues to illumine the lived reality and theological significance of religious life; see *Finding the Treasure: Locating Catholic Religious Life in a New Ecclesial and Cultural Context.* Her discussion of celibacy is found in *Selling All: Commitment, Consecrated Celibacy and Community in Catholic Religious Life.* Sean Sammon's *An Undivided Heart: Making Sense of Celibate Chastity* offers an informed and honest look at the experience of consecrated celibacy today. Barbara Fiand's *Refocusing the Vision: Religious Life into the Future* examines the transformations facing religious life today. In *Poverty, Celibacy, and Obedience: A Radical Option for Life,* Diarmuid O'Murchu explores the positive dimensions of human consciousness that these religious vows both express and safeguard.

After Vatican II, a renewed dialogue about the meaning of celibacy sprang up in the church. Donald Goergan's classic treatise on sexuality and celibacy, *The Sexual Celibate*, was followed by Philip Keane's discussion of celibacy in his *Sexual Morality*. This dialogue continues today in Joan Chittister, *The Fire in These Ashes*; Michael Crosby, *Celibacy: Means of Control or Mandate of the Heart?*; Donald Cozzens, *The Changing Face of the Priesthood*; Richard Sipe, *Celibacy: A Way of Loving, Living, and Serving*; and Heinz Vogels, *Celibacy: Gift or Law*. See also the issue devoted to celibacy that appeared as a supplement to the Jesuit spirituality journal *The Way*.

Edward Schillebeeckx traces the appearance of celibacy as a requirement for priesthood in his book *Ministry*. Jo Ann McNamara examines the early history of consecrated celibacy among women in *A New Song: Celibate Women in the First Three Christian Centuries*.

10

Always Our Children? Young Catholics Consider the Pastoral Message

Barbara Jean Daly Horell

On a crisp morning in the Bronx, brown leaves curling in gutters, translucent yellows and reds clinging tenaciously overhead, more than a hundred U.S. Catholics gathered to consider issues of sexuality and faith in our post-scandal, postmodern age. This Pastoral Conference on Human Sexuality in the Roman Catholic Tradition raised questions about the diverse ways in which Catholics connect their sexual identity and experiences with their spiritual formation and Christian life-praxis. In the ensuing years, the questions addressed during those autumn days have gradually taken on greater clarity and meaning for me. I've collected anecdotes and conducted surveys of Catholics, Protestants, and Jews across four generations and three continents, including individuals who define their sexual orientations as heterosexual, homosexual, and bisexual, as well as some transgendered individuals.

My inquiry has led me back to those autumn days on Fordham University's Rose Hill campus, and to a particular question raised by Fran Ferder, F.S.P.A., and John Heagle in one of their workshops. There they discussed the mixed welcome that homosexual individuals sometimes receive within their local and regional Catholic faith communities. Ferder and Heagle's question, simply put, was this: "Always Our Children?" The addition of a simple question mark to the title of the 1997 USCCB Pastoral[1] invited conference participants and their faith communities to question their current attitudes and practices, to reflect critically on whether they have been as welcoming to homosexual persons as they could be, and to consider whether we as a church need to imagine new possibilities[2] for growth in charity and hospitality. In their inimitably gentle fashion, Ferder and Heagle proposed a powerful movement forward in the way Catholics think about homosexual individuals. They challenged us to move away from a mere rejection of bigotry and

149

fear to consider attitudes that carry potential for new ways of being together in community. Ferder and Heagle's question mark continues to invite us: to explore homosexuality *per se* (and not just in relation to the dominant culture) as a human orientation that the bishops themselves describe as "innate" (AOC 2:6);[3] to grapple with understanding the purpose (Aquinas's *telos*) for which homosexuality came from the Creator's hand; and to foster the kind of spiritual maturity necessary for *all* Christians to live fully their "innate" sexual identity as "a gift from God." (AOC 1:3, 5:2.2)

This kind of questioning is, of course, true to the spirit of pastoral reflection and dialogue for which pastoral messages are conceived and written. *Always Our Children* achieves this spirit of dialogue most effectively by means of its many kind words of welcome and Christian concern. The "compassionate and empathetic"[4] tone of the pastoral, reflective in many respects of the generous spirit of Christ's gospel, establishes a level of respectful intimacy with readers that encourages companionable dialogue about current practices in our families and Christian communities.[5]

Three questions sum up what I have heard from contemporary American Catholics whom I engaged in companionable dialogue about the Catholic bishops' pastoral teaching on homosexual Christians and their place as part of the Body of Christ:[6]

1. Why do U.S. bishops, in *Always Our Children*, assume that the discovery of a homosexual orientation is painful or difficult for the person's family? What is so painful about being homosexual that educating *society* out of its prejudices won't cure?
2. If homosexual orientation is, according to the bishops, "innate," why do the bishops advise parents that "it may be appropriate and necessary that your child receive professional help, including counseling"? (AOC 3:5) What do the bishops and parents expect homosexual children to accomplish by means of therapy? What would be reasonable to expect?
3. Why are committed, monogamous, and vital (*life-giving*) relationships that include sexual expression considered "objectively immoral" for homosexual individuals? And, to take it one step further, why do our bishops proscribe public leadership in the Catholic Church for homosexual Catholics living in committed, monogamous, life-giving relationships?

I. WHY ASSUME DIFFICULTY?
WHERE DOES THE PAIN COME FROM?

Always Our Children expresses in heartfelt words the church's concern for parents who struggle to accept a child who is homosexual. To the parents they write, "Our message speaks of accepting yourself . . . accepting and loving your child as a gift of God; and accepting the full truth of God's revelation about the dignity of the human person and the meaning of human sexuality" (AOC 1:3).

And yet the bishops' compassion seems to falter in subtle ways. The preface, for example, comes across as lacking real confidence in its message that homosexual persons are "gifts from God." The very first sentence of *Always Our Children* states: "The purpose of this pastoral message is to reach out to parents who are trying to cope with the discovery of homosexuality in a child who is an adolescent or an adult" (AOC Preface:1). This initial statement lays out the program and attitudes contained throughout the rest of the document. It also provoked controversy among the Catholic university students and the youth ministers with whom I spoke. Despite the pastoral's words of comfort in the face of what the bishops call a "difficult" situation, my survey respondents were troubled (AOC 1:1). They asked "Why do the bishops assume that a homosexual orientation would be painful for family members?" "Why use the word 'cope'?" "To me, the word 'coping' in the first sentence has a very large negative connotation and . . . does not fit the topic." One young woman writes, "I do feel that [homosexuality] is a topic that needs to be handled by the church." She goes on to say, however, that before the bishops can adequately address this complex issue they will need to entertain "the idea that being homosexual may not be the worst thing in the world to the person and his/her family."

Careful reading of the document does seem to admit a bias: the U.S. bishops appear to operate from an assumption that parents are bound to experience pain or, at least, serious confusion when faced with the discovery that their child is homosexual. The bishops write, "Do not expect that all tensions can or will be resolved" (AOC 2:9); "Your child may need you and the family now more than ever" (AOC 3:3); and, "It is essential for you to remain open to the possibility that your son or daughter is struggling to understand and accept a basic homosexual orientation" (AOC 3:5). Where does this underlying negativity come from?

In one of my conversations it was suggested that younger Catholics will most likely become more cautious about homosexuality as they mature and perhaps become parents themselves. An alternative explanation might suggest that young Catholics today have not received adequate moral formation. But neither of these hypotheses account for the fact that so many of the pastoral ministers I consulted—several of whom are the contemporaries of bishops in both age and education—raised similar questions. Furthermore, almost everyone I spoke to was operating out of the kind of compassion and love that transcends differences of sexual orientation, a fact that bespeaks an appropriate level of moral maturity.

Those most troubled by the document's assumption of negativity toward homosexual persons were the youngest Catholics with whom I worked. They even wondered about the choice of topic in this pastoral, considering homosexuality to be almost a non-issue. They drew attention to issues they considered far more pressing. "Why don't bishops and priests focus on things like sexual harassment or date rape" and the disastrous effects these can have on human development and faith? They wonder why "we rarely hear" the bishops address, for example, the impact of incest or emotional neglect in Christian families. Of course, the bishops have and, I hope, will continue to address these and other topics that young adults consider so poignant. (For example, see U.S. Catholic Bishops, *When I Call for Help*.[7]) I wonder, though, why earnest, educated young Catholics do not hear the bishops when they speak on the subjects most relevant to youth?

In short, young Catholics and their pastoral mentors seem to be confused by the overall tone and message of *Always Our Children* in two specific ways. First, they notice what seems to be a conflict between the intended message of hope and comfort in the pastoral letter and the subtle negativity toward homosexual individuals that seeps into the text unexpectedly. Many young Catholics today seek to understand the bishops' concerns and wonder why our leaders struggle with what seems (bringing us to the second source of confusion) to be almost a non-issue. They are astonished that homosexuality and "homogenital" intimacy (assuming lifelong fidelity that they consider comparable to marriage) should have any unusual impact on the life of the community of faith as a whole.

In the face of these concerns, it seems that the pastoral message is, at least, "out of sync" with the concerns and experiences of young Catholics today. One has to wonder if the bishops know something that well-educated young Catholics and their ministers don't. What is the grievous need that prompts the USCCB (and, indeed, the worldwide church) to address this particular pastoral issue repeatedly?[8] How is it that, contrary to wide experience, the difficulties attending to homosexuality outweighs, for our bishops, some apparently graver issues that concern U.S. Catholics today? Given the focus of *Always Our Children* (not to mention the recent Vatican investigation of homosexuality within the culture of U.S. seminaries) it seems fair to conclude that, for the authors of *Always Our Children*, fear and rejection seem likely responses to learning that a loved one is homosexual.

Perhaps a more poignant issue in relation to the *fear* expressed by our Catholic leaders is the very real possibility that older Catholic parents, and probably a segment of contemporary Catholic parents of youth and young adults, have indeed rejected—or at least distanced themselves from—their homosexual children. The issue is real, despite the tolerant ideals of contemporary youth. What does this issue tell us about the spiritual formation of Catholic parents? Shouldn't they have learned as small children that Christians are called to imitate the unconditional love of Christ? If adults have not achieved this basic level of Christian maturity, what does this suggest about the effectiveness of religious formation in our parishes and schools?

Finally, it is also important to consider the breach between our bishops' concerns and the overriding spiritual issues of younger Catholics. What responsibility do U.S. bishops bear, not only to bridge this gap and address the serious concerns of contemporary Catholics, but also to look at their own assumptions about homosexual persons and about the private intimacies that bar these individuals from priesthood, the diaconate, and other active leadership roles in the church? Could it be that the bishops are asking (and attempting to answer) the wrong questions, at this stage of our history as a people of God, for forming and sustaining Catholic faith in the United States?

II. RESPONDING TO HOMOSEXUAL CHILDREN: WHY THERAPY?

Even a cursory reading of *Always Our Children* raises another perplexing question: "If homosexual orientation is 'innate,' coming to individuals from the hand of the Creator, why does the pastoral hold out psychological therapy as a kind of *hope* for parents of homosexual adolescents and young adults?"[9] What is the point of advising that homosexual individuals, any more than their heterosexual counterparts, undertake psychological counseling as they develop sexual awareness in their adolescence? The document advises parents to respect "a person's freedom to choose or refuse therapy directed toward changing a homosexual orientation. Given the present state of medical and psychological knowledge, there is no guarantee that such therapy will succeed" (AOC 3:10). This statement implies that *Always Our Children* proposes psychological counseling primarily for the purpose of dissuading young Catholics from a homosexual orientation. If such is indeed the bishops' intention (or if the bishops allow such a misinterpretation to stand unchallenged), parents could easily be deluded into thinking that they can (or *should?*) alter their child's sexual identity. This kind of attitude could be quite damaging to our youth.

Does anyone doubt that American teenagers, at the peak of self-consciousness and sensitivity to parental disapproval, would react (in spades!) against a parent's suggestion that they aren't "really" homosexual? It doesn't take a lot of imagination to recognize how many ways that scenario could go wrong. On the one hand, adolescents who operate primarily from a need to please their parents are likely to conceal or repress their sexuality out of fear of losing parental approval. If a pattern of repression becomes established, the child is susceptible to entrenched self-rejection and its battery of attendant mental health issues. On the other hand, the development of a

child into an adult requires that the adolescent "pull away," establish independence as a human being distinct from her or his parents. As the analogy
of "pulling" suggests, this process can be difficult. To add to that struggle an
apparent rejection of the child's emerging identity (by suggesting the child
undertake therapy to reconsider his or her sexual identity) is liable to put a
serious strain upon the parent-child relationship precisely when that relationship is most vulnerable. For example, the child might run away from
home, separating her or himself from the family's (presumably) emotional
and financial stability just when these resources are most needed for successful growth into adulthood. Or the child might develop entrenched patterns
of defiance that lead to experimentation with drugs, alcohol, or casual sex
and the attendant risks of such behavior. Or, out of a need to "prove" him or
herself the child might act out in ways that are physically or mentally (and
also spiritually) unhealthy, and in the process become alienated from not
only family and friends, but also from God and the faith community. The importance of parental support during adolescence cannot be understated, and
the breakdown of authenticity in the parent-child relationship at this point
can have serious and long-lasting consequences.

Considering the possibilities for a negative impact on a young person, a
parent who tries, directly or through a willing counselor, to change a child's
sexual orientation surely risks pushing that child toward dangerous patterns
of behavior. Fortunately, reputable therapists in the United States today are
unlikely to jeopardize their patients in this way. It disturbs many U.S.
Catholics, however, that their bishops seem to endorse this possibility in *Always Our Children*.

What is certain, however, is that there are situations in which therapy is
highly useful and appropriate. A competent therapist has the ability to
mentor young people in (among other things): discerning sexual orientation and gender identity; exploring options for pursuing or channeling sexual energies appropriately; and seeking ongoing support for living a healthy
lifestyle. Parents and family members too might benefit from the support
of a good counselor. Given (1) a good match between the needs of the
client (whether parent or child) and the abilities of the therapist, (2) an essential respect for the spiritual dimensions of the human person, and (3)
the parents' unconditional love and support for the child, therapy can be an
extraordinary process not only for developing emotional health but for
growing in holiness as well.

III. CHASTITY, CELIBACY, AND THE CHRISTIAN LIFE

Kelly,[10] a senior at a New England Catholic university, shared with me that
she thinks celibacy can be freeing, and I agree. "Doesn't self-sacrifice really

liberate the spirit?" Certainly. But I marvel inside to hear Kelly articulate this mystery at such a tender age. Kelly talks openly and easily about life as a celibate homosexual.

I think it's the ease that puzzles me. I've never known a path to holiness that lacks some sense of struggle—it seems to be the human way. Yet it is true that very young children often show remarkable spiritual acumen. It's possible that Kelly has the wisdom of Therese of Liseux or Joan of Arc. Or perhaps Kelly is mouthing words that others have supplied. In either case, Kelly's position—while spiritually true and profound for one who has obtained the maturity to embrace celibacy as a path of freedom—does not provide much in the way of healthy guidance for *most* young Catholics. As one campus minister writes,

> I am the mother of four (soon to be five) children. Recently my husband and I have begun the process of talking to our thirteen-year-old son about sex, relationships, and moral choices. If he is straight . . . the church's teachings on sexuality and marriage offer me much I can use by way of counseling him in this difficult area of moral and physical growth. I can speak with confidence and conviction about the church's teachings on the joys of sexual intimacy, the importance of chastity, and the holiness of marriage. But if he is gay, this letter, and the larger church teaching it is based on, offers me little I can use. If my child is gay, I can no longer hold up Christian marriage as . . . ideal. I cannot even offer monogamy . . . as a life-giving option for him to choose. If I am true to the church's teaching, I can offer him only an artificially imposed lifelong celibacy. Celibacy offered this way is not so much a way to live out our sexuality creatively, but a way to avoid sin.

My sense is that Kelly—and others of Kelly's generation who value and earnestly pursue spiritual growth—seeks a way to make sense of a catechism that summarily dismisses the right of homosexuals to choose how best to live out their sexuality.

Compared to the majority of young Catholics today, Kelly is, of course, extraordinary. By contrast, consider the situation of most contemporary adolescent children and young adults. On the one hand, for one hundred thousand years the evolutionary process (*nature*) has favored early and frequent sexual activity. Until the last century, it was vitally important for youth to begin having children. Conspiring with the direction of evolution, society (and the Catholic Church) has, in the past, measured a woman's value by how devotedly she spent her life raising children to adulthood. The status of a young man depended upon his virility and ability to provide for the resultant family. Adolescents and young adults have been "hard wired," biologically and socially, to have sex in their teens and twenties.

Society is changing, but evolution cannot keep pace. The human species cannot, in one or two generations, adapt to the new historical situation that we now face, including medical advances that prolong human life-expectancy, low infant and childhood mortality rates, and the resultant burgeoning population of the earth. But until nature catches up with human longevity, many teenagers will have sex, and virtually all teenagers will *desire* to have sex.

Flying in the face of these *natural* tendencies, parents and faith communities insist (rightly) that contemporary adolescents lack the emotional or spiritual maturity to engage in the kind of healthy intimacy required for a long-term, committed sexual relationship that nurtures growth in holiness. Children are, therefore, counseled to discipline their inbred tendencies and "wait."

How likely is it that, in every case, discipline will prevail over one hundred thousand years of evolutionary impulse? And even among young people who achieve such discipline, how much longer would it take for them to achieve the spiritual self-mastery that allows them to recognize and embrace celibacy as something that is ultimately freeing? Pastoral experience is clear: the hurdle of teenage chastity is difficult (at best) for adolescents. Statistics tell us that almost 50 percent of teenagers in the United States do not clear that hurdle. What are the chances, then, that young adults or adolescents are likely to achieve a level of spiritual self-mastery that can embrace lifelong celibacy without misgiving or resentment? Are they not more likely to feel trapped into a lifestyle (celibacy) they have not freely chosen? And how likely is it that, given no alternative to lifelong celibacy, homosexual Catholics will trust the outstretched hand of welcome that *Always Our Children* extends? Are they not more likely to approach that welcome with doubt, or even fear that the hand of welcome will "let go," just when they lean into its embrace?

Like Kelly, all of our homosexual brothers and sisters are hungry for spiritual nourishment. How can we ask them to operate from a level of spiritual maturity that they are unlikely to be ready for? There must be more we can offer them.

And what happens if, out of sincere love of Jesus and the church, someone like Kelly attempts the path of celibacy toward spiritual maturity? Unless that person is really ready to embrace celibacy, pastoral experience shows that, sooner or later, that path leads to frustration over the dichotomy between the body's needs and the spirit's aspirations. My pastoral sense tells me that, at least for earnest young Catholics like Kelly, if young people set foot to the path of lifelong celibacy before they are truly ready, they must close their minds to the inner struggle that resists that path. If I am correct, at the heart of their spiritual journey will be a kind of inner blindness or self-deception. Can self-deception lead to the One who called Himself "the Truth"? Can spiritual blindness lead to the One who chastised the Pharisees for their spiritual blindness? Furthermore, from the viewpoint of the social sciences, *pretended* maturity is not a likely path to *actual* maturity. As much as we might wish otherwise, we are forced to take life's paths one step at a time. The standards we set for our young people must take this truth into account.

None of this is intended as a judgment against young Catholics who, like Kelly, are striving to be faithful to the church and to grow in personal holiness. I admire Kelly's courage, candor, and dedication to living a chaste life. And, as Thomas Merton reminds us, the desire to walk in faith pleases God. Kelly's longing for "the freedom of the children of God" (Romans 8:21) is itself a sign of holiness. Still, the blind acceptance of celibacy, unaccompanied by the maturity to adequately understand either sexual intimacy or sexuality sublimated in a celibate lifestyle, is unlikely to be truly life giving and life sustaining, in the broader sense of those concepts. In God's grace, all paths may eventually lead to spiritual maturity, but in the experience of many, enforced celibacy is neither the only nor the preferred path.

Shouldn't these questions raise concerns among Catholic leaders? How can we continue to advise our homosexual youth that the only path of virtue (for them) mandates celibacy? Many Catholics ask whether, despite honorable intentions, documents like *Always Our Children* and the *Catechism of the Catholic Church* succeed only in exposing our youngest brothers and sisters to serious spiritual hazards—despair over the improbability of living a holy life; the hypocrisy of trying to take on a celibate lifestyle when one doesn't feel ready or called to that choice; bitterness about the lack of life-giving options within the community of faith; the negative self-image that can result from a perceived failure to measure up to the church's standards; heretical concepts of an exacting landlord God; and so many other of those pitfalls that Jesus our Lord most strongly opposed in his own time. Matthew's gospel reminds us that "if anyone causes one of these little ones who believe in me to sin, it would be better for that one to have a large millstone hung around the neck and to be drowned in the depths of the sea," but "whoever welcomes a little child like this in my name welcomes me" (Matthew 18:5-7).

By defining "homogenital activity" as "objectively immoral," we as Catholics deny our homosexual children any reasonable possibility of fulfilling their innate desire for sexually active human intimacy. Are we then not also neglecting our responsibility to inspire the next generation of young Christians? Could it be that we're risking not only the health and happiness of these our children, but also the health and holiness of future communities of faith? How can we faithfully foster a new generation of Catholics if (to many contemporary Catholics) our catechism seems unjust, in that what we offer our heterosexual children (marriage and sexual fulfillment) is not only out of reach for our homosexual children but is actually considered bad ("objectively immoral") for them?

Since none of Jesus' teachings in the gospel really address issues of homosexual intimacy, we have to glean from what we do know about his ministry to guide us. Does the position of *Always Our Children*, in regard to the mandate of lifelong celibacy for everyone whom God created with a homosexual orientation, seem a likely position for Christ to espouse?

By denying our homosexual children all hope for the same healthy and holy life choice that is available to our heterosexual children, are we being good mentors of the next generation? Can it be in anyone's best interest to discourage all hope of achieving a satisfying, even sacramental, sexual union for significant numbers of young Catholics? Is it realistic to expect that every single homosexual Catholic will have the capacity, either by inclination or by education, to tread the arduous road to the spiritual freedom that celibacy can offer? And if they do not have this capacity, what internal terrors are we exposing them to?

IV. LIVING A CHASTE LIFE

Defining Chastity

Let us take a step back for a moment to recap the document's position on chastity and consider the issue in another way. *Always Our Children* relies on the definition of chastity developed in *The Catechism of the Catholic Church*. In his article, "Homosexuality and Chastity," Joseph A. Selling summarizes how the *Catechism* understands the virtue of chastity.

> It would seem that there are only two forms of chastity that are being proposed by the teaching of the *Catechism*: conjugal chastity which encompasses the engagement of genital sexual activity in the context of the marital relationship; and the practice of chastity by unmarried persons, which apparently excludes all forms of sexual activity whatsoever.[11]

More than 50 percent of the pastoral ministers consulted on this project found the document's definition of chastity to be too limited to be useful in pastoral ministry. One religious educator asserted that chastity should be considered in the larger context of human relationships and their impact on human communities, and not by an *a priori* list of situations in which sexual intercourse can be considered chaste.

Selling agrees:

> The general definition of chastity in paragraph 2337 [of the *Catechism*] seems to be a very open one, referring to the successful integration of human sexuality and placing this in the context of interpersonal relationships. When the *Catechism* comes to describe what it calls the "various forms of chastity," however,

we find a different approach. Most of these forms of chastity refer to the total abstention from erotic activity. . . . It is almost as if chastity referred to turning something on and off. When celibate and unmarried, the light is red. . . . When one is married, sex is okay (as long as one does nothing to impede conception).[12]

Seiling rightly disputes an understanding of sexuality (and the virtue of chastity) that reduces sexuality to its "physical and biological dimensions." He recognizes that the church needs to be consistent in its consideration of virtue as involving the whole person, including psychological, social, political, and spiritual dimensions. He further states that "the cardinal virtue that governs our relationships with others is justice. Therefore any relevant definition of chastity must combine aspects of both temperance and justice in order to respond to the very meaning of sexuality that goes beyond the merely biological observation of sexual differentiation."[13]

Paradoxically, it is precisely in that section of *Always Our Children* that felt the least "fair" to young Catholics that the document also hints at moving toward a more holistic understanding of chastity and discusses chastity within the broader context of communal relationships. By proscribing public leadership in the church for those who are known to engage in homosexual intimacies, the church seems to recognize the impact of sexual relationships on the life of the community itself, albeit in a very negative way. Sadly, the bishops target for exclusion precisely those homosexual individuals who desire most to live in honesty and integrity with their God-given identity and to bring their personhood to fulfillment by placing their gifts in the service of the Catholic Christian community.

Most of the young Catholics in my studies were amazed at the ironic rejection of homosexual individuals who continue beyond puberty to want to be active in the church. And, when asked to understand this issue from the perspective of protecting the church against scandal, young Catholics continued to wonder at the bishops' apparent lack of tolerance for human difference. Specifically, even though they did *not* agree that "homogenital behavior" was necessarily sinful, they tried to understand the point of view of *Always Our Children* where it prohibits homosexual persons from entering any public form of Catholic leadership. In making this attempt, they raised two points that I think the community of faith should consider. First, in the case of lay leadership, young Catholics wondered why sexual sins seem to present greater obstacles to public ministry than other kinds of sins, and whether pastors don't seem more concerned about *homosexual* relationships between unmarried persons than they do about *heterosexual* relationships between unmarried persons. In the experience of some young Catholics, cohabiting heterosexuals are not prohibited from, for example, proclaiming the Word in liturgy or providing companionship to sick members of the parish. Second, the young Catholics with whom I spoke raised questions about the gifts of homosexual persons. They asked, "Why doesn't our church welcome into the priesthood and the diaconate homosexual persons who are striving to live good and holy lives?"

Defining Life

As previously noted, the section of *Always Our Children* that "unpacks" the virtue of chastity for homosexual individuals concludes, "The Church teaches that homogenital behavior is objectively immoral" (AOC 3:8).[14] The document goes on at length to assure us that neither the person nor the orientation is considered objectively immoral: only that *acting upon, or actualizing* the inherent (and logically, God-given) desire for same-sex genital expression of that orientation is objectively immoral. The document gives two reasons for this conclusion: (1) "It is God's plan that sexual intercourse occur only within the context of marriage," and (2) "Every act of intercourse must be open to the possible creation of new human life."

These teachings raise powerful questions for American Catholics, and at the root of their questions is the way our leaders define life. The only life that counts, it seems, is the life that can be conceived in a woman's womb. Many young Catholics point out that the focus on literal conception seems unnecessarily narrow and flat.[15] One woman, a doctoral candidate in pastoral theology, expresses fundamental disagreement with this limited understanding of life. "It seems to me," she argues, "that there are numerous situations within which the sharing of human love, including that of a sexual nature, can be argued to be chaste and life-giving without . . . having the potential to co-create human life." To another Catholic minister, the idea that "homogenital" behavior could never foster human life flies in the face of her own experience. She lifts up for consideration the spiritual vitality she herself has received through her friends, a homosexual couple, who extend life-giving hospitality in such a way that everyone, child and adult alike, is made to feel welcome, invited, safe, and unconditionally loved in their home. She tells us that the relationship this couple shares fosters exactly the kind of vitality (in each of them individually and together as a couple) that overflows into the life of the community to encourage faith, hope, love, and unity. Another lay ecclesial minister summarizes the argument well:

> I would argue that many relationships exist, with sexual dimensions, heterosexual as well as homosexual, in which the co-creation of human life is impossible. [Yet,] these relationships remain life-giving, and, in fact, contribute to the blossoming humanity of the persons involved. The idea that homosexual persons are incapable of maintaining chaste (faithful) relationships of a sexual nature, relationships that contribute to the development of their personhood, is insulting and demeaning.

To consider the same question from yet another angle, if "genital behavior" is only chaste when it is open to the procreation of children, why does the church not teach married couples to discontinue sexual relations when one partner is, or becomes, infertile? Such an expectation would be absurd, of course, because the discovery of infertility in a young couple—or the movement into infertility for an older couple—is one of those moments in which greater sexual intimacy will help sustain life and marital vitality. And, of course, in cases in which children are still desired, the church wisely counsels adoption as a means to foster new life within the family.[16] So how is this different from homosexual couples who generously raise their own adopted children? For some Catholic men and women, it does not seem very different at all.[17]

A Double Standard for the Family of Faith?

Questions about what it means to live a chaste life lead ultimately to basic questions of justice and love. One mother and minister notices that the document is called *Always Our Children*. It invokes, she reminds us, the traditional image of church as mother or parent. "What kind of 'mother' is the church," she asks, "if she offers some of her children the option of marriage, but denies it to others?" Can such a church be considered just? Does such a church embody the unconditional and perfect love of God? "Which of you, if [your child] . . . asks for bread, will give a stone? . . . If you, then, though you are evil, know how to give good gifts to your children, how much more will your Father in heaven give good gifts to those who ask!" (Mt 7:9, 11).

Now, some will suggest that God's love *is* perfect, because God predisposes homosexual individuals to a celibate lifestyle. By this logic, the teaching of the church merely identifies what *must be* (in the final analysis) natural to homosexual lovers because they cannot conceive children together.[18] Yet, only a tiny percentage of homosexual individuals identify celibacy as "natural" for them. Are we open, as church, to having a genuine conversation about what we can discern to be "natural" or in accord with the God-given nature of homosexual persons? Or are we bound by a definition of what is "natural" for human beings that is determined before we listen to the voices of all those who are always our children?

V. HOMOSEXUAL INTIMACY: THE SENSE OF THE FAITHFUL FROM SCRIPTURE AND TRADITION

The experience of committed Christians, both homosexual and heterosexual, tells us that all persons are made with a sexual nature that, per se, seeks its *immediate* end in one of two ways: (1) sexual fulfillment by means of sexual activity or (2) celibacy, by means of sublimating sexual energies. Either way, human sexuality seeks its *final* end in God. According to Aquinas's teleological construct of human nature and activity, is it logical to insist that homosexual lovers are unable, through an intimacy enhanced by sexual activity, to obtain the *final* end of their sexuality (intimacy with God our Creator) simply because one of the *intermediate* ends of *heterosexual* intimacy (i.e., procreation) is not available to them?

The second *intermediate* end of human sexuality is the comfort and nurture of human persons. The experience of celibate singles and childless couples bears witness that procreation is not a *necessary* step toward the *final* end of sexuality (which is union with God). Why then, does the magisterium teach that "homogenital" behavior is objectively immoral? Is it not logical to assume that homosexual intimacy has the same loving potential to carry our homosexual brothers and sisters along a path similar to that of married heterosexual couples, through the human comfort and nurture of human sexual intimacy to its ultimate *telos* in God?

But in considering the bishops' characterization of "homogenital" behavior as "objectively immoral," we must also recognize another bedrock idea upon which their position rests: biblical literalism.[19] Because homosexual persons were outcast in biblical times, fundamentalist Christians of every denomination continue to denounce homosexual practices. Now, the case against biblical literalism has been argued definitively by popes, councils, scripture scholars, and Jesus himself,[20] yet biblical literalism continues to creep into theological and pastoral pronouncements. The Bible stems from a heterosexually dominant society. Therefore the paradigm of human sexuality in the creation stories,[21] for example, is necessarily heterosexual. But Jesus taught us to look past the literal meaning of the Hebrew Scriptures and to consider the heart of God's *relationship* with humankind described there.[22]

It was the genius of Israel more than three thousand years ago to recognize and respond to God's covenant invitation as understood in terms of a code of justice dependent for its meaning upon God's love affair with a people. The radical insight that drives the Torah and that remains the foundation of Judaism and Christianity today is the understanding that God does *not* love where or as we love. Power, money, fame, sex appeal: Israel had none of these things. God wants kings like David and Hittites like Uriah, prophets like Elijah and sinners like Rahab to fall in love with Him. Throughout history God has called widows and patriarchs, the wealthy and the homeless, to the same standards of justice rooted in right *relationship* with Her.

More than ten centuries after Moses the lawgiver, Jesus of Nazareth took this insight and tore it wide open for all time. New Testament evidence attests to the profound love Jesus had for the law.[23] He knew the heart and soul of the law to be God's love and God's gift to the world. As such, Jesus honored and kept the law above everything except the one thing for which the law was created: the people. Jesus knew God's passionate love for God's people so intimately because it was embodied in his own flesh and blood, historically. Jesus, as Son of God, knew of God's love for him in a way that no one before or since has known it. And he came to know that God's love could not be fully contained by one people, by any temple or priesthood, or even by the law itself. As Christians, we believe that Jesus the Christ knew God's love to its core because *he himself was both that love and that love's gift.*

Since the time of Jesus, the world has cradled more kinds of fundamentalism than we have names for the hatred it can espouse. Thank God that *Always Our Children* sees, on one level, beyond the literalism that teaches us to pick and choose which laws in the Torah code to idolize. To begin with, the pastoral letter refuses to foster this kind of rejection. It is a good beginning. But does it go far enough?

Here we return to one of the rock-bottom concerns that burden many contemporary Catholics, young and old. Can we tell—at least, from this pastoral letter—whether our Catholic bishops faithfully model the profound love that Jesus the Christ demonstrated for all? As a church, we have grown significantly in universal charity since the time of the Roman Empire. We have, for the most part, come to understand that the passionate desire of God for God's people is not limited to Christians or Jews or Muslims. And we profess, now, to know that God abhors slavery and genocide, so we seem to be facing down the specter of racism. We now name sexism a sin, although it remains open to debate whether and where sexism exists in our church. What does *Always Our Children* tell us, in 2007, about God's love for homosexual persons? What does the document suggest about Catholic leaders and the community of faith as we grow in Christian love for those whom God created to desire sexual intimacy with those of their own gender?

One lay pastoral minister raises this question most poignantly. She asks, "What kind of parent would refuse to offer the same gifts and opportunities— the same love—to all their children?" Alexander McCall Smith raises a similar question in his 1998 novel, *The No. 1 Ladies' Detective Agency,* in which a wise woman of Africa has a conversation with her wealthy client:

> Mr. Patel: "I make no distinction between my children. They are all the same. Equal-equal."
>
> "That's the best way to do it," said Mma Ramotswe. "If you favour one, then that leads to a great deal of bitterness."
>
> "You can say that again, oh yes," said Mr. Patel. "Children notice when their parents give two sweets to one and one to another. They can count same as us."[24]

Could we admire a father who would lavish gifts on one beloved child but withdraw his support from the rest of the family? Could we approve of a mother who would favor one child over another or discriminate among her children when sharing her time and resources? Is God that kind of parent? Is the church?

When the bishops teach that "to live and love chastely is to understand that 'only within marriage does sexual intercourse fully symbolize the Creator's dual design, as an act of covenant love, with the potential of co-creating new human life,'" are they engaging in the kind of legalism Jesus criticized in some of the Pharisees of his time? (AOC 6:6). And when, from this starting point, our leaders apply human logic to deduce that "homogenital behavior is objectively immoral," are they clinging to the kind of human wisdom that Paul argues against so effectively in the initial chapters of 1 Corinthians? The whole power of the Hebrew Scriptures and the ministry of Christ rests on understanding that the law is based upon God's love and made to be a vehicle for God's love. If we cling to our human wisdom when it conflicts with the passion of God for humanity, do we not act as the leaders of Jerusalem acted in Jesus' time?

Sexual fulfillment connects human beings in the deepest union of bodies, hearts, minds, and souls. It changes people dramatically. When sexual fulfillment opens persons to loving union with God, it opens spiritual paths that have no parallel. Our definition of the human virtue of chastity must include in its scope (and does, within marriage) the path of sexual fulfillment as one of two holy ways in which our sexuality draws us into encounters with Christ, who is The Way. Committed, faithful sexual intimacy strives to bring us along this path; it opens us to God's love in a unique and wholly personal way. This is sacramental union in its most profound form.

More succinctly, the magisterial logic, both in *Always Our Children* and in *The Catechism of the Catholic Church*, does not "wash" with educated American Catholics in the twenty-first century. They are asking whether the bishops would have us believe that God is a parent who plays favorites, who graces heterosexual couples with a path of sanctity that is closed to God's homosexual children.

Finally, is it possible that our Christian faith communities might benefit from a new model of understanding God's love for us? For two millennia, understanding God as *Abba* has inspired people to great depths of compassion and justice. But, as Karl Rahner recognized,[25] Vatican II set forth new challenges for Catholics: challenges to a greater maturity and accountability in our communities of faith than we have known in the past. He described Vatican II as the Catholic Church's moment of transition to maturity. Perhaps, then, now is the time to embrace a more adult model of God's love. What would happen in our communities if we as a church moved from relating to God primarily as parent toward relating to God as consummate lover? The bond of intimacy that the Eucharist symbolizes and makes real is a bond of physical unity, much like the bond of sexual union.

Christian husbands and wives have the privilege of joining Teresa of Avila and the author of Song of Songs in recognizing that ecstatic union with God is an encounter that reaches into the depths of human sexuality and transforms it into mysticism. Similarly, sexual intercourse at its best intertwines souls with the Divine Lover in ways unapproachable by any other means. Sex is both a witness to union with God and an act that makes real that bond of love with God. So why shouldn't anyone, of any sexual orientation, who cannot or will not choose celibacy, strive to follow this sacramental path? And why would God, who is passionately in love with humankind, choose to restrict this path *carte blanche*?

That's what many young Catholics want to know.

APPENDIX TO *ALWAYS OUR CHILDREN*:
YOUNG CATHOLICS CONSIDER THE PASTORAL MESSAGE.
SURVEY AND DISCUSSION QUESTIONS

"Perfect love casts out fear."

(1 John 4:18)

Keep in mind that "the purpose of this pastoral message is to reach out to parents who are trying to cope with the discovery of homosexuality in" an adolescent or adult child. "The message is not a treatise on homosexuality. It is not a systematic presentation of the Church's moral teaching." At the same time, pastoral guidance does give expression to attitudes and practices that lie at the heart of the Church's social and moral teaching.

Please read the document *Always Our Children* and answer the following questions in a few sentences or a paragraph. (Feel free to answer as fully, or as succinctly, as you prefer.)

1. How would you characterize the overall tone of the pastoral message, *Always Our Children*? Does it achieve its intention to "speak words of faith, hope, and love"? What leads you to this impression?

2. In your reading of *Always Our Children*, what are some of the overall attitudes toward gay and lesbian Catholics you see reflected, either explicitly or implicitly, in the document? What leads you to this conclusion? Give one or two examples, if you can.

3. Choose one of the following statements from *Always Our Children* and then answer the following questions: What are the implications of the teaching expressed for homosexual individuals in the Catholic Church? Do you agree with the teaching expressed? Why or why not?

   A. "God expects everyone to strive for the perfection of love, but to achieve it gradually through stages of moral growth."

B. "To live and love chastely is to understand that 'only within marriage does sexual intercourse fully symbolize the Creator's dual design, as an act of covenant love, with the potential of co-creating new human life.'"

C. "Homogenital behavior is objectively immoral," but "a homosexual orientation . . . is not immoral in itself."

4. Does the pastoral message *Always Our Children* represent or reflect a positive moment in the Catholic Church's relationship with its people? What, in the document, encourages you to remain a faithful and active member of the Catholic Church? What, in the document, seems discouraging to you?

5. Please feel free to add any further comments or observations inspired by your reading of *Always Our Children*.

NOTES

1. Committee on Marriage and Family, National Conference of Catholic Bishops, *Always Our Children: A Pastoral Message to Parents of Homosexual Children and Suggestions for Pastoral Ministers* [AOC] (Washington, D.C.: United States Catholic Conference [USCC], 1997). For convenience and in accord with traditional usage, when citing from this document I refer to sections by number (beginning with section 1, "A Critical Moment, A Time of Grace," immediately following the Preface), followed by a colon and paragraph number.

2. *Always Our Children* describes itself as intending "to speak words of faith, hope, and love to parents who need the church's loving presence at a time which may be one of the most challenging in their lives." The very hospitality implicit in the statement's intent invites open conversation and holds out the hope for freedom of dialogue. AOC, Preface:2.

3. *Always Our Children* cites the Sacred Congregation for the Doctrine of the Faith, *Declaration on Certain Questions Concerning Sexual Ethics: Persona Humana*, December 29, 1975 (Washington, D.C.: USCC, 1977), no. 8: "The meaning and implications of the term homosexual orientation are not universally agreed upon. Church teaching acknowledges a distinction between a homosexual 'tendency,' which proves to be 'transitory,' and 'homosexuals who are definitively such because of some kind of innate instinct.'" Moreover, Christine Gudorf introduces us to research that substantiates the "genetic support for homosexuality at least as a predisposition." She also addresses research that indicates "there is clearly some environmental influence as well." Gudorf, "A New Moral Discourse on Sexuality," in this volume, 62. *Always Our Children* seems to accept the plasticity of "homosexual tendencies" that Gudorf discusses, but the bishops also conclude that "it seems appropriate to understand sexual orientation (heterosexual or homosexual) as a deep-seated dimension of one's personality and to recognize its relative stability in a person." AOC 2:6.

4. This quotation and many others in this chapter come from participants in a survey and colloquium held in June 2006. The survey is available as an appendix to

this chapter. Some of these individuals would permit me to cite them by name, but out of concern for possible repercussions in pastoral or professional situations, I have chosen to omit specific citations to individuals. Nonetheless I am indebted to each of them for their thought-provoking comments and questions by which they helped me to sift through anecdotal evidence and to identify those strands of insight and experience that comprise the core of the quandaries that emerged in our study of *Always Our Children*. Thanks are especially owed to Kathleen Conger, Gina Donnarummo, Kerin Fullam, Basia Horelik, Patricia Leonard Pasley, and Eleanor Sauers.

5. For example, the document intentionally asks family members to reflect upon the parental love of God for his children, insisting that homosexual children be accepted as "gifts of God" and permanent members of the faith community. AOC 1:3, 5:2.3, Conclusion:3.

6. The scope of this chapter is to raise questions for further theological, spiritual, and pastoral study. These questions are not intended to exhaust the issue, but to isolate some compelling questions that suggest promising avenues of inquiry.

7. USCC, *When I Call for Help: A Pastoral Response to Domestic Violence Against Women* (Washington, D.C.: USCC, 2002).

8. In Vatican and USCCB statements it is clear that the weight given to the issue of homosexuality stems from concern over what is believed to be a devaluation of marriage and a threat to family life. See United States Conference of Catholic Bishops [USCCB], *Promote, Preserve, Protect Marriage*, public statement, September 9, 2003, available online: www.nccbuscc.org/comm/archives/2003/03-179.shtml (accessed August 15, 2006); Congregation for the Doctrine of the Faith, *Considerations Regarding Proposals to Give Legal Recognition to Unions Between Homosexual Persons*, June 3, 2003, available online: www.vatican.va/roman_curia/congregations/cfaith /documents/rc_con_cfaithdoc_20030731 homosexual-unions_en.html (accessed August 15, 2006); Pontifical Council for the Family, *Family, Marriage and "De Facto" Unions*, July 26, 2000 (Washington, D.C.: USCC, 2001); Pontifical Council for the Family, *Truth and Meaning of Human Sexuality: Guidelines for Education with the Family*, November 21, 1995 (Washington, D.C.: USCC, 1996). Contrariwise, I was surprised that no one among those who engaged me in conversation about *Always Our Children* considered homosexual unions to pose any "threat" to the dignity of marriage.

9. In 1997, *Always Our Children* merely advised therapy for children who might be growing into a homosexual orientation. By contrast, only two years earlier the Vatican's *Truth and Meaning of Human Sexuality*, paragraph 104, turns therapy into a moral imperative: "If parents notice the appearance of this tendency or of related behavior in their children, during childhood or adolescence, they *should* seek help from expert qualified persons in order to obtain all possible assistance." (Emphasis mine.)

10. Kelly's name has been changed and gender obscured for reasons of privacy.

11. Joseph A. Selling, "Homosexuality and Chastity: An Alternative Moral Criterion," *New Theology Review* 11 (1998): 64.

12. Ibid., 66.

13. Ibid., 67.

14. Vatican statements flesh out their perspective on the "sin" of "homogenital" acts in *Truth and Meaning in Human Sexuality*, paragraph 104: "Homosexual unions

are also totally lacking in the conjugal dimension, which represents the human and ordered form of sexuality. Sexual relations *are human* when and insofar as they express and promote the mutual assistance of the sexes in marriage and are open to the transmission of new life." (Emphasis mine.) Is it possible that sexual relations are human that promote, but do not *express*, the mutual assistance of the sexes? Is it feasible to consider that homosexual persons living in lifelong partnerships could lend support and fellowship to married couples?

15. In other parts of the document, the bishops introduce greater nuance into their presentation of the nature of sexuality and relationships. For example, they write, "Chastity means integrating one's thoughts, feelings, and actions, in the area of human sexuality, in a way that values and respects one's own dignity and that of others." Unfortunately, this respect does not extend to the feelings and thoughts that are inherent in a homosexual orientation: to engage sexually fulfilling, faithful, and monogamous relationships.

16. In *Follow the Way of Love*, the U.S. bishops write, "We share the pain of couples who struggle without success to conceive a child. We admire and encourage families who adopt a child, become foster parents, or care for an elderly or disabled relative in their homes." USCC, *Follow the Way of Love: A Pastoral Message of the U.S. Catholic Bishops to Families on the Occasion of the United Nations 1994 International Year of the Family*, November 17, 1993 (Washington, D.C.: USCC, 1994).

17. These same men and women are greatly disheartened by the decision of the Commonwealth of Massachusetts to allow Catholic Charities to deny services to homosexual couples seeking to adopt a child. I imagine that they would also raise questions about the Congregation for the Doctrine of the Faith's statement indicating that "allowing children to be adopted by persons living in [same-sex] unions would actually mean doing violence to these children, in the sense that their condition of dependency would be used to place them in an environment that is not conducive to their full human development." *Considerations Regarding Proposals to Give Legal Recognition to Unions Between Homosexual Persons*, paragraph 7.

18. Those who argue in this way rely on a very limited understanding of natural law and a narrow reading of scripture to reinforce their point of view. Case in point: "These truths about marriage are present in the order of nature and can be perceived by the light of human reason. They have been confirmed by divine Revelation in Sacred Scripture." USCCB, *Between Man and Woman: Questions and Answers about Marriage and Same-Sex Unions*, November 12, 2003 (Washington, D.C.: USCCB, 2003).

19. Unfortunately, the length of this work allows only a cursory treatment of the biblical argument that, put crudely, "It's Adam and Eve, not Adam and Steve." It can easily be argued, from the perspective of biblical scholarship, that we often overturn Bronze Age constructs of morality when scientific or historical evidence reveals them to be inherently repressive, or based on a faulty understanding of the world and/or God. For example, although slavery is condoned in many scriptural texts, slavery has long been understood to be an "objectively immoral" practice because it denies the intrinsic worth of every human being.

20. See especially, Pope Paul VI, *Divino Afflante Spiritu: Encyclical Letter on the Promotion of Biblical Studies*, September 30, 1943, available online: www.vatican.va/holy _father/pius_xii/encyclicals/documents/hf_p-xii_enc_30091943_divino-afflante -spiritu_en.html (accessed August 15, 2006); *Dei Verbum: Dogmatic Constitution on Di-*

vine Revelation, Solemnly Promulgated by His Holiness Pope Paul VI, November 18, 1965, in *Vatican Council II: A Completely Revised Translation in Inclusive Language,* ed. Austin Flannery, O.P., (Northport, NY: Costello Publishing Company, 1988); and Pontifical Biblical Commission, *The Interpretation of the Bible in the Church,* March 18, 1993, available online: www.ewtn.com/library/CURIA/PBCINTER.HTM (accessed August 15, 2006). *The Catechism of the Catholic Church* similarly states, in paragraph 100 (including a quote from *Dei Verbum* 12:2): "In order to discover the sacred authors' intention, the reader must take into account the conditions of their time and culture, the literary genres in use at that time, and the modes of feeling, speaking, and narrating then current. 'For the fact is that truth is differently presented and expressed in the various types of historical writing, in prophetical and poetical texts, and in other forms of literary expression.'" (Emphasis in original.) *The Catechism of the Catholic Church,* promulgated by Pope John Paul II, October 11, 1992 (New York: Doubleday, Image Books, 1994). Furthermore, the late Raymond E. Brown presented one of the most cohesive and comprehensive cases against biblical literalism that I am aware of. In particular, his illumination of biblical literalism as counter to the incarnational nature of Christianity (i.e., being founded upon the belief that, historically, God became human and chooses to operate in history through human beings) continues to be highly relevant in understanding the problems of biblical literalism. See *Reading the Gospels with the Church: From Christmas through Easter* (Cincinnati, OH: St. Anthony Messenger Press, 1996), 77–86.

21. The exclusive prerogative of conjugal sexuality is "rooted in the biblical account of man and woman created in the image of God and made for union with one another (Gen. 2–3)." AOC 6:6, and elsewhere.

22. The biblical creation stories are some of the most complex passages in the Bible, joining theological and pastoral insights from at least four different centuries. To take these stories as paradigmatic for all human sexuality certainly has historical precedent. Still, for twenty-six centuries or more, the mythology depicted in these stories similarly set historical precedent for belief in a flat earth. Since the time of Galileo, the magisterium has reconsidered this point of view and no longer insists that the sun rotates around the earth. Similarly, it seems reasonable to question whether these texts must continue to stand as the incontrovertible and exhaustive paradigm of all that can be considered "human" in human sexuality.

23. For example, in Matthew's gospel's Sermon on the Mount (the gospel of Matthew chapters 5–7), we see Jesus affirming that he has "not come to abolish [the Law and the Prophets] but to fulfill them," and precisely then (in the next verses) Jesus goes on to reinterpret the law for the purpose of revealing those human attitudes and relationships that (1) have primacy over literal execution of laws and (2) give laws their truest meaning (Mt. 5:17–20 and 5:21ff).

24. Alexander McCall Smith, *The No. 1 Ladies' Detective Agency* (New York: Anchor Books, 1998), 100.

25. Karl Rahner, "A Basic Interpretation of Vatican II," *Theological Studies* 40 (1979), 716–27.

11

A Tortured Trio: Sexuality, Adolescence, and Moral Theology

Julie Collins

As part of his "Rules for Discernment," St. Ignatius Loyola tells us that if we are paralyzed by a decision—torn as to which way to go—we ought to consider our deathbed. Imagine you are dying. Now, facing your imminent demise, how do the choices before you look? Not exactly "cheery" advice, but as our Basque mystic knew, there is nothing like using our imagination to get us in touch with what is "really real."

I have my own version of this fantasy. I have this strong sense that when we arrive at the "pearly gates" Jesus is going to ask us only one question: *Who* did you bring with you? Who has tasted heaven because you lived? In other words, *what was the quality of your love life?*

The last breath we take may be an odd place to begin a conversation about the tortured trio—sexuality, adolescence, and moral theology—but to me it frames the topic perfectly. Teenagers need to hear that their sexual choices are about love and they are about eternity: nothing more, nothing less.

Placing sex in the context of love and eternity usually works with adolescents. They are, by nature, romantics. Even the males, by the end of high school, are fascinated with the question of romantic love: What is it? How does one stay in love? Can love be trusted?

They are also fascinated with eternity because they are desperate to know the meaning of life. What is life all about? Does life have a meaning, a purpose, or is this world all just a bad joke? Teenagers may have never read Sartre but, at their core, most of them realize that what we believe about death illuminates what we believe about life. The Resurrection—*my* resurrection—tells me that my choices in life are of gut-wrenching significance and my body contains within it the possibility of unimaginable glory.

Check it out: the resurrection means that sex can never be "just physical" because there is no such thing! Our bodies are on nothing less than a celestial
trajectory. (Forgive the "teen-speak" but the rejection of Platonic dualism
demands some emphasis!)

For all these reasons, I often begin my course asking for a vote: "How
many of you would like to have a holy friend?" This question is usually
greeted with a nervous giggle because to many of them it is a laughable contradiction: a *holy* teenager?! But we plow ahead and I insist on hands in the
air; this is a vote! After that, we brainstorm and I carefully record on the
board *why* a holy friend is attractive to some of them and unattractive to
others. I make very little comment and although they are usually eager to
rebut some of the "pros" and "cons" being offered by their classmates, I insist that we just listen respectfully to each other's reasons. When everyone's
reasons are all on the board, we can discuss them.

What is usually staring back at us is fascinating and creates a fertile discussion. The focus of my facilitation is simply to invite them to discover
what our attitudes about holiness reveal. Here are some of the assumptions
that consistently emerge from this adolescent consideration:

1. Holiness is about perfection; teens are experimenting, trying to learn
   about the world and about other people. We make mistakes. Therefore, a teenager cannot be holy.
2. A holy friend would be a sort of moral policeman; he could be judg-
   mental.
3. A holy friend would be boring—not interested in "fun."
4. A holy friend would be helpful, loyal, kind, trustworthy.
5. A holy friend would be a good example.

After we have worked with this question, I ask the young men before me
the logical follow up: "Would you like to have a holy girlfriend?" The reaction is an instant of stunned silence and then much hilarity. But we peel
that response apart and try again to get at the attitudes that make this question seem like such an impossibility. Like clockwork, some young man will
opine: "I don't want a holy girlfriend, Ms. Collins, but I think I might want
a holy *wife*." As you can imagine, I rejoice when this pearl falls into my lap
because it allows so much theology to be unpacked.

This "holy friend/holy girlfriend" discussion allows a class in moral theology to focus on the first hurdle: Why should you care about the rules of
the game if you really don't care about winning? Or to put it another way:
"This sanctity thing—what is in it for me?" This can seem like a rather crass,
childish way of approaching the Christian life, but let's remember what we
are up against, let's remember the message contemporary Western culture is
sending teens:

1. Religious people are anti-sex, anti-pleasure, anti-fun.
2. Religious people are just like your parents—they want to control you and tell you what to do.

Face it: we catechists, pastors, and campus ministers have a terrible public relations problem. Before they will listen to us about sexuality or any other topic, we have to convince young people that holy people are happy people. We have to convince them that holiness is about love and that loving people (with apologies to Barbara Streisand!) are the happiest, luckiest people in the world.

We also have to convince them that the church is not interested in controlling them or limiting their freedom. The goal is not control; the goal is, in fact, our happiness in this life and in the next. One can get at that through the natural law argument: in our nature, in our very DNA, is our need for God. I often use a very simple metaphor to explain this:

> We are made for God, we are made for Love, the way our lungs are made for oxygen. You are perfectly free to choose to smoke, or to live in a smog-ridden environment; no one will stop you and your lungs will still wring whatever oxygen they can from the tainted air. But over time, the very cells in your body will become distorted. Cancer, emphysema, heart disease will follow. The same is true about our relationship with God.

> The Judeo-Christian tradition would say that every human being has a need for God, a need for love, that is equivalent to our need for oxygen. Neither God nor the Church is punishing us when we reject God/Love any more than God is punishing us when we get lung cancer. The illness is simply a product of our choosing to smoke cigarettes. Our spiritual disintegration is also the product of countless choices, countless decisions to violate our nature.

If a young adult can touch this truth about sin, real liberation can follow. But often, what first has to be challenged is the teen's image of God. Over the last fifteen years, I've had the privilege of directing high school seniors in a semester-long experience of the Spiritual Exercises of St. Ignatius Loyola. Like their elders, when young adults pray the First Week of the Exercises, they too, can taste the reality of sin—both in the world and in their private lives. Just as with older retreatants, this realization can be stunning and ultimately, life-changing. But over the years it has become clear to me that retreatants under twenty-five come at sin from a slightly different perspective.

Young adults tend to fall somewhere on a spectrum with regard to their own personal view of sin. At one extreme, you can find the classic, "God is out to get me" perfectionist who is forever nitpicking at his or her moral life. Far opposite from this anxious soul is the teen who has domesticated

God, turning the Creator of the Milky Way into a sort of heavenly teddy bear. Their divine plush toy is always available for cuddling and consolation but easily tossed in the corner when pleasure, vanity, or the "me first" ethic beckons. On an intellectual level, this believer would never question that personal sin exists or that he or she is capable of sinning. But at a gut level, there is no fear of sin, no sense of what it costs.

People born decades after Vatican II tend, often unconsciously, to live their moral lives closer to this extreme. The good news is that they do not generally see God as a harsh, exacting judge, always demanding, impossible to satisfy. The *bad* news is that this generation has taken St. John's declaration that "God is love" to mean: "God is a wimp." They will proclaim absolutely that God's love for them is unconditional. But when they affirm that "God will always love me," unknowingly, they have added a two-part subtext:

1. God loves everyone. Thus, God's love is rather generic, not based on profound knowledge. It is not intimate, not personal. If prodded a little and asked to describe their image of God, what a director sometimes discovers is a theist who has not experienced a personal God. God is imagined more as a "force" than a person.
2. Since God will always forgive me, there must be no consequences, really, to sin. I can always "kiss and make up with God." This is a variation on that old-time slander against the Church of Rome: "You Catholics think you can just go out and sin, no problem, and then just take care of it in confession." Alas, Catholics under the age of twenty-five don't usually couple their carefree attitude toward sin with much time in the confessional!

The other challenge created by the domesticated, divine teddy bear is a sort of spiritual schizophrenia. What religious educators and campus ministers discover is that it is perfectly possible to have a young person who is very active in retreats, liturgies, and service while at the same time parts of his or her personal life are morally chaotic. During the week, these high school or college students work hard. Their academic performance is well above average and they are very committed to sports and other extracurricular activities. The weekends, however, are a whirl of substance abuse, genital sex, and generally reckless behavior.

The reasons for this "Dr. Jekyll and Mr. Hyde" phenomenon are legion: stress, peer pressure, and adolescent rebellion. But when one begins to direct the prayer of these young adults, the revelation of their "secret" lives can be shocking; and all the more so because, simultaneously, their prayer life can be generous, graced, and fervent! Even youth ministers who thought themselves in touch with the lives of their flock can be stunned to discover that the accomplished young man or woman sitting in front of them is morally color-blind.

This moral blindness often springs from a tragic confusion over the nature of love and the consequent adolescent interpretation of St. Augustine's advice: "Love and do what you will." Everyone who teaches morality to teens has heard the cry: "Sex is OK if two people really love each other." This can be a jewel tossed into the teacher's lap as long as it is handled gently.[1] I usually affirm that yes, sex is about love and I remind my students what they already know: our culture says that casual sex is just *recreation*. And what moral elements are there to recreation? "You want to play tennis, I want to play tennis. How 'bout I meet you at the court at 4:00 and we'll play tennis?" This attitude explains why the only moral issue from popular culture's point of view is consent and fair disclosure. Is the sexual intercourse consensual? Is it between two adults who are physically healthy?

At this point it is helpful to remind students that sexual intimacy is part of the language we speak with our bodies. "Body language" may be a late twentieth-century concept but human beings have known for eons that touch speaks. Whether it is the handshake that tells you I won't harm you (because if I give you my right hand, you know that I have no weapon!), or the kiss on the cheek you give Great Aunt Susie every Christmas, increasing physical intimacy conveys greater passion, greater attachment, greater commitment. Sex is meaningful because touch is a language. And touch is a moral issue because we can tell the truth with our bodies or we can tell lies.

"So, Ms. Collins, if we really love each other, if we are really telling the truth, it must be OK for us to sleep together . . . ?"

My answer focuses on that mysterious reality: time. Can you say to your beloved: "I'll love you for six months?" Or even, "I've loved you for two years?"

Sounds silly, doesn't it? Love, by definition, is forever. We don't place a time limit on it; we don't even think about it having an expiration date. But if we are too young or too busy with college or graduate school, if we are not in a place to make a commitment to someone, if we cannot marry him or her, there is a problem. If we choose to be sexually intimate outside of a permanent commitment, "I'll love you for six months" is exactly what we are saying.

This conversation usually rings true for teens because they are all familiar with the transitory nature of most adolescent relationships. They know that for people their age, love is rarely "forever." And frankly, this mystifies them—especially if they have ever imagined themselves to be in love. How is it possible that all the passion and even adoration they showered on their beloved dissolved into banality? How is it possible that someone who promised them "forever" walked away from them—seemingly without a pang?

These heartbreaking questions make teenagers quite receptive to a conversation about the distinction between real love and infatuation. In *The Road Less Traveled*, M. Scott Peck does an admirable job distinguishing between real love and falling in love, or infatuation. While acknowledging the impossibility of defining anything as sublime as love, Peck proposes a sort of working definition: Love "is the will to extend one's self for the purpose of nurturing one's own or another person's spiritual growth."[2] I find this definition helpful because it invites students to consider the complexity of the word "will." "Will" is desire combined with *action*. "Will" is all about choice.[3]

The idea that love is a choice liberates it from simple emotion and reminds young people that they, personally, *know* something about love. When they come home tired and hungry from an athletic practice and their mom asks them to go back out into rush-hour traffic to pick up their sister from her piano lesson, and somehow these teenagers manage to smile and say, "Sure, let me grab a Coke and then I'm out the door," that is love. When they cheerfully stay on the phone while a close friend revisits for the umpteenth time why s/he is *desperate* to go to the prom with the current class teen god or goddess, that, too, is love.

Love, at its core, springs from a self-sacrificing commitment that is sweetened by emotion but not dependent on it. Romantic, sexual love is fired by passion but is driven by a profound, unflinching knowledge of the Beloved: "I know who and what you are and I love you unconditionally."

This is, of course, the love for which teenagers—whether male or female—hunger. But the path toward it—especially if they do not grasp the difference between love and infatuation—can be perilous. If they confuse real love for the "false fire" that is infatuation,[4] their sexual choices are likely to be questionable.

And here is it critical to verbalize what teens before the 1960s heard with some frequency: chastity is challenging. Waiting is tough. We do fall in love; we do become infatuated with people, and sexual desire, like clockwork, follows. This is good, this is holy, and this is what it means to be human. But there is a difference between sexual desire and lust. And lust is something we can all fall into so easily. It is so easy to use another person as a means to a self-centered end: *my* ego gratification, my sexual pleasure.

Our culture, our airways, are dripping with invitations to lust. It is the greatest poverty of the last half-century: lust and sexual desire have become conflated! Teenagers almost always think that they are the same thing and believe the church is in vehement opposition to the pleasure that our sexuality offers. ("And so *why* should I listen to these asexual killjoys!?")

When the distinction between lust and sexual desire is explained to them, teens are often relieved. For as inured as this present generation is to guilt, they have felt rather hopeless and even angry: "I am always having sexual thoughts and feelings—it is just impossible to manage to do what the church asks of me!"

An explanation of lust, like a conversation about any of the deadly sins, demands some nuance. I often use it, in fact, to drive home the reality that most sins exist on a spectrum of seriousness: taking a pencil off the principal's secretary's desk is theft and so is making off with your grandmother's retirement, but one is clearly more devastating than the other. "Reading" *Playboy* is a form of lust and so is a liaison with a prostitute. They are the same but also different.

Talking about "low level" lust is helpful in driving home the focus of Christian morality and the nexus between morality and holiness: What is the quality of your loving? Are you using people? Are you telling the truth with your body as well as with your words?

The lust conversation also allows me to insert a great piece of wisdom from the twelve-step literature: H.A.L.T—hungry, angry, lonely, or tired. A simple but profound truth: when we are in a tough emotional or physical space we are likely to make questionable moral choices. With increased self-knowledge, with real consciousness of our feelings and our patterns, we can see moral pitfalls before they engulf us. We can stop, attend to our real needs, and make better choices.

St. Ignatius Loyola was, as always, right: know your patterns of consolation; know your patterns of desolation. (The Evil One does!) Be in touch with your own needs, know how to evaluate the purity of your motives. Chastity is ultimately a commitment to real love—of God, self, and others. And only the Holy Spirit can help us sort out what attempts at intimacy are self-serving and what are genuine and selfless.

Sexuality, encompassing all of the senses, reveals to us a Lover-God who is so enamored with flesh that he dignified it with his own life. But we have to help young people grasp that, like Prometheus, they must acknowledge the power of passion's fire or be inevitably singed by it.

NOTES

1. Ignatius Loyola felt passionately that the minister did not *bring* God to people. God was already at work in the person's life. Thus, one could avoid the pitfall of the "Messiah complex" and be present to people in a gentle, contemplative way. The moral health of the next generation is not in our hands—it is in God's. As Doncoeur notes in *The Heart of Ignatius*, 114, Luis Gonzales recorded this bit of Ignatian advice:

> The members of the Society should be like guardian angels to those with whom they deal and who are entrusted to them in two ways, first helping them as much as possible to eternal salvation, second, after they have done all they could, not being disturbed or losing their serenity when the others do not advance.

2. M. Scott Peck, *The Road Less Traveled*, 81.

3. Ibid., 83.

4. See Thomas J. Tyrrell, *Urgent Longings*, 17–18. Tyrrell asserts that the etymological roots of "infatuation" could be *ignis fatuus* or "false fire." He says: "An *ignis fatuus* was known to the nomadic tribes and pilgrims who crossed the desert in caravans guided by the only signposts that were reasonably dependable, the stars. . . . Often the desert pilgrims would observe what appeared to be the flickering light of a campfire. This becoming light was such a strong inducement to depart from the chosen route that even seasoned travelers would have to discipline themselves to be guided only by their planned route and their knowledge of the stars."

SELECTED BIBLIOGRAPHY

Doncoeur, Paul. *The Heart of Ignatius: The Ignatian Concepts of the Honor and Service of God.* Translated by Henry St. C. Lavin. Baltimore: Helicon Press, 1959.

Peck, M. Scott. *The Road Less Traveled: A New Psychology of Love, Traditional Values and Spiritual Growth.* New York: Simon & Schuster, 1978.

Tyrrell, Thomas J. *Urgent Longings: Reflections on the Experience of Infatuation, Human Intimacy, and Contemplative Love.* Whitinsville, MA: Affirmation Books, 1980.

12

Cohabitation: A Reassessment

Kieran Scott

Marriage in the Christian tradition is a remarkably flexible institution. Marriage customs have changed. Ceremonies have developed. Historically, there has not been one standard path into marriage for Catholics. Entry more often reflected local custom than universal Christian norms. In the second millennium, marriage became a sacrament. The requirement of a church representative at the ceremony and the stipulation of two conditions, consent and consummation, for a valid marriage became definitive only at the Council of Trent (1563) after centuries of debate.

Today our contemporary understanding of marriage as covenant is a post–Vatican II development. The role of friendship, equality of partners, and just love in marital relations has come to the fore with renewed emphasis in our current theology of marriage and sexuality.[1] Furthermore, the church has made exit from marriage permissible, through the annulment process, under an expanded array of conditions. The story of Christian marriage, then, is not one of stasis but of flexibility and development. That is the meaning of authentic tradition.

The question at the heart of the chapter is: Can this sense of tradition assist us in dealing constructively with the pervasive reality of premarital cohabitation in our society? Can it enable us to reframe the issue? Can an inclusive meaning of marriage encompass premarital cohabitation? The prefix before marital would seem to exclude it. On the other hand, could the question be reconsidered if set in a larger developmental marital framework that has emerged in the latter half of the twentieth century? Within this broader context, could the intention of the couple to marry be seen as having already embarked on the process? Could the (possible) next

step be the sacramentalization of the marriage? And, during this in-
between time, could the sexual activity of the couple be loving, faithful,
and morally responsible?

This chapter seeks to answer these questions with a fresh moral reassessment. Some may read the proposal as accommodating to the spirit of the
age. However, tradition is the basis for the argument put forth here. The
conviction is: the Christian tradition deeply and richly reclaimed can be a
wise guide in our postmodern marital situation.

Widespread cohabitation is a fairly recent phenomenon. It has become a
major social phenomenon in the past twenty-five years. Its upsurge spans
both sides of the Atlantic Ocean, and even most parts of the Western in-
dustrialized world. Churches seem perplexed, if not paralyzed, in their response to the phenomenon. Pastoral ministers are still learning how to address the issue in marriage preparation. Many of them identify cohabitation
as the most difficult issue they deal with in marriage preparation programs
and pre-marriage counseling.[2]

This chapter, then, takes a fresh look at cohabitation. It makes some critical distinctions as a way of seeking a moral reconsideration of the issue.
First, a framework is set for our proposal by offering a stage theory of marriage. Second, current social science research is presented on the topic.
Third, some traditional pastoral solutions by the churches are described. Finally, a moral reassessment of the issue is proposed in light of historical
precedent and contemporary personal and pastoral needs.

A STAGE THEORY OF MARRIAGE

The celebration of a couple's marriage in church is generally the high point
of their growing union. It is the point of no return. It solemnizes this union
as the couples mutually administer the sacrament. The assumption, however, that marriage begins at this point is false. This assumption has gravely
weakened our theology of marriage, and the efforts of the churches in com-
mending marriage and ministering to couples in postmodern times. A wide
and deep sense of our own Christian history tells us: the marriage nuptial
in church is not the beginning of marriage. Contemporary psychological
theory, legal proposals, and faith development perspectives support this
historical perspective.

Evelyn and James Whitehead, in *Marrying Well*,[3] write about the demise
of marriage as a state and its survival as a journey. Marriage as a stable state
is gone. Divorce functions in our consciousness as one of the outcomes of
marriage. Married couples find fidelity a new and unexpected challenge.
New resources are needed to navigate the unexpected turns, detours, and
passages. These continuing shifts and challenges give marriage the appear-

ance of journeying. It is not a location in life, a place where we live, but rather a relational pattern of movement, a way we travel through life.

The Whiteheads capture well this rich developmental psychological perspective. They write: "Understood as an institution, marriage has been a state that one either did or did not inhabit. Legally, a person is either married or not married; there is no in-between. The Christian Church, influenced by this legal orientation toward marriage, came to view marriage as an either/or situation." They proceed to note: "Outside this well-defined state no sexual sharing was permitted; once inside this institution, one could even demand one's sexual rights. There seemed no gradualness or development in this commitment; one was either in or out. The period of engagement and of marriage preparation were anomalies; little effective attention and ministry could be given to these 'borderline' events."[4] The fundamental thesis of the Whiteheads' is to oppose this legal framework and to propose marriage as relational process. In theological language, marriage is a personal covenant between individuals.

Some decades earlier, Margaret Mead sensed the emergence of some crucial cultural changes that were impacting marriage. In particular, she named shifting attitudes toward sex and commitment. Sex, for most Americans, has become a natural activity, like eating and sleeping. "We have come to believe also," she wrote, "that asking physically mature young people to postpone sex until their middle twenties is neither fair nor feasible. . . . [Also] we believe in commitment, but we do not believe that commitments are irrevocable."[5] The succeeding years would bear out Mead's observations. She discerned an emerging gap between belief and experience, between precept and practice in relation to the style of marriage at the time. She asked: "How can we invest marriage forms with new meaning?"[6] Can we create new patterns that would: 1) give young couples a better chance to come to know each other, and 2) give children a better chance to grow up in an enduring family? In response to her own questions, Mead proposed marriage in two steps.

We need two forms of marriage, Mead wrote: an *individual marriage* and a *parental marriage*. One can develop into the other—though it need not. Each has its own possibilities and special forms of responsibility.

The first step in marriage would be the *individual marriage*. It might be called a "student marriage" or a "companionate marriage." It would be a licensed union, a serious commitment, entered into in public and validated and protected by law, and, for some, by religion. The central obligation of the couple to each other would be an ethical, not an economic one. Each partner would have a deep and continuing concern for the happiness and well being of the other as long as they wished to stay together. Children and commitment to future parenting are not part of this marital form. In the individual marriage, the couple has a chance to know each other, grow into each other's life, and develop meaningful relationships of choice. It could also open the way to a more complex marital form, namely, a *parental marriage*, or it may allow the couple to part without guilt or recrimination.

The *parental marriage* is the second step in Mead's analysis of marriage. It is explicitly directed toward the founding of a family. This second type of marriage always follows on an *individual marriage*—no matter what stage in life. It would have its own license, ceremony, and responsibilities. It would be more difficult to contract. The couple needs to demonstrate their economic ability to support a child and marital skills to foster a quality marital relationship. This would be a marriage that looks to a lifetime relationship with links to the wider community.

While I have reservations with some of Mead's proposal, I affirm three aspects of it. First, her concern that couples have a better chance to come to know each other; second, her concern that children have a better chance to grow up in an enduring family; and third, her recognition that marriage is a development journey.

On the canonical and liturgical levels, there has also been a growing awareness of the depth and development of faith in relation to Christian marriage. The issue tends to surface when a baptized Catholic couple requests a nuptial for their church wedding. The couple is ready to enter into the covenant of marriage with each other. However, they may not possess a faith sufficiently alive to affirm that their relationship is a reflection of the love of Christ and the church. In other words, they are unable to state that their marriage is an explicit participation in that covenant. The only choice facing the couple at this stage is: celebrate a sacrament in which they really do not believe or enter a marriage relationship not recognized by the Christian community.

James Schmeiser[7] describes a marriage program initiated by the diocese of Autun, France that permits these baptized Catholic couples a further option in order to respond to this situation. The Autun diocesan pastoral team believes it was important to develop a notion of church as "catechumenal" or as a "place of welcome and freedom." This would offer each person a way of experiencing himself/herself as he/she is and provide a structure that offers a real choice. The diocese proposed diverse forms of reflection and celebration in accordance with different situations. It would recognize different choices and respond to these choices. No longer would there be only two possibilities: sacramental marriage in the church or civil marriage. The diocese of Autun proposed three forms of marriage.

The first form of marriage is *civil marriage*. The marriage takes place at city hall and is registered with the state. The church recognizes the value of this commitment and its permanence. The married couples are welcomed publicly in church. An implicit affirmation or openness to faith is required; in as much as they are one with family and friends, for whom faith is a living reality.

The second form of marriage is *welcomed civil marriage*. This may not be the most appropriate naming, but it follows the civil marriage. In this case, the baptized couple believes in God but is very distant from church practice and is not receptive to celebrating the sacrament of marriage. It has little or no meaning for them. Yet, they desire a religious ethos and a religious manner of expressing their commitment and personal beliefs before family and friends. The church welcomes and opens itself to the couple, helps them to reflect upon their faith and discover the realities of their love, as it testifies to its own faith. The couple is asked to declare their intentions before the community. The celebration may take place with the full participation of the assembly in the ritual. The ritual has a rich religious dimension to it. But it is not the sacrament of marriage. The marriage, however, is registered in a special church register.

The third form of marriage is *sacramental marriage*. This is celebrated by a couple of deep faith. They wish to symbolize the covenant of Christ and the church. The Gospel will guide their married life. It will be a sacrament. The couple celebrates their sacramental love before the community. The community, in turn, commits itself to support them.

In these three forms of marriage, then, a *civil marriage* is seen as a true and important step; a *welcome civil marriage* provides a religious ceremony, which is recognized as nonsacramental; and the *sacramental marriage* is an explicit form of covenantal grace. As Schmeiser notes, "This approach recognizes possible growth within the marital relationship. There is a recognition of various stages of marriage."[8]

SOCIAL SCIENCE RESEARCH AND COHABITATION

As indicated above, the emergence on various levels of a stage theory of marriage sets the framework for an ethical reassessment of cohabitation. Before we turn to this reexamination, however, we need to get a clear and accurate handle on the scope of cohabitation. The social sciences offer us extensive empirical information on the phenomenon.

Cohabitation is pervasive and growing. In the United States, between 1970 and 1980, Census Bureau data recorded a tripling in the number of cohabitating couples to over 1.5 million. Between 1980 and 1990, there was a further increase of 80 percent, to 2.9 million couples. In 1990, unofficially, there were actually between three and eight million cohabitating couples. Similar figures and trends have been found in the United Kingdom.[9]

Cohabitation is common both before marriage and after it. A little over half of all first marriages are preceded by cohabitation.[10] This statistic is as true of Catholics as other group.[11] The trend crosses all age groups and all first-world countries. Some additional pertinent data is worth noting:

- Cohabitants are as likely to return to singleness as to enter marriage.[12]
- Slightly more than half of couples in first-time cohabitation never marry.[13]
- The median duration of cohabitation is one to three years. One-third of couples cohabit for less than a year. Sixteen percent live with their partner for more than five years.
- Half of all cohabiting couples are young, unmarried or not yet married, and childless.
- Persons with lower levels of education and earning power cohabit more often and marry less often.
- Some people choose cohabitation as an alternative to marriage, not as a "trial" for it.
- Cohabitation is more likely to occur where religious belief is weak. However, there is no difference in frequency of cohabitation by religious denomination.
- Cohabiters may be more likely to divorce than people who marry directly from the single state. They divorce at a rate of 50 percent higher.
- Cohabiters with plans to marry report no significant difference in relationship quality to married people.
- The reasons for cohabitation vary: the growing secularization and individualization in first-world countries; sexual, social, and economic changes; peer pressure; fear of long-term commitment; desire to test the relationship; waiting to conclude higher education.

This cumulative data indicates one striking fact—cohabitation, as a contemporary phenomenon, is having a profound impact on marriage and family in postmodern times. Lost in the data, however, is adequate attention to different forms of cohabitation. Three types can be distinguished. First, there is temporary or casual cohabitation. This is entered with little thought or commitment. The second type is conscious preparation for marriage, a "trial run" as it were. The third type functions as a substitute for marriage.[14] These distinctions will be vital in our ethical reassessment of cohabitation and the needed pastoral responses of the churches. Let us turn first to the traditional responses of religious bodies to cohabitating couples.

TRADITIONAL PASTORAL SOLUTIONS

Cohabitation is disapproved in all the official documents of the Christian churches and by many Christian theologians. The official belief is that people should not have sexual intercourse before they marry. This teaching, however, is widely disregarded by church members (practicing and nonpracticing) and, as noted above, almost universally disregarded. In spite of this mismatch between traditional church teaching and the convictions and practices of its members, official church teaching cannot bring itself to sanction cohabitation before marriage. The unanimous teaching of the churches remains: sexual intercourse must be confined to marriage.[15]

The Roman Catholic Church condemns cohabitation.[16] Such a relationship is seen as a false sign, contradicting the meaning of a sexual relationship. It violates the church's teaching about sexual love and marriage. It is condemned under the rubric of "free union" or "trial marriage" and is considered a grave offense against the dignity of marriage. Intimate sexual expression is fitting only when commitment has been formally and liturgically expressed. All carnal activity outside the marital union is considered fornication and gravely sinful. However, there is acknowledgment of the pastoral difficulty in dealing with this issue. Two extremes are to be avoided: (1) immediately confronting the couple and condemning their behavior; and (2) ignoring the cohabitation aspect of their relationship. A middle road is suggested as the wisest strategy: integrate general correction with understanding and compassion; use it as a "teachable moment" in such a way as to smooth the path for them to regularize their situation. The assumption is that they are in a disordered state of sexuality, a state of sin.[17]

The Orthodox churches also strongly disapprove of cohabitation. Officially, they are reluctant to raise the question of sexual activity outside of marriage. The response from the evangelical churches is generally the same, and the Lutheran, Presbyterian, and Episcopalian churches take a similar position. They all affirm sexual intercourse properly belongs exclusively within marriage. Some committee reports, however, from a number of these churches seek pastoral accommodation to living together. However, there is near-unanimous consensus in all official teachings: living together before marriage is wrong.

This traditional position is based on a threefold argument:

1. It situates sexual intercourse within the context of the bond of marriage. Any nonmarital sexual intercourse then is wrong. Cohabitation, in this situation, is a sign of lack of discipline and giving in to the spirit of the times.
2. Cohabitation is a threat to marriage and family. Marriage, as Christians understand it, is a communal event undertaken with the intention of unlimited commitment. Cohabitation, on the other hand, tends to be private, lacking communal sanction and unlimited commitment.
3. Cohabitants tend to create less stable relationships when converted into marriage.[18]

For a constructive reassessment of cohabitation, the concerns expressed in this traditional argument need to be heard, given additional consideration, and, at the same time, outweighed by a most persuasive counterargument. This is the task of the rest of this chapter.

COHABITATION RECONSIDERED

Contemporary theology (and religious studies) has to perform a double act of listening. It must listen to the voices of its traditions and the voices surrounding those traditions. It must be able to make connections between the Christian tradition and ordinary life—if the gospel is to be capable of touching and transforming people. In light of the topic at hand, a Christian theology of marriage must take seriously both the Christian traditions of marriage and the difficult challenges facing marriage today. High on the list of these challenges is the phenomenon of cohabitation. Adrian Thatcher offers a serious, substantive, and lucid vision of marriage.[19] What is creative about his proposal is that it incorporates some forms of cohabitation. I am indebted to Thatcher in opening up this new (yet old) perspective in his groundbreaking work.

Key to Thatcher's proposal is his basic distinction between two types of cohabitation. There is a form of cohabitation within which the couple intends to marry. They are engaged and on their way to the altar. This is prenuptial cohabitation. There is also a form of cohabitation where the couple has no plans to marry. Here cohabitation is an alternative to marriage. It is nonnuptial cohabitation. For Thatcher, there is a qualitative difference between the two forms. They are not equal, and there ought to be a corresponding difference in moral judgment about the two types of relationship. It seems unjust to bring those who intend to marry and those who do not under the same rubric, namely, fornication.

However, Thatcher offers a still stronger argument for treating engaged couples in a different category from those who merely live together. His argument is an historical one. We could also call it deeply conservative, that is, preserving deep strands within the tradition. In Christian history, there are two traditions regarding the beginning of marriage. The traditional or conventional view is that a marriage begins with a wedding. An earlier Christian view, however, is that marriage begins with a pledging and binding of the couple to each other with a promise to marry. (The quaint-sounding term betrothal captures the meaning of this view better than our own current term engagement.) This nuptial pledging of the couple was followed later by the marriage ceremony. Sexual experience regularly began after the couple's pledge to marry (i.e., betrothal) and before the wedding ceremony (i.e., the nuptial). This premodern distinction between spousal (pledging) and nuptial (wedding) has largely been forgotten today. Yet, it holds the key as to when marriage begins. Does marriage begin with the wedding or is the entry into marriage a staged process, with the wedding marking the "solemnization" of a life commitment . . . already well begun?

Thatcher offers us a meticulously documented history on the question.[20] The widespread belief that a marriage begins with a wedding, he demonstrates, was not so much a religious or theological issue but a class matter. From the mid-eighteenth century onward, in England and Wales, the middle and upper classes had the political clout to enforce the new marriage laws requiring the registration and ceremonial ritualization of marriage. Also, new courtship procedures in the upper classes required prenuptial virginity of brides—for social rather than moral reasons. However, for most of Christian history, marriage did not begin with the wedding. The entry into marriage has been by spousal pledge or/and betrothal ceremony. John Gillis proceeds to note, "Betrothal constituted the recognized rite of transition from friends to lovers, conferring on the couple the right to sexual as well as social intimacy."[21] Sex began at the moment of engagement. The marriage in church came later, often triggered by the pregnancy. Half of all brides in Britain and North America were pregnant at their weddings in the eighteenth century.[22] So premarital sex is not simply a modern phenomenon. The only significant difference is that throughout most of Christian history it was mostly and truly premarital, i.e., it was part of the process of marrying. But with the current loss of the central importance of the spousal pledge (and betrothal rite), Adrian Thatcher claims, "Gone with it is the sense of entry into marriage as a process, liturgically marked and celebrated and sometimes revocable in cases of serious difficulty or incompatibility. Gone too is much of the social recognition of the in-between status of the couple."[23]

Thatcher's agenda is to recover this earlier (and biblical) understanding of the entry into marriage. It is essential, he believes, to the future of marriage in the new millennium. It also holds the possibility of transforming the perception of cohabitation with the intention to marry, from the domain of sin and fornication to the domain of marital beginnings of mutual growth and religious development. Crucial, of course, to this transformation is the distinction between forms of cohabitation. It is laissez-faire, promiscuous, nonnuptial cohabitation that is damaging to the couple (and to any children they may have). On the other hand, faithful committed cohabitants with a clear intention of getting married are qualitatively different. They ought also to be considered, in Christian ethics, morally different.

Finally, Thatcher asks: How can the churches pastorally support this moral reassessment? He proposes the reintroduction of betrothal (the pledging of the couple), as well as the ritual betrothal, and of seeing betrothal as already part of the process of marriage. Thatcher argues that marriage itself is a process and a liturgically celebrated engagement could become a significant symbol of the beginning of that process. This, in many ways, is a premodern solution to our postmodern marriage crisis.

The operating assumption in Thatcher's approach, then, is that the meaning of marriage already belongs to premarital cohabiters. By their intention to marry they have already embarked on the process that leads to the solemnization of their marriage. Unlike most cohabitating couples, betrothal was "emphatically premised by the intention to marry." It was never an end in itself. It was open "to the probability of future marriage." It honored the sacredness of marriage.

In premodern times, betrothal could last up to two years. It served valuable functions. The couple had the opportunity to grow intimately together. The couple's families and the community came together to support the upcoming marriage. Couples discovered whether their union could produce children. Churches supported these unions. And they also supported breaking them under certain conditions.

Today, however, the formal process around marriage generally only takes one day, the wedding day. The reclaiming of the notion—and the ritual—of betrothal helps us to see marriage again not as a simple event, but as a "process." This, in turn, would enable couples to begin to explore the sacred dimensions of their bond before they solidify their union for life. It would support them in the process of linking the various stages of their relationship. And, of vital importance, it would help couples to weave their relationship into the larger social fabric of family, community, and church. In this regard, Adrian Thatcher concludes: "If the entry into marriage were accepted as a process which involved, as steps within it, betrothal and ceremony, the anomalies presented to the church by cohabitees could be more easily handled. Furthermore, the actual availability of a betrothal liturgy or liturgies would help considerably in providing the missing language, which renders cohabitation socially problematic. It would also meet the concern that, while marriages are public, cohabitation is private.[24] A betrothal ceremony would provide precisely the public language and community dimension which are currently properties of weddings."[25] In a word, it would be a public act, with public legitimation.

We can summarize some conclusions from this study. First, Christian morality should not assume that all premarital sex is wrong. It is not. Nor ought we to assume that the nuptial has always been normative. It has not. Second, to distinguish between pre-nuptial and nonnuptial forms of cohabitation, we must open up the possibility of a moral reassessment of the issue. Third, there is no longer any provision for a two-staged entry into marriage, engagement and ritual solemnization. Some current practices of cohabitation could be read as a return to earlier premodern sensibilities rather than as a rejection of Christian marriage. And, finally, reclaiming the notion and the ritual practice of betrothal may be of service to the Christian churches in the construction of a postmodern theology of entry into marriage.

Every piece of sociological data indicates cohabitation is not going away. Even though the official teaching of the Catholic Church is opposed to it, Catholics cohabitate on a par with other groups in our society. Our Christian churches have more to offer than opposition and condemnation. This chapter offers a practical method of dealing with the issue. It also offers an interpretative framework to reassess cohabitation as a viable moral option.

NOTES

1. See Margaret Farley, *Just Love: A Framework for Christian Sexual Ethics* (New York: Continuum, 2006).

2. NCCB Committee on Marriage and Family, *Marriage Preparation and Cohabiting Couples: Information Report on New Realities and Pastoral Practices* (Washington, D.C.: NCCB, 1999).

3. Evelyn and James Whitehead, *Marrying Well: Possibilities in Christian Marriage Today*. (New York: Doubleday, 1981).

4. Ibid., 98.

5. Margaret Mead, "Marriage in Two Steps," in *The Family in Search of a Future*, ed. Herbert Otto (New York: Appleton Century Crofts, 1970), 76–78.

6. Ibid., 76.

7. James A. Schmeiser, "Marriage: New Alternatives," *Worship* 55, no.1 (1981): 23–34.

8. Ibid., 33.

9. See Adrian Thatcher, *Living Together and Christian Ethics* (Cambridge: Cambridge University Press, 2002).

10. See Larry Bumpass and Hsien Hen Lu, "Trends in Cohabitation and Trends for Children's Family Contexts in the United States," *Population Studies* 54 (2005): 7.

11. See Randall Jay Woodard, "Cohabitation and Entry into Marriage: Two Diverse Trajectories and the Future of Catholic Theology," in *New Horizons in Theology*, ed. Terrance W. Tilley, 198–213 (Maryknoll, NY: Orbis, 2005).

12. Thatcher, *Living Together and Christian Ethics*, 7.

13. NCCB Committee on Marriage and Family, *Marriage Preparation and Cohabiting Couples: Information Report on New Realities and Pastoral Practices.*

14. Adrian Thatcher, *Marriage After Modernity* (New York: New York University Press, 1999).

15. Adrian Thatcher, *Living Together and Christian Ethics*, 41.

16. See *The Catechism of the Catholic Church*, promulgated by Pope John Paul II, October 11, 1992 (New York: Doubleday, Image Books, 1994), #2391.

17. NCCB Marriage and Family Committee, *Marriage Preparation and Cohabiting Couples: Information Report on New Realities and Pastoral Practices.*

18. Adrian Thatcher, *Marriage After Modernity*, 106.

19. Adrian Thatcher, *Living Together and Christian Ethics*, and *Marriage After Modernity*.

20. Adrian Thatcher, *Marriage After Modernity*.

21. John Gillis, *For Better, For Worse: British Marriages, 1600 to the Present* (Oxford: Oxford University Press, 1985), 47.

22. See Lawrence Stone, "Passionate Attachments in the West in Historical Perspective," in *Perspectives on Marriage*, Second Edition, ed. Kieran Scott and Michael Warren, 129–38 (New York: Oxford University Press, 2001).

23. Adrian Thatcher, *Living Together and Christian Ethics*, 46.

24. See Jo McGowan, "Marriage versus Living Together," in *Perspectives on Marriage*, Second Edition, 83–87.

25. Adrian Thatcher, *Marriage After Modernity*, 131.

13

Sexuality and the Church: Finding Our Way

Harold D. Horell

I have been preoccupied with "sexuality" and "sex" for the past three years. That is, I have been attentive to every conversation or program that discusses sexuality, and this has heightened my awareness of the many ways "sex" is understood in contemporary cultures. My preoccupation began when Vincent Novak, S.J., who was then dean of the Fordham University Graduate School of Religion and Religious Education, invited me to attend a meeting to discuss human sexuality. That meeting led to the development of the Fordham University Conference on Human Sexuality in the Roman Catholic Tradition on October 28–29, 2004.

One winter day in 2006, I happened to encounter two very different discussions of human sexuality. First, I watched a television show about polyamory. A polyamorous relationship is, ideally, a deep, romantic, and committed relationship involving more than two fully consenting adults. On this television show people talked openly about their polyamorous relationships and sexuality. Second, that evening I attended a liturgical rite in which a woman took vows as a "consecrated virgin in the world." This ancient rite, during which a woman commits her life to service in the world that is intensified by a pledge of perpetual virginity, was common in the early church, fell into disuse and was then restored within the Catholic Church on May 31, 1970.[1]

By seeking to understand polyamorous relationships, consecrated virginity, and other expressions of sexuality, I have become more and more convinced that Fran Ferder and John Heagle are correct in their observation that "for the last half-century human sexuality has undergone what might best be described as a 'sea change'—a major historical transition—in our culture and in our religious institutions."[2] To use the vernacular of our postmodern era, people today are *constructing* new ways of being sexual and new paradigms of sexuality; or, as in the case of consecrated virgins, they are reclaiming older paradigms of sexuality that had fallen from active use. Now, this is hardly a new insight. Anyone who observes contemporary trends is likely to grant the validity of this point. However, I suggest that if we examine contemporary discussions of "sex" and "sexuality," we discover that the changes in how sexuality is understood are much broader and deeper than we might at first imagine. There is a unique degree of openness and adaptability in the ways people understand and express their sexuality in our present socio-cultural milieu. In some cases, such as in polyamory and consecrated virginity, we find new or reclaimed forms of sexual life. In other instances, such as in marriages, cohabitation, single lifestyles, and celibacy, there have been gradual yet meaningful changes in the ways people embody a sense of sexuality.

The church has two basic options in responding to changing views of sexuality. We can either ignore the sexual signs of our times or we can acknowledge and respond to them. We may choose to ignore them, thinking that the church has lost its credibility to speak about issues of sexuality because of the recent crisis of sexual abuse.[3] Or we can ignore them because we believe that questions about sexuality have been raised and answered, that established answers to questions about sexual issues remain adequate, and that additional discussion is not necessary. From such a perspective, even though times may be changing, the teaching role of the church can still be met by reasserting established understandings of married, single, and ordained life, and marital and celibate sexuality. Or we can ignore changing views of sexuality because they are too dangerous to consider. Despite the many positive understandings of sexuality within our faith traditions and culture, a deep suspicion of sexuality remains within the church and broader society. This suspicion leads some people to lash out against those who discuss sexuality and sexual issues. Catholic theologians, in particular, who express a willingness to raise critically reflective questions about sexuality are likely to be pressured or threatened. As Christine Gudorf explains, "Many persons have taken great risks and endured great suffering at the hands of our mother church in order to contribute to a transformation toward a more humane, more loving sexual theology."[4]

Why, then, should we as Catholic Christians acknowledge and respond to changing views of sexuality? I contend that changing views of sexuality place us at a crossroads today. On the one hand, we can allow the currents of contemporary culture to continue to carry us along, so that we can watch and then react to how these currents affect the ways sex and sexuality are understood in church and society. On the other hand, there is another path: a path suggested by the contributors to this book. Ferder and Heagle write about "the need for a renewed theology and spirituality of human sexuality," and Gudorf calls for "a new moral discourse on sex." Similarly, Sidney Callahan claims that "the struggle is now joined to develop a new integrated and coherent view of sexuality that is true to the Gospel."[5]

In this chapter, I draw together insights from Ferder and Heagle, Gudorf, Callahan, the other authors of this book, and other sources to outline how we as Catholic Christians can examine, in the light of our Christian faith, contemporary views about sexuality. I suggest that we cannot afford to be silent about or dismissive of the broad-ranging changes in human sexuality. And, we cannot let anti-sexual attitudes within the church and broader society keep us from reflecting on human sexuality. Because our sexuality is so very much a part of who we are as persons, we need to be attentive to our sense of sexuality and how contemporary understandings of sexuality affect us as persons. From a Christian faith perspective, we need to reflect openly on how our sexuality and our spirituality are interrelated and can be integrated with one another in a mature personality.

ON ADOPTING A POSTMODERN
FRAMEWORK OF ANALYSIS

I suggest above that we situate changing understandings of sexuality within the ebb and flow of our multifaceted and often ambiguous postmodern age. I also contend that by adopting a postmodern approach we can develop: (1) a better understanding of the difficulties we encounter today in discussing sexuality; and (2) an initial appreciation for the contribution the essays in this collection make in addressing these difficulties.[6] To move into a postmodern pastoral approach, I suggest that we think of sexuality as a construct, as something that we as human beings fashion to help us make sense of our lives and world. From a postmodern perspective, sexuality is never simply a dimension of human persons and relationships. Rather, we experience sexuality as part of life and the world because of personal and social constructions/understandings of sexuality that we have internalized. From a postmodern perspective, the question we need to raise is: Are current constructs of sexuality adequate, and, if they are not, how can we reconstruct them so that they are grounded in our faith convictions and are truly life-sustaining in our contemporary era?

Some people will object to my approach, arguing that postmodernity cannot provide an adequate pastoral or moral perspective. Specifically, there are two noteworthy arguments that have, in various formulations, been leveled against postmodernity. The first argument may be called "the negativist challenge." There are those who argue that the currents of cultural postmodernity have been primarily, if not completely, negative and need to be resisted or overcome. Second, it has been suggested that postmodernity's greatest weakness is that it fosters an ethical relativism that is problematic and, ultimately, incoherent. Both of these arguments need to be considered before I outline a postmodern approach to understanding human sexuality.

The Negativist Challenge

It must be admitted that there is, beyond doubt, a trivializing dimension to postmodernity.[7] The currents of trivializing postmodernity lead us to focus on how our lives are based on chance and uncertainty rather than on secure knowledge. They highlight the fact it can be difficult to make comparisons among competing and conflicting ways of viewing the world. Generally, trivializing dimensions of postmodernity can lead us to question whether or not our lives can have a sense of meaning and value beyond our particular life contexts. They may also promote skeptical, even nihilistic, critique of any broad criteria for evaluating the potential of human thought and activity. From a trivializing postmodern perspective, and in contrast with the moral sensibilities of many people today, polyamory, marriage, celibacy, and even casual sexual expression without commitment might all be seen as on par with one another. That is, these four options could be seen as equally legitimate ways to *construct* an understanding of sexuality, each offering a chance for either fulfillment or frustration.[8] Overall, it can be argued that a postmodern, radical historicist perspective is too negative, defeatist, nihilistic, and vacuous a starting point for theological or moral analysis.

Ethical Relativism

Ethical relativism is the belief that the moral claims and worldviews of particular persons and groups are *always* dependent upon the persons and groups holding them. From a postmodern ethical relativist perspective, moral outlooks are constructed by particular persons and groups and pertain only to those persons or groups. Moreover, to claim that moral views are always dependent on particular perspectives is to imply that they are *never* expressive of transcendent, universal, or objective moral value, and that, consequently, there are no overarching standards to which we can appeal to make comparisons among differing moral outlooks.[9] For example, a person with a trivializing postmodern perspective might hold that some people opt for mutual sexual intimacy while others opt for sexual bondage and domination, and that these perspectives can only be judged in terms of whether or not they are internally coherent and, on a subjective level, provide sexually fulfilling experiences for those who adopt them.

However, many people in our contemporary era, including many Christians, hold that there are universal moral standards; and that our sense of morality is rooted in a sensitivity to life, especially human life, that goes beyond or transcends specific situations, and should be present in all situations. In our postmodern age we need to recognize that a moral awareness of the value of life may be expressed in a variety of differing ways, and that we will never be able to offer a universally agreed upon account of moral sensitivity. Yet it is reasonable to suppose that just as we are bodily beings, and just as we are thinking and feeling beings, we are beings who are sensitive and responsive to life—and that this sensitivity is indicative of a trans-situational, transcendent valuing of life that is part of all that we are and do. For instance, Richard Kearney expresses such a transcendent valuing of life when he claims that beyond all relativistic, postmodern preoccupations with internal, subjective webs of belief, there lies "the resistant ethical relation of the 'face to face.'"[10] Moreover, because of this sense of a transcendent valuing of life, an argument can be made from a Christian or a contemporary Western perspective that in all instances mutual, life-affirming sexual intimacy has a *prima facie* praiseworthy quality, while destructive, nonlife-affirming, sexual domination is always morally problematic. In the final analysis, a moral framework that does not provide rational criteria for discerning or judging how specific moral perspectives compare to one another in terms of their respective abilities to express a respect for persons as living beings is deficient.

A second criticism of ethical relativism is that it is intellectually incoherent. Moral relativists reject all totalizing moral claims. They contend that we *cannot step beyond* particular moral standpoints and judge them in terms of transcendent or universal moral standards. However, moral relativism is itself a totalizing standard insofar as the relativist *claims, at least implicitly, to have stepped beyond* the moral perspectives and worldviews of all particular persons and groups and determined that all moral stances are *always* dependent upon the persons and groups holding them. Thus, the relativist position is intellectually inconsistent and, thus, incoherent.

A Postmodern Starting Point

Despite the critiques of postmodernity, I offer three reasons for beginning with our contemporary postmodern condition as a starting point for an analysis of human sexuality. First, there is a side to postmodernity that its critics too often ignore. Beyond the limitations of "trivializing postmodernity" there is what can be called "searching or questing postmodernity." Rather than seeing the currents of postmodernity as a burden that trivializes life, questing postmoderns tend to see postmodernity as an opportunity to be more honest about our world and ourselves than we could be in the past, and, consequently, more open to new possibilities.[11] For example, when I discussed sexuality with some of the consecrated virgins who attended the consecration rite I mentioned above, one of them remarked that she felt frustrated when she tried to envision her life in terms of a vowed religious life, single life, or marriage. She insightfully critiqued (we might, from a postmodern perspective, say that she skillfully deconstructed) the view that these three lifestyle choices could ever provide a comprehensive vision of human sexuality. She spoke excitedly about the new possibilities she imagined when she learned about the option of becoming consecrated for service in the world. As I listened to her, I realized that she embraced the postmodern challenge to construct new understandings of sexuality. Moreover, her outlook on life was hopeful and positive, rather than being trivializing or negative. Generally, I suggest that while we need to be aware of the negative dimensions of postmodernity, we can at the same time recognize that a postmodern outlook need not be trivializing or relativistic. Rather, a postmodern stance can offer us a standpoint for critical reflection upon our present-day understandings of sexuality.

Second, from a theological perspective I contend that an openness to the critically reflective attitude found in postmodern spiritual questing can help us to discern God's active presence in the world—and God's call to review and, as need be, reimagine our understandings of sex and sexuality so that the spiritual meaning of sexuality is made known more fully in the way we experience our sexuality. Those who reject postmodern currents of thought and action too often diminish our appreciation for the presence of God in our contemporary postmodern culture, and, as a result, they often add to, rather than counter, the trivializing tendencies of our times.[12] In contrast, I suggest that if we truly believe that our God is a God who continues to dwell among us and who will often surprise us with life-giving possibilities beyond what we might at first imagine, then we need to: (1) work to distinguish the positive, searching dimensions of postmodernity from the negative and trivializing dimensions of contemporary culture; (2) be open to recognizing what is genuinely good within the currents of postmodern change; and (3) be willing to discern how God may be enabling and requiring us to construct new paradigms for thought and action—including paradigms for human sexuality.

Third, I opt for a postmodern perspective because ethical relativism is not the only postmodern moral stance, and because nonrelativistic postmodern stances offer an insightful way, and perhaps the most insightful way at the present time, to understand and approach the challenges we as Christians face in addressing questions about sexuality. More fully, as people have responded to or reacted against the currents of postmodern change and have critiqued ethical relativism, another moral perspective has emerged as expressive of the postmodern outlook. This other postmodern moral stance is what can be called "moral perspectivism."[13] From a perspectivist stance our moral viewpoints are constructed within the context of our specific time and place and generally retain a grounding within this specific context to a significant extent. However, a perspectivist can reject ethical relativism. From a perspectivist viewpoint there simply is no way we can step back from our grounding within a specific time and place to offer the kind of totalizing judgments that a relativist wants to try to justify. More importantly, a fully developed perspectivist stance offers a very different outlook on life than a relativist moral perspective. From a perspectivist stance, the relativist worldview is *too limited*. It is not able to express a hopeful outlook that enables us to envision possibilities for greater human flourishing. Additionally, moral relativism does not provide ways of envisioning a sense of trans-situational, trans-historical, and transcendent valuing.

The overly narrow perspective of relativism can be seen by examining a number of central tenants of a relativist perspective. Specifically, from a relativist stance, values are temporary and limited. For instance, from a relativistic viewpoint we might think of values as tools that we use in structuring human relationships. Yet, tools break and wear out, at which point they are discarded. Or a new relational task may require us to get a new tool/value. Similarly, relativists often think of life as contingent and limited. Our lives are what they are, for a relativist, because of happenstance. Things could be otherwise than what they are. Moreover, from this perspective our lives and our social worlds are like humanly-made and self-contained islands floating on an unfathomable and chaotic sea. Sometime we will be able to throw a line from one island to another (that is, find a connection between two differing ways of looking at life and the world). Other times we will not.[14] Overall, a relativist vision diminishes our ability to construct a meaningful sense of life.

Christian Perspectivism

It is beyond the scope of this chapter to offer a fully developed account of perspectivism as a standpoint for Christian pastoral analysis. Yet, in order to differentiate a perspectivist stance from a relativistic outlook and to indicate how perspectivism can provide a framework for understanding human sexuality, I sketch a few basic features of a Christian perspectivist position.[15] These are the central notions of *the deeply Christian* and *the classic*. From a perspectivist stance, we begin with a sense of the situatedness of human values and, specifically for Christians, the grounding of our moral values within our personal and communal faith perspectives. Our goal in addressing pastoral and moral issues is to draw from the wisdom of our Christian Scriptures and traditions and to be open to the fuller realization of God's Reign in our midst as we strive to express a *deeply Christian* perspective in the present; that is, to embody a way of life that: (1) addresses present life situations effectively in the light of our Christian faith; and (2) faithfully expresses of the heart of our faith.

From a perspectivist stance, we construct moral values. Yet, they are not mere tools. They are expressions of the wisdom of our faith traditions, and they are expressive of a transcendent valuing. From a pespectivist stance, values help us to structure our lives. On the one hand, they ground us in the wisdom of our faith traditions and connect us with others in a community in which these values are shared. On the other hand, as we strive to be more just and loving and to realize core moral values moral fully in our lives, we look toward the future. From a faith perspective, our efforts to realize moral values more fully should be grounded in openness to discerning what God is enabling and requiring of us as specific persons in the concrete circumstances of our lives. Thus, from a Christian perspectivist stance, our lives are not based on happenstance. Rather, Christian perspectivists can embrace the core Christian conviction that our lives are lived in response to God's call. We can also affirm the core Christian conviction that we are called to be cocreators with God in the ongoing creation of the world, and that we are called to help to bridge the gaps among people by constructing frameworks of meaning that enable people to understand one another and work together.

The second construct needed for a Christian postmodern perspectivist stance is the notion of the classic, an idea developed by David Tracy and based on a distinction between the origins and the effects of the resources of Christian faith traditions. Tracy first notes that classic works of art or literature, while they have their origin in a specific time and place, can have an effect or influence far beyond that time and place. For instance, Harper Lee's novel *To Kill a Mockingbird* chronicles how a specific family responded to racial prejudice in a small, southern United States town in the mid-twentieth century. Yet, it is a classic of literature because the portrayals of integrity and respect for human dignity have inspired people living in diverse life situations. Tracy then suggests that some of the resources of Christian faith traditions can have a value beyond the boundaries of Christian communities and in some cases can become "classics" when they help people in diverse life contexts express their deepest thoughts and feelings or express possibilities for human living that can be applied in a variety of situations. For instance, Pope Leo XII's *Rerum Novarum* can be considered a classic of social ethics because its analysis of the rights of workers has affirmed the moral sensibilities of many people of good will and has been used to foster moral consensus among people of diverse religious, social, and political backgrounds. Similarly, understandings of "human dignity," "the common good," and "solidarity" that are grounded in Christian faith convictions have become basic moral principles within our society because they can and have been used to express the moral sensibilities of people (Christian and non-Christian alike) in a variety of life situations.[16]

Overall, Christian faith is directed outward from the church toward the world, toward welcoming and working to realize more fully the Reign of God, the values of God's peace and justice, within the world. While we remain committed, postmodern, perspectivist Catholic Christians who are always grounded within our specific faith perspectives, we also need to be open to dialogue with others as we explore the extent to which our pastoral and moral convictions (and the moral convictions of others) have a *classic* quality—that is, are constructs that can express a trans-situational and transcendent valuing and that can help us to express the significance of Christian faith in the world.

The Church and Human Sexuality Today

A postmodern, perspectivist, Catholic Christian viewpoint can help us to see more clearly the issues raised for the church by changing understandings of human sexuality today. *To begin, we as a church more often than not seem unable, sadly, to foster conversations about how to construct deeply Christian understandings of sex and sexuality.* In fact, there are few if any places in the church today where Catholics can engage in authentic dialogue about how to develop/construct deeply Christian approaches to sexuality and sexual issues. Rather, Catholics' understandings of sexuality are often marked today by confusion and incoherence. More fully, as John S. Grabowski notes,

> [Many] Catholics experience a kind of disconnect between their faith and the experience of sexuality. . . . Numerous studies, polls, and surveys highlight the fact that there is a disturbing gap between official Catholic teaching regarding sexuality and the actual beliefs and practices of large numbers of the baptized. This is not simply true of the contentious issue of birth regulation, but also of other issues such as extramarital sex, homogenital activity, the use of reproductive technologies, such as artificial insemination or in vitro fertilization, and even abortion.[17]

The lived sense of sexuality of many Catholics is becoming increasingly removed from church teaching and Christian faith. Catholics who raise critically reflective questions concerning official church teaching about sexuality are likely to be accused of disloyalty to the church, faithlessness, immorality, or worse. And, on the generally rare instances when issues such as birth regulation and homosexuality are discussed within Catholic communities, the exchanges are often acrimonious.

On a broader level, *it seems inconceivable to many people today, both within and beyond the church, that Catholic Christians could express an insight or understanding about sexuality that could have a classic quality—that is, that could be expressive of an insight that could help Catholics, as well as others, make sense of their sexuality.* As a result, there is a growing sense within the church that sexuality is an area in which our faith does not provide adequate guidance for us or offer substantial insights that we can share within the broader culture.

Re-envisioning Sexuality

One of the great strengths of the chapters in this collection is that they provide us with places to begin to foster conversations about how we can develop *deeply Christian* understandings of sex and sexuality today. For example, at the heart of Ferder and Heagle's chapter is the insight that a deeply Christian understanding of sexuality will need to explore the spiritual promise of sexuality, and that it may be possible to move beyond the confusions and discord of current church discussions of sexual issues by beginning a conversation about how our faith can inform and even transform our sense of sexuality. Callahan also offers a fruitful approach. She suggests that in discussing sexuality and ministry we look to the future, and that, perhaps, a renewed dialogue about sexuality within the church can begin by asking what we want to pass on to future generations.

Another strength of the chapters in this collection is that they offer perspectives that could enable us to present a Christian view on sexuality within the broader culture. For instance, in focusing on Christian sexual maturity, Cecero suggests how Christians can be part of a broad social conversation about sexual maturity and make a distinctive contribution from a Christian faith perspective. Similarly, in drawing insight from Christian faith traditions and the biological and social sciences to outline possibilities for a new moral discourse about sexuality, Gudorf crafts an approach to sexual ethics that can contribute to the renewal of conversations about sexuality both within and beyond our Christian faith communities.

Overall, all of the chapters in this collection offer potential starting places for fruitful dialogue about sexuality.

Moreover, I contend that we can respond even more fully to the confused and incoherent views on sexuality within our contemporary church by undertaking a complete postmodern review of present-day understandings of sexuality. Rather than being suspicious of postmodernity, I suggest that a postmodern perspective can help us to envision clearly how we as church need to approach and respond to the changing views of sexuality in our church and world today. And, to outline a way of responding to changing views of sexuality, I draw insights from the chapters in this collection and other resources to provide, in the next four sections, a framework for structuring a new conversation about sexuality within the church today.[18] I suggest that we need to begin with an assessment of how sexuality is presently understood/constructed. Then I contend that we need to reflect on our current situation to try to make sense of it and determine how we should, ideally, respond—that is, how we can construct understandings of sexuality that provide pastoral and moral guidance and that enable us to flourish as persons and to realize more fully the spiritual promise of sexuality. Next, I claim that we need to determine what we can do in our parishes, dioceses, and other religious institutions, such as Catholic colleges and universities, to begin to address changing understandings of sexuality and the difficulties caused by these changes. Finally, I consider the questions: How can we begin contributing to the development of a renewed sense of sexuality within the church? What can we then do to sustain our efforts to develop a renewed theological understanding of human sexuality?

I do not claim that the framework I offer for structuring a conversation about sexuality is the only possible framework we could adopt to help us understand and respond as church to the ways sexuality is understood and expressed today. Additionally, there are many places where my analysis could be developed more fully. Still, my hope is that the framework of inquiry and analysis in this chapter is developed fully enough to suggest how we can construct holistic and healthy senses of sexuality that can enable us to express the spiritual promise of sexuality and embody authentic Christian senses of sexuality in our postmodern world. I believe that we must strive to develop understandings of sexuality that are deeply Christian and, at the same time, have the potential to resonate with people of other faith and philosophical convictions. This would enable us to contribute to contemporary social efforts to distinguish between what is life-giving and what is not life-giving in our sexual perspectives and practices.

DEVELOPING A GREATER AWARENESS OF THE SEXUAL SIGNS OF OUR TIMES

Pastoral and moral assessment begins with awareness; specifically, with attention to the salient features of a situation—that is, the aspects that come to the fore as we attend carefully to a situation. If we are to contribute to the development of more life-giving and life-sustaining understandings of sexuality, we need to begin by fostering a conversation that will encourage greater awareness of how people construct senses of sexuality today. However, this is a more complicated task than it might first appear. In the case of sexuality there are not paradigmatic constructions of sexuality. Rather, there are intertwining *layers of meaning*. In contemporary understandings of sexuality, these layers of meaning are combined in various ways. We can begin to understand contemporary conceptions and expressions of sexuality when we begin to peel back and explore these layers of meaning.

New Expressions of Sexuality

The surface layer of meaning, as already noted, consists of the new ways of expressing human sexuality that have emerged as part of the major historical transition in sexuality. In addition to polyamorous relationships and consecrated virgins in the world, we find today, as noted in the earlier chapters, re-envisioned or renewed understandings of sexuality within marriages, new ways of understanding and expressing sexuality among single people, a variety of forms of cohabitation, more developed and clearly articulated understandings of sexuality from the perspectives of homosexual persons, renewed understandings of celibate sexuality, and many other constructs of human sexuality.

A Crisis in Human Sexuality

Once we look beyond the new expressions of sexuality in contemporary society, we find another layer of meaning, a layer that often makes it difficult to understand and evaluate these new forms of sexuality. This second layer of meaning, as Ferder and Heagle note, is a crisis in human sexuality, both in our culture and our religious institutions. At the core of this crisis is what Ferder and Heagle describe as a "shame-based dualism."[19] Building on the analysis of the earlier chapters and my own observations and reflections, I suggest that we can summarize this dualism as follows. On the one hand, in our culture we often reduce sexuality to genital sexuality, and then regard genital sexual expression as a recreational commodity. More fully, sex is often seen as a recreational activity—like bowling or going to the movies—that, perhaps, offers a bit more stimulation than other forms of recreation. At the same time, popular culture often promotes the notion that a person should strive to have many genital sexual experiences with multiple partners, sort of like trying a variety of dishes and flavors at the local ice cream parlor. Hence, sex becomes just another consumer commodity in a culture in which nearly everything is turned into a product to be consumed. (Examples of sexuality reduced to genital sexuality as a recreational commodity can be found in the hit television shows *Friends*, *Will and Grace*, *That 70s Show*, and many other primetime series. Observation of undergraduate weekend activities on college campuses also often reveals the presence of this attitude among many young adults.[20]) Overall, when sexuality is reduced to a recreational commodity people are treated as sex objects, and there is a lack of sensitivity to persons as living beings worthy of respect.

On the other hand, there is what we can call the "superhero asexual stance." As one strand of the current crisis of human sexuality, the superhero asexual stance is problematic because it fails to respect the goodness and integrity of human persons as embodied and relational beings. A paradigmatic example from popular culture of this position is found in the *Spiderman* movies of the past few years. In the first movie, young Peter Parker (portrayed by Toby Maguire) struggles to discern how best to use his superhero spider powers. He reasons that those who are close to him will always be in danger and that being too closely attached to particular people will interfere with his ability to be of service to humankind as a whole. Parker then strives to sever close ties with others, including his romantic interest Mary Jane Watson (portrayed by Kirsten Dunst). This sense of the incompatibility of intimate relationships and service to humankind is then illustrated further in the stormy relationship between Parker and Watson in the second *Spiderman* movie.

More subtle portrayals of the "asexual superhero stance" saturate popular culture. For instance, consider the contrast that is frequently drawn between the characters of Gil Grisson (William Petersen) and Catherine Willows (Marg Helgenberger) on the CBS evening drama *CSI* (short for "Crime Scene Investigation," with both Petersen and Helgenberger playing crime scene investigators). In a fifth season episode entitled "Weeping Willows," Catherine flirts with a man in a bar, exchanges a brief kiss with him, but then says "goodnight" and goes home alone. When the man later becomes a suspect in a murder investigation, Catherine's reputation and credibility are threatened because of her passing acquaintance with the man. Near the end of the episode Catherine and Grisson have a discussion in which Catherine asserts that she did nothing wrong, that she went to a bar the night she met the murder suspect because she needed "a little human contact." In his response Grisson notes that contact among people always has the potential to create compromising situations and that because of this he does not go out. In the end, Grisson stands alone as the solitary asexual hero who has distanced himself from others so that he can be a dedicated servant of humanity. In contrast, Catherine Willows, tainted by her sexuality, limps away to an isolated corner and weeps.

Unfortunately, the Christian churches also often embody unhealthy sexual attitudes and contribute to the contemporary crisis of sexuality. In fact, Christian history offers many examples of limited and reductionistic approaches toward sexuality that have impoverished and continue to impoverish both the church and the broader society. For instance, as Callahan notes, "It was the involuntary and seemingly uncontrollable nature of emotional and sexual response that worried St. Augustine and led him (along with his modern followers) to think of sexuality as shameful." Augustine distrusted human pleasure because he thought that experiencing pleasure could diminish our rational control of our actions. He also saw pleasure as being antithetical to authentic human and spiritual growth. Moreover, since pleasure often accompanies sexual intercourse, Augustine taught that intercourse in

marriage was at least venially sinful.[21] Based on over twenty-five years of experience as a lay ecclesial minister in a number of settings, I suggest that an
Augustinian distrust and denigration of the body and sexuality is still found
among many Christians.

There are also parallels within the church to the contemporary cultural
image of the asexual superhero. For instance, from the late Middle Ages to
the present a somewhat common topic in preaching and religious education has been "the counsels of perfection," especially when the focus is on
"vocations"—with a "vocation" understood narrowly as a calling to ordained priesthood or religious life, and excluding a call to the married or
single states of life. The counsels of perfection are a call to voluntary
poverty, chastity (usually presented as a renunciation of marriage and a
commitment to celibacy), and obedience (that is, obedience to established
authority or renunciation of any desire for worldly honors and authority).[22]
While the counsels of perfection are being re-envisioned today and have
provided fruitful guidance for some, they have been and continue to be
used to foster unhealthy images of sexuality.[23] Specifically, they are used to
present an image of the perfect person as the asexual/celibate individual
who is dedicated to a life of serving the people of the church and the world,
and who stands in sharp contrast to the implicitly "imperfect" people who
are unable to resist the lures of sexual intimacy and deep friendships with
specific persons.

Negative understandings of sexuality have also often reinforced patriarchal attitudes and prejudice against women in the church. Women have
been, and sometimes still are, seen as unequal to men. Generally, attitudes
toward sexuality—and the distorting affects of these attitudes upon understandings of marriage, Christian service, and gender and gender roles within
the church—have been significant, and continue to have an influence on
how people are educated in Christian faith within the church today. As Gudorf notes:

> We are still teaching a sexual code based in fear of the body and of sexuality,
> in understandings of sexual virtue as repression of bodily desires by the force
> of the rational will, on physicality, especially sexuality, as an obstacle to spiri-
> tuality, and on women as lacking reason and only possessing the image of God
> through connection to men. The churches have disowned the Mosaic law's as-
> sumption of male ownership of women and children, Luther's understanding
> that women are like nails in the wall, prohibited by their nature from moving
> outside their domestic situation, and Aquinas's teaching that females are mis-
> begotten males, produced from male embryos by physical or mental debility
> in the father, or by moist winds off the Mediterranean. But we continue to
> teach most of the moral code which was founded upon such thinking.[24]

In summary, in both the broader society and the church sexuality is often
reduced to genital sexuality and regarded as basic—yet base and irresistible

for most people. That is, sexuality is seen as a basic dimension of human life, yet it is often regarded as base and of lesser value than rationality or rational control. While the broader society often fosters the attitude that we should give in to the base desires of carnal sexuality and gain from them what pleasures we can, the church has often encouraged people to strive to resist and, if possible, overcome the desires of the flesh. Moreover, in both the broader society and the church there are images of those who do overcome the "lure" of genital sexuality and who are then seen as truly praiseworthy people who have freed themselves from the lower dimensions of life so that they can be of genuine service to others. Running throughout these contemporary, negative sexual attitudes is a failure to respect persons as persons and a lack of respect for the goodness of the human body and bodily integrity.

The negative understandings of sexuality in society and the church add to the trivializing of life in contemporary culture. Because we have often made sexuality a thing of shame there is often too little honest talk about sexuality, including between parents and their children.[25] Also, there are often very few examples of committed, loving, married sexuality in popular culture today. Too often genital sexuality is sensationalized or made to appear as irresistibly attractive, especially when it involves risk. This has contributed to a high rate of premature and self-centered sexual activity among adolescents that can inhibit their psychological and emotional maturation. On a psychological level, unhealthy attitudes toward sexuality often lead to lifetraps. As Cecero explains, lifetraps are "maladaptive schemes such as abandonment, emotional deprivation, and mistrust, which are core thoughts/beliefs/body sensations which endure through life and cause emotional distress and interpersonal problems."[26] Insofar as unhealthy senses of sexuality can hinder the development of a sense of self and authentic human relationships, they can contribute to lifetraps that significantly impoverish the lives of persons and communities. Unhealthy and negative attitudes about sexuality and the prejudices against women that they sometimes foster or reinforce have also contributed to the prevalence of violence, including sexual violence, against women and children. Within the church a failure to understand and foster sexual maturity has contributed to the personal and sexual malformation of ministers and the recent crisis of sexual abuse within the church.[27]

Two Temptations

Whenever our sensitivity to the negative aspects of a complex pastoral situation is especially salient, we need to be aware of two temptations that can distort our pastoral awareness. First, there is a temptation to be blinded by the negative. That is, when the negative features of a situation are especially prominent, we may at times be only able to focus on these features, and as a result we will miss any positive dimensions of a situation. For instance, as already noted, in being overwhelmed by the negative dimensions of contemporary postmodern culture, some people fail to see the positive, questing, life-giving dimensions of our present age. Second, when the negative aspects of a situation are especially salient there is often a temptation to bring our awareness to premature closure. This rush to closure is sometimes an effort to escape a seemingly overwhelming situation. At other times it may involve giving in to an anxious sense that we need to move quickly to an evaluative judgment and/or toward the development of a strategy for addressing the situation.

I suggest that if we observe the sexual signs of our times closely we can find many examples, in both the broader society and the church, of giving in to, at the same time, the temptation to be blinded by the negative and the temptation to seek premature closure in addressing issues concerning human sexuality. For instance, within the church there is sometimes a tendency to adopt a primarily (if not totally) countercultural sexual ethics that stresses official church teachings and places Catholics in conflict with the broader world. This countercultural stance builds upon a strong reaction *against* unhealthy forms of sexuality as well as a tendency to *focus only on the negative* aspects of the contemporary changes in sexuality, or to associate all contemporary changes in how sexuality is understood with the negative layer of meaning in contemporary constructions of sexuality.[28] What advocates of this countercultural stance fail to consider, of course, is whether or not there are positive dimensions to contemporary constructions of human sexuality. Moreover, I suggest that if we are *nonanxiously present to contemporary culture* we find a significant number of positive, potentially life-giving and life-affirming expressions of sexuality, and that these positive expressions of sexuality constitute a third layer of meaning in the construction of contemporary forms of sexuality.

Movements Toward Health and Renewal

Even in aspects of the culture that contribute to the trivializing of life, there is often an impulse toward health and renewal. For example, while sexuality is reduced to genital sexuality as a recreational commodity on television shows such as *Will and Grace* and *Friends*, the main characters of these shows are also driven by a hunger to move beyond the trivializing of life in contemporary culture and to find the deeper significance of their sexuality.

Moreover, when we move beyond popular culture and attend carefully to how people embody a sense of sexuality today we can also recognize many essentially positive and healthy expressions of sexuality in people's every-

day lives. For instance, within many marriages and especially Christian marriages today, there has been a renewed celebration of the potential for married sexuality to be synergistic and spiritually nourishing.[29] As Callahan
notes, "Married people have experienced the truth that unity and love are
recreated and nourished by sexual intercourse." And Gudorf's comments reflect a renewed and positive understanding of marriage in contemporary
culture when she remarks that "being with the loved one makes one feel
more real, more alive, more loving, more at peace with oneself. These are
spiritual qualities, qualities for which all humans hunger. All love puts us
in touch with ultimate reality."[30] (It should be noted that while marriage is
often a healthier and more mutually enriching way of life than it has been
in the past, there are also greater pressures on many contemporary marriages because of the loss of extended family supports, the demands of
work, and/or a greater need to supervise or provide structured activities for
children.)

One of the great strengths of the chapters in this collection is that the authors strive to present balanced approaches to understanding human sexuality. All of the authors have a realistic sense of the crisis in sexuality. At the
same time, they resist the temptation to bring their pastoral awareness to
premature closure and are open to exploring positive resources from contemporary culture. Thus, the authors move well beyond an awareness of the
trivializing tendencies of our times as they uncover significant positive expressions and understandings of sexuality in contemporary culture. For instance, Gudorf notes that in constructing a new moral discourse on sexuality "we need to look to the sciences, both biological and social sciences, for
data about human sexuality." She then explores groundbreaking research
on men's and women's sexuality, male/female sex differences, and homosexuality. To the many resources Gudorf mentions, I add that for insight
into understanding human sexual responses and preferences we can turn to
the studies by Masters and Johnson, and Bell, Weinberg, and Hammersmith.[31] While we need to examine scientific research in the light of the wisdom of our Christian faith traditions, this research can aid us in developing
an honest and accurate sense of present understandings/constructions of
human sexuality, and the biological, social, and psychological contexts that
shape these constructions.

In focusing on the positive resources from contemporary culture, Cecero's chapter deserves special mention. I commented earlier in this chapter on the image of the asexual superhero and its antithesis, the image of
the person "tainted" by her/his sexuality. These images contribute to the unhealthy attitudes about sexuality found in both contemporary culture and
the church. Cecero's analysis enables us to recognize that the images are
specious. He notes that modern psychosocial theories of development have
shown that to reach mature adult sexuality we need to be able to express

ourselves fully in close relationships with a minimum of anxiety, and that
this ability for close relationships is what then enables us to care for and
guide others.

Drawing insight from Cecero's analysis we can note that, because of their
shunning of close relationships and consequent lack of relational abilities,
people who strive to be asexual superheroes are not likely to be mature
enough to care effectively for others or to develop the insights into human
behavior that would enable them to observe, understand and respond in
healthy and life-giving ways to social situations. Cecero's analysis also outlines how we can integrate our sexuality into a mature sense of self, and
avoid falling into the lifetraps that are likely to develop when sexual energy
is regarded as an irrational force that is difficult to control. Overall, Cecero's
analysis helps to heighten our awareness of many genuinely positive and
healthy understandings of human sexuality in contemporary humanistic
and scientific scholarship. We need to have an awareness of these understandings and have some sense of the contributions they can make to contemporary constructions of sexuality if we are to develop fully our reading
of the sexual signs of our times.

Next, in reading the sexual signs of our times we must recognize that
while the church has contributed to the present crisis of sexuality, our Christian Scriptures, traditions, and communities offer tremendous resources for
fostering *healthy* understandings of sexuality. Foremost among these resources is the respect for the human body that is at the core of Jewish and
Christian faith traditions. The opening chapter of our Scriptures (Gen 1:27)
tells us that as embodied beings we are made in the image and likeness of
God, and as embodied beings created by God we are fundamentally good.
In the New Testament, we learn of a God who came to dwell bodily among
us, and one of our enduring images of what it means to be church is that
when we gather together inspired by the Holy Spirit we are the Body of
Christ (1 Cor. 12:27). As Callahan notes, "The Christian good news about
sexuality began when Jesus was born of woman and became fully human.
God validates embodied life."[32] Generally, an understanding of the blessed-
ness of the body and the body as revelatory of the spiritual dimensions of
our lives and world contributes to the positive understanding of sexuality
found in many Christian sexual practices today.

The contributors to this collection explore some of the many resources
from our faith traditions that contribute to positive and healthy contemporary understandings of sexuality. I will not repeat all that they have written.
However, I make special note of the image of the divine mystery of the human person found among Christians today. To begin, Gudorf comments
that "within the mystical tradition we find a useful sexual tradition emanating, interestingly enough, from persons who were almost exclusively

celibate. But many of the mystics used very sexual language—even orgasmic language—to describe the relationship between the mystic soul and God."[33] There is often a freedom, even a playfulness, in the mystical traditions to use many images and analogies, at times even sexual analogies, to lead us beyond any attempts to try to make definitive claims about God and instead learn to experience, albeit in a limited way, the reality of God. Moreover, just as the mystical traditions help us to develop a richer understanding of God as Mystery, they can also help us to deepen our appreciation for the mystery of the human person as made in God's image and reflective of the Mystery Who is God. Now, in my pastoral experience and in attending to discussions of sexuality among Christians, I have been struck by how the mystical traditions, a Christian sense of mystery, and a respect for the mystery of the human person as a bodily and sexual person have contributed significantly to positive understandings of sexuality in contemporary culture. Cecero voices an insight that is shared by many people when he notes that, "From a Christian perspective, sexuality continually challenges us to acknowledge the divine mystery that we are as human beings."[34]

Conclusion

In this chapter, I have tried to offer a basic framework for outlining how sexuality is understood in our times. I commented on: (1) new ways of understanding and expressing human sexuality; (2) our contemporary crisis of sexuality, negative understanding of sexuality, and tendencies that can distort our pastoral awareness in responding to negative understandings of sexuality; and (3) the many positive expressions of sexuality that we find today. I suggest that we need broad-ranging discussions within the church about how these three strands of meaning are combined as people construct understandings of sexuality.

As a guide for such discussions we can turn to Kieran Scott's chapter on cohabitation. Scott discusses the changing realities of cohabitation in contemporary society (one of the new ways of expressing human sexuality and, as such, part of what I have called the first strand of sexual meaning in our world today). In his analysis he distinguishes between negative and positive strands of meaning woven into practices of cohabitation. Through this analysis Scott is able to foster a deeper awareness of cohabitation as a form of sexual life today. Scott's chapter illustrates how, in striving to develop a richer sense of the sexual signs of our times, we need to engage in conversations about the ways our senses of human sexuality are constructed from the various strands of sexual meaning found within our broader society and church, being careful, in particular, to distinguish between positive and negative strands.

TOWARD A NEW IDEAL: REFLECTING ON
THE SPIRITUAL PROMISE OF SEXUALITY TODAY

If we are to engage in a genuine conversation about sexuality within the church, we need to be able to move beyond awareness to reflection. That is, we need at some point to move beyond examining how the various strands of sexual meaning found today are combined in constructing senses of sexuality, and begin to reflect upon how we should, *ideally*, combine strands of sexual meaning so that we can strive to be more intentionally life-giving and life-sustaining in expressing our sexuality.

Inadequate Models of Ethical Reflection

The difficulty we encounter, however, is that our present pastoral and moral frameworks for ethical reflection are inadequate. In "A New Moral Discourse on Sexuality," Christine Gudorf provides a provocative analysis of these inadequacies. She notes that many of the difficulties with present-day official church teachings are due to "the anti-sexual heritage of the church."[35] For instance, the teachings that vowed virginity is morally superior to marriage and that "all sexual matters are grave" are rooted to some extent in the idea that sexual energies are irrational forces that we need to avoid, if possible, or at least strive strenuously to control. Thus, some official church sexual teachings prove to be inadequate guides for pastoral reflection about sexuality and sexual issues because they are part of the problem. These teachings are among the negative influencing factors that prevent the church from constructing whole and healthy understandings of sex and sexuality at the present time.

Additionally, some of our official church teachings neither resonate with the life experiences of a majority of faithful Catholics nor provide adequate guidance for them as they strive to develop a sense of sexuality and sexual maturity that is informed by their Christian faith. For instance, in commenting on the teaching of "the inseparability of the unitive and procreative aspects of human sexuality," Gudorf notes that "the vast majority of U.S. Catholics have been convinced that sexual intercourse and procreation are not only separable, but *that such separation has become normative.*"[36] In my pastoral experience, I have found many couples who have sincerely tried to embrace this teaching, but find that it is ultimately incompatible with their sense of themselves, their relationship, and their vision of a Christian family. Generally, this and other official teachings about sexuality have contributed significantly to the disconnect between many Catholics and official church sexual teaching.

Caught between Two Fears

The failure of the church to provide adequate guides for ethical reflection has led us to be caught between two fears. On the one hand, there are many people who do not feel safe discussing or reflecting upon their sexuality with pastoral leaders or within their faith communities because they do not accept one or more of the official church sexual teachings. Many married couples who regulate birth in proscribed ways, single people (especially young adults), gay and lesbian persons, those who are separated and divorced, and many others are often afraid to talk within the church about how they experience and express their sexuality. On the other hand, there is a sense among a significant number of Catholics that we need to be very cautious in discussing sexuality lest we risk being swept away by the deconstructive, relativistic, and trivializing forces of our postmodern age. Some Catholics claim that we need to hold firmly to official church teachings as a secure foundation for pastoral and ethical reflection. Others contend that the first step in moving forward is to develop new church teachings that could provide a renewed foundation for reflection on sexual issues. A significant number of Catholics fear what could happen if the church began to raise critical questions about official church teachings without a solid foundation for ethical reflection. And, while disputes about the foundations of sexual ethics rage, the church as a whole is left without adequate guidance for pastoral and ethical reflection about sexuality and sexual issues.

Moving beyond Fear

I propose that what is needed today is an effort to move beyond our fears about sexuality within the church. I have already suggested that we can begin by creating forums where people can converse about sexuality based upon their Christian faith. To do this, we need a much more nuanced awareness of how sexuality is constructed in the church and broader society today. First, we need to be willing to reflect critically upon present-day, official church sexual teachings and be open to developing a sense of when these teachings are based upon positive strands of meaning and when they are not. Second, rather than continuing to doubt the good will, sincerity, intelligence, maturity, or faith commitment of the majority of Catholics who question or reject one or more official church sexual teachings, or presuming that these Catholics' moral sensibilities have been invalidated by the trivializing forces of contemporary culture, the time has come to listen to all Christians who are willing to contribute to discussions about the spiritual promise of sexuality. We need to be open to recognizing how people are embracing a positive postmodern quest to construct new, more life-giving, and *deeply Christian* expressions of sexuality for our contemporary age.[37] Even when we disagree with official church sexual teachings or disagree strongly with one another, we need to be aware of the possibility that there are positive strands of meaning and value found within a wide variety of contemporary constructions of sexuality. Moreover, if forums to discuss sexuality are to dispel the fears that have prevented authentic dialogue within the church, they need to be all-inclusive. All people who have tried to develop or who are striving to develop a sense of sexuality that is informed by their faith should have opportunities to discuss their sincere efforts to embody positive, life-giving strands of meaning from our faith traditions and our broader culture in their sense of sexuality. This practice would address the fear, noted above, about whether sexuality can be discussed *safely* within the church.

The second fear noted above is the fear that we will be left without adequate guidance for pastoral and ethical reflection if critically reflective questioning becomes too vigorous. We can address this fear by adopting a postmodern, perspectivist, Catholic Christian viewpoint. An understanding of Christian perspectivism enables us to recognize that we do not have to choose between a reactive and nonreflective countercultural/sectarian stance or being swept away by the deconstructive, relativistic, and trivializing forces of our postmodern age. It also provides us with a path that is between the *hard* foundationalism of moral stances grounded in established church sexual teachings and the nonfoundationalism of radically historicist, deconstructive, and trivializing postmodernity. A Christian perspectivist stance is, in essence, a *soft* foundationalism. From a Christian perspectivist stance we begin with the resources of our faith traditions, knowing that these are limited resources, but also knowing that these resources have and can continue to express a sense of trans-historical and transcendent valuing, including a recognition of the value and dignity of the human person, that can guide us in addressing pressing pastoral issues.

Foundational Aspects of Ethical Reflection

In formulating a Christian perspectivist stance to guide pastoral reflection we can begin with the recognition that when we sort reflectively through the data of pastoral awareness we find that our pastoral perspectives always have two basic features. On the one hand, there are foundational elements. On the other hand, there are fissures and cracks. We can envision these two features as established structures/constraints and growth edges. In exploring foundational structures for reflecting on human sexuality, a useful starting point is Gudorf's observation that "human sexuality is constructed, but individuals never get to be sole contractors in that construction. They in effect inherit partially built structures."[38] Essentially, in adopting a perspectivist stance we can begin with a sense of the constraints that come built into our personal, social, and faith perspectives.

I suggest that when we sort through the strands of meaning that shape contemporary understandings of sexuality, we find biological, psychological, social, moral, and theological constraints that provide a foundation for critical reflection about sexuality. As Gudorf points out, "Not only individual genes but chromosomal patterns, hormonal levels, brain patterns, and other biological aspects contribute to sexual identity and behavior." The understandings of sexuality that we construct need to be guided by an awareness of these biological realities. On a social level, "relations with one's family, friends, religious community, and culture" guide how we construct understandings of sexuality.[39] Similarly, Cecero notes that, from a psychological perspective, there are developmental tasks and challenges that must be addressed if we are to mature sexually. Our efforts to construct understandings of sexuality must certainly be guided by an awareness of these developmental markers.

There are also foundational guides for pastoral and ethical reflection about sexuality that we can draw from our postmodern culture. Specifically, as noted above, in reacting against the trivializing dimensions of postmodernity there have been affirmations of a sensitivity to life as a basis for understanding the trans-situational and transcendent dimension of morality. Additionally, there are many examples we can draw upon of people who embrace postmodernity in a hopeful way, and find within postmodernity resources for constructing more life-giving and life-sustaining patterns and practices. These positive understanding of postmodern morality must be part of the foundation for contemporary pastoral reflection upon sexuality if we are to avoid drifting toward the trivializing dimensions of contemporary culture.

Finally, and most importantly, as noted in the preceding section, our Christian Scriptures, traditions, and communities offer tremendous resources for fostering healthy understandings of sexuality. These resources suggest images, examples, and basic frameworks of meaning that we can draw upon to help us discern the signs of God's presence in our lives as sexual beings. Our goal as Christians must be to remain faithful to the wisdom of our faith traditions while we construct understandings and practices of sexuality that enable us to make meaningful and morally responsible connections between our Christian faith and our everyday lives as embodied, sexual persons. Stated differently, we need to draw from the richness of our faith traditions as we reflect upon the spiritual promise of our sexuality in our lives and world today. Ultimately, the biological, social, psychological, and moral guides for constructing understandings of sexuality need to inform our efforts to reflect upon how our sexuality can lead us to be more open to accepting God's loving presence in our lives and the world.

The "Growth Edge" of Contemporary Ethical Reflection

Once we look beyond the foundational givens of our Christian faith perspectives, we need to identify the fissures, gaps, and unanswered questions
within our understandings. To identify areas of incompleteness is to name
the "growth edges" of reflection. If we can address these gaps and questions
we can continue to grow and to present a viable way of making sense of the
world. Now, I suggest that if we are to sustain pastoral reflection about sex
and sexuality within our church, there are at least five major "growth edges"
that we must address.

First, there is a need to clarify what we mean by sexuality. Ferder and Heagle opt for a broad and inclusive understanding of sexuality and comment
on how our sense of sexuality is impoverished when it is reduced to genital
sexuality. In contrast, Callahan warns us about the dangers of "blurring sex
with all forms of embodiment."[40] Generally, we need to develop an understanding of sexuality that is focused enough to enable us to distinguish sexual from nonsexual relationships, but broad enough to provide a lens for
reflecting upon the various expressions of sexuality found in married life,
celibacy, single life styles, nonmarital relationships, vowed religious life,
and consecrated virginity. Our understanding of sexuality also needs to be
able to guide us in understanding how mature, generative energies that enable a person to care for others and engage in life-giving service within the
world are related to, or part of, a person's sexuality. Ultimately, we need to
develop understandings of sexuality that provide ways of articulating how
our sexuality and our spirituality can be integrated with one another.

Second, to foster genuine critical reflection about sexuality within the
church we need, as Cecero notes, to find a balance between reconciliation
and openness to prophetic challenge. On the one hand, there is "a need for
reconciliation for those who are estranged from the church because of its
sexual teaching."[41] On the other hand, Christian faith always has a
prophetic dimension. If we are truly open to the power and presence of God
in our lives we will be called to recognize and move beyond any unhealthy
and sinful dimensions of our personal and social expressions of sexuality.
Hence, we need to raise the question: How can we create safe spaces for
sharing life experiences and fostering pastoral and ethical reflection about
sexuality that also maintain an openness to the prophetic challenge of our
faith—that is, a radical openness to discerning the power and presence of
God in our lives?

Third, there is a need for a fuller understanding of the relationship between sexuality and virtue. On the one hand, virtues are qualities of character. Since the time of Thomas Aquinas the church has taught that the primary sexual virtue is chastity, and chastity is understood today as involving
"the successful integration of sexuality within the person."[42] Today we need

to reflect critically on how Christian understandings of chastity have contributed to both positive and negative understandings of sexuality within the church. We also need to discuss how we can articulate understandings of chastity and other virtuous qualities of character that can guide us as we reflect upon what it means to be persons of sexual integrity in our postmodern era.

On the other hand, virtues are relational qualities. And chastity is not just a personal quality of character, it is a relational quality or quality of love that enables us to relate sexually to others in temperate and just ways. However, as Ferder and Heagle note, there has often been too little discussion in the contemporary church about "sexual injustice," in particular about "the evil of sexual abuse, forced sex, and domestic violence."[43] I suggest that there is a need for a renewed discussion today not just about sexual injustice, but also about sexual justice—that is, about how our understandings of chastity and other virtues can provide guides for reflecting on how we should relate temperately and justly to one another as sexual beings. We also need to articulate an understanding of sexual justice that can guide us in addressing sexual abuse and violence.

Fourth, to sustain pastoral and ethical reflection about sexuality in the church today, we need to emphasize the importance of sexuality education. To a certain extent, pastoral and moral theologians are analysts. We often focus on analyzing specific issues in order to provide resources that can be accessed when these issues arise, or we strive to clarify the parameters of pastoral awareness and reflection within a specific context. Yet, there is also an educational dimension to the ministry of the pastoral theologian. This educational component is especially important when addressing issues of sexuality. Because people have not had opportunities within the church to discuss sexuality and reflect on how we as a church can make sense of sexuality, there is a great need for pastoral theologians to focus on the educational tasks of helping people to name and reflect on their experiences of sexuality, examine their sexual experiences in the light of the positive resources of our faith traditions, and then move toward the development of a richer sense of responsible moral agency in making sense of their sexuality from a faith perspective. Generally, we need to create educational forums for discussion where people can develop fuller senses of their own sexuality within the context of a Catholic Christian community. We also need to be attentive to possibilities for distilling the insights and wisdom of these educational forums into new sexual teachings to guide ethical reflection about sexuality.

Fifth, I suggest that we need to attend carefully to how we present the processes of pastoral awareness and reflection. More fully, pastoral awareness and reflection entail, essentially, focusing on the signs of the times and considering how best to respond in the light of Christian faith. At the present time, pastoral awareness and reflection about sexuality within the church (as often presented, for instance, in the sacrament of reconciliation, preaching, marriage preparation, and religious education) are most often envisioned as the processes by means of which we look at the circumstances of our lives, consider the sexual teachings of the church, and then reflect upon how we can gradually and prayerfully (and with prudent attention to pastoral circumstances) conform our lives as fully as possible to the ideals presented within church sexual teaching. However, this model does not honor fully the insights of people's experience, and fails to recognize how church sexual teaching is at times grounded in questionable presumptions about human sexuality.

I suggest that in striving to encourage pastoral awareness and reflection in our postmodern age, we focus on honoring people's life experiences and emphasize the importance of critical inquiry. Moreover, we can initiate processes of pastoral awareness and reflection about sexuality from a Christian perspective by asking: How does faith shape our experience of sexuality, and how, ideally, should faith shape our experience of our sexuality so that the way we think about and express our sexuality can be *deeply Christian*? Such a way of leading into awareness and reflection honors the unique degree of openness and adaptability available to people in our postmodern age.

However, to develop pastoral reflection fully, we need to go beyond this to ask: How can we compare and contrast our efforts to express our sexuality with the efforts of others, past and present, to express a *deeply Christian* understanding of sexuality? How can we reflect critically upon our understanding of sexuality in the light of all available resources, especially the resources of our faith traditions? The goal of such questioning should be to lead us to reflect upon our experience of sexuality in order to gain a sense of what resonates with the most life-giving and life-sustaining insights of Christian faith traditions.

We also need to ask another critically reflective question—specifically, what aspects of our deeply Christian expressions of our sexuality have a potentially *classic quality* that could lead us toward dialogue with people from other faith and philosophical traditions? This last question can help us develop a more universally inclusive perspective and is especially important in our increasingly pluralistic postmodern age.

Overall, I suggest that a Christian perspectivist viewpoint can help us to move beyond the fears and confusions within the church that too often stifle critical reflection and fruitful inquiry. It can also enable us to embrace the positive search for meaning and value at the core of cultural postmodernity, and provide a way for entering into conversations about sexuality within the broader society.

TOWARD A RENEWED PASTORAL RESPONSE:
DISCERNING OUR WAY FORWARD

From a pastoral perspective, we must move beyond reflection in order to realize a concrete pastoral good. Specifically, to address a concrete situation
we need to consider what pastoral commitments we *can* make that will enable us to work to realize a positive outcome, goal, or good in a given situation. While reflection focuses on considering what we *should* do to respond
to a situation, commitment making is concerned with what we *can* do to
address a pastoral issue. Our pastoral commitments are based on our pastoral awareness and reflection. Yet, the process of making a pastoral commitment moves beyond awareness and reflection to involvement and the
personal or social embodiment of moral virtue.

In the last section I claimed that if we are to foster pastoral and ethical reflection about sexuality within the church today, all people who have tried
to develop or who are striving to develop a sense of sexuality that is informed by faith *should* have one or more forums where they can discuss and
reflect upon their experiences of sexuality. As we move beyond reflection
and consider making pastoral commitments we must ask: How *can* we as
church provide such forums for discussion?

As a guide for considering how we can respond to changing understandings of sexuality, I offer the following outline of areas in which we can commit to working to renew our theology of sexuality and strive to realize more
fully the spiritual promise of sexuality.

Marriage Enrichment, Marriage Preparation, and
Outreach to Cohabiting Couples

Gudorf contends that, "Sex—good, frequent mutually pleasurable—is as
vitally important to the vocation of marriage as reception of the Eucharist
is to membership in the church community." Would our faith communities
change if we took Gudorf's words to heart? Consider: How many homilies
on the importance of the Eucharist have you heard in the past five years?
How many homilies have you heard on the importance of marital sexual
pleasure in the past five years? I suggest that if we are to address contemporary issues and concerns about sexuality we need to place much greater
emphasis on marriage enrichment, with a specific focus on the importance
of marital sexuality. We need to talk much more openly about sexuality in
our faith communities, and we need to create forums where couples can
talk about their relationship and sexuality and learn more about the rich resources in both the broader society and in the church for developing their
sense of sexuality. Note well, to create a truly safe space for sharing, exploration, and growth in faith, we will need to set aside problematic church

teachings to allow a respect for the body, the mystery of sexuality, and the other positive resources of our faith traditions to guide these discussions. However, these sessions would also need to foster critical reflection about what is and is not life giving and positive in our contemporary expressions of sexuality. Christian faith communities can also do more to address the social pressures that bear down upon families so that there is more time and a more relaxed environment within families for relationships among family members to develop and mature.

If we create more open environments for discussing sexuality in our faith communities, we will also have a base from which we can build in providing sexuality education for couples in our communities who are preparing for marriage. Generally, as Gudorf notes, there is a need to provide more adequate sexuality education in most marriage preparation programs. Additionally, as Kieran Scott argues, if we are to provide adequate marriage preparation, we need to question the church prohibition of cohabitation and bring a more nuanced understanding of the forms of cohabitation to marriage preparation processes. Finally, if we can learn to address issues of cohabitation more fully in providing marriage preparation, we would then be prepared to engage in outreach to cohabiting couples within or on the margins of our faith communities.

Preaching and Parish Life

I suggest that every person who preaches regularly needs a preaching preparation group consisting of persons and couples who represent a variety of life styles. By discussing upcoming liturgical readings the groups can help homilists become more sensitive to the diverse life experiences of the members of their congregations. When readings focus or touch upon issues of sexuality, homilists can be guided by their group in considering how they might strive to nurture a positive and healthy sense of sexuality as they address these readings.

As Kieran Scott notes in his response to John Cecero's chapter, "Our sexual lives are lived in the context of social institutions." Our sexual lives can be shaped both positively and negatively by the social institutions to which we belong.[44] Consequently, there is a value to having parish pastoral councils or other parish groups review the ways their faith community affects people's sense of sexuality. Questions that could be asked in such a review include: Are there any groups whose special needs and concerns are not addressed or not addressed adequately in parish life—perhaps, young single people, divorced persons, single parent families, or gay and lesbian persons or couples? How is "family" defined within the parish, and are all ways of life included in this definition? Discussion of the review could then be a springboard for broader conversations about how sexuality is understood by people within the parish. These reviews could also contribute to efforts to distinguish positive from negative strands of meaning in the ways sexuality is constructed in our faith communities, and would provide opportunities to reflect critically on how our parishes may be called to strive to formulate more life-affirming constructs of sexuality in our institutional life.

Sacramental Reconciliation and Pastoral Care and Counseling

Sacramental reconciliation provides unique opportunities for both sexual healing and sexuality education. When sexual issues are brought up during the sacrament, confessors can use such graced moments to discuss the effects of unhealthy sexual influences in our society and to educate people about positive resources for developing a fuller sense of sexuality. However, confessors need also to provide safe spaces for people to share their sexual experiences and to be genuinely respectful of people's efforts to live lives of sexual integrity.

Opportunities for sexual healing and sexuality education may also arise when sexual issues are brought up during pastoral care or counseling. Additionally, pastoral care or counseling sessions may offer venues for discussing how people are affected by the new ways of understanding and expressing human sexuality that have emerged as part of the major historical transition in sexuality.

To guide parish ministers, we need to create forums for discussing what is and is not sexually sinful, and for assessing the gravity of sexual sins. Based upon my pastoral experience, I suggest that there are many parish priests and lay ecclesial ministers who have a more refined sense of sexual sin and sexual flourishing than what is provided by current, official church sexual teachings. However, at the present time there are few opportunities for these parish ministers to share either the wisdom of their experiences or their frustrations and perplexities in addressing issues of sexuality.

Adolescent Religious Education, Youth Ministry, and Young Adult Ministry

Julie Collins provides a model for adolescent religious education in her chapter in this volume. She begins with students' life experiences and engages them in critical reflection about sexuality. She outlines how the resources of Christian faith traditions can be introduced in a dialogical way as students are encouraged to develop a sense of responsible moral agency that is informed by Christian faith.

Most of the components of a Comprehensive Youth Ministry program provide opportunities for nurturing a richer sense of sexuality and addressing the effects of unhealthy expressions of sexuality in both the broader society and the church.[45] For example, discussions of Community Life can include a focus on relationships and sexuality. When talking about Pastoral Care the effects of unhealthy sexual influences can be reviewed. Sexuality education can be included when the focus is on Catechesis, and sexual justice can be covered when exploring Justice and Service. However, to nurture a healthy sense of sexuality, youth ministers need, like Collins, to focus first on creating a safe space for students to share their life experiences and then engage in critical reflection upon their experiences in the light of the positive resources of our Christian faith traditions.

A number of the chapters in this collection point out that increasing numbers of people are remaining single throughout their twenties and into their thirties. Many of these young adults enter into sexually intimate relationships. At the present time, there are few forums within which young adults can discuss their sexuality, and many Christian young adults today feel a disconnect between their sense of sexuality and their faith.

Developmentally, the challenge of young adulthood is expressed in the question, "What am I going to do with my life?" That is, as people emerge into young adulthood, they have a new sense of themselves, and a major concern is where they will be in ten years, twenty years, fifty years, and beyond. Hence, young adulthood is the first time in life when people are ready, existentially, to think critically about what legacy they want to leave and what sense of an eternal destiny they want to incorporate into their lives.[46] Tragically, many Christian faith communities provide little pastoral outreach to young adults. Still, this developmental stage offers a tremendous opportunity for Christian faith communities to connect with young adults and to provide forums within which they can reflect critically on how they want to develop their sense of sexuality over the course of their lives in the light of a sense of the transcendent dimension of Christian faith.

Responding to Gay and Lesbian Christians

In *Always Our Children*, the Catholic Bishops of the United States took an initial step toward recognizing the presence of homosexual persons in our faith communities and affirming their dignity and worth as persons created in the image of God. However, as Barbara Jean Daly Horell remarks in her chapter, much more needs to be done before homosexual Christians will feel truly welcome in our faith communities. Generally, there is a great need to provide opportunities for gay and lesbian persons of faith to discuss their sexuality and how they integrate their sexuality and spirituality, and for Christian communities to listen and learn from their gay and lesbian members.

Outreach to Separated, Divorced, and Widowed Catholics, and Mature Single Adults

Many faith communities have pastoral programming to address the needs of separated and divorced Catholics, widowed Catholics, and mature single adults. Where such programming does not exist, it needs to be created if we are to be all-inclusive in our efforts as church to provide forums for discussions about sexuality. Moreover, as part of pastoral outreach to persons within these groups, we need to set aside problematic Church sexual teachings and allow some of the positive resources of our faith traditions to guide these discussions.

Family Sexuality Education

Discussions about sexuality in the areas mentioned above would spill over in many cases into family life, where discussions of sexuality could take place in a more intimate setting. Generally, if we create a more open environment in the church for discussing sexuality and our parishes support parents in their efforts to talk about sexual issues with their children, parents would be able to take better advantage of the opportunities they have to encourage their children to develop healthy and spiritually-centered understandings of sexuality.

The Formation of Ordained and Ecclesial Lay Ministers

The church has suffered greatly because we have and to some extent continue to separate the spiritual formation of pastoral ministers from their on-going development as sexual persons. Hence, as part of the professional, personal, and spiritual formation of all pastoral ministers within the church we need to create discussion forums where those preparing for ministry and those already working in ministry can discuss their sexuality, the relationship between their sexuality and their spirituality, and connections among their spirituality, their sexuality, and their ministry. Special attention, I suggest, needs to be given to continuing to foster the gift of celibacy in the church today. However, to discuss celibacy honestly we need to be willing, as Evelyn Eaton Whitehead and James D. Whitehead remark, to "disengage" the lifestyle of celibacy from the ministry of priesthood.[47] Only then will we be open to a renewed and re-envisioned appreciation of the gift of celibacy in consecrated virginity, vowed religious life, and parish ministry.

Pastoral Theological Reflection and Catholic Colleges and Universities

Pastoral theologians can play a threefold role in nurturing forums for discussions of sexuality within the church: an initiatory role, a critically reflective

role, and a learning role. First, pastoral theologians are in a unique position
to bring together the resources of our faith traditions and insights from the
social and biological sciences in addressing the need for more sustained discussions about sexuality, and to help initiate and structure forums for discussions.

Second, Catholic colleges and universities throughout the world have become the critical reflective intelligence of the church. They provide a context that is a step beyond the pressures normally present in the life of a faith
community. And within this context there can be a freedom to explore new
ideas and new forms of life. Hence, theologians working within or in collaboration with colleges and universities are in a position to create forums
for discussing newly emerging forms of sexual life that either have not significantly impacted parish life or that have been (or could be) disruptive to
the life of a faith community. Some of the new forms of life, such as consecrated virginity in the world, show great promise in contributing to renewed
understandings of sexuality in the church. Still, they could benefit from critically reflective examination in order to help those who have adopted these
forms cope with the negative and anti-sexual attitudes in the broader society and the church.

In other instances, new forms of sexual life reveal themselves to be problematic. Those who profess polyamory, for example, often show too little
an understanding of the challenge, if not impossibility, of maintaining mature sexual intimacy when persons look beyond dyadic relationships to intimate triadic and quadratic unions. (Put differently, mutual and intimate
one-to-one relationships, while greatly rewarding, take a great deal of effort to maintain. It is not possible to maintain truly intimate threesomes
and foursomes.) Generally, pastoral forums within college and university
settings would provide the best arena within the church in which to reflect
critically on new forms of sexual life that are built upon questionable presumptions.

There are also new forms of sexual life that we know too little about, and
that, as a result, it is difficult to respond to pastorally today. For example,
we do not have a clear understanding in either the broader society or the
church of the unique biological, psychological, emotional, and spiritual dimensions of trans-sexuality. Pastoral theological reflection within Catholic
colleges and universities could provide a foundation for developing resources that could help trans-sexual members of the church—and perhaps
trans-sexual persons beyond the church—to live lives that are both sexually
and spiritually fulfilling.

Finally, pastoral theologians can also contribute to the church as a learning church. If we can create a variety of forums for discussing sexuality
within the church, these forums will undoubtedly generate a wealth of insights and new understandings. Pastoral theologians, in sustained conver-

sation with pastoral leaders, could play a role in drawing together the insights of discussions about sexuality. Building upon these insights, bishops would then have the responsibility of formulating new sexual teachings to guide the church.

In summary, I have outlined how we as a church can embrace an open, questing postmodern spirit and use it to create discussions about sexuality that could enable us to begin to respond to the unique degree of sexual openness and adaptability in our world today from a distinctly Christian perspective.

GETTING STARTED AND SUSTAINING OURSELVES ON THE JOURNEY

As we consider all that could be involved in fostering a new dialogue about sexuality in the church today, it could become overwhelming. In order to avoid being overwhelmed we need to keep in mind that the task of developing a renewed theological understanding of human sexuality is a task for the whole church and not for any specific person or group within the church. As individuals and members of specific faith communities, the question we need to ask is: In what way or ways is God enabling and requiring me (or us) to begin to work to renew understandings of sexuality within the church? We need to discern where in our personal relationships, our ministry, our teaching, our writing, or other areas of our lives we may experience a call to seek a renewed sense of sexuality. We need to discern whether or not in adult religious education, sacramental ministry, religious education, or in some other area we experience opportunities and a call to address issues of sexuality more fully than we have in the past. And we need to be open to changes in this call as our lives and ministries unfold.

When we are involved in efforts to work toward a renewed theological understanding of sexuality, we may face the challenge of sustaining ourselves in our efforts. In most ministerial efforts, we face the temptation to give into "tunnel vision"—that is, the danger of becoming so caught up in what we are doing to address a situation that we lose sight of the broader framework of meaning and value that sustains our efforts. However, there are several things we can do to proactively avoid or, if need be, to respond to the temptation to tunnel vision in working toward a renewed theology of sexuality in the church.

First, we can build alliances with others. Those who are addressing issues that are similar to our own can often offer insights that are directly relevant to our own ministerial efforts. Those who are addressing sexual issues and concerns in another area of ministry may help us to maintain a sense of the larger whole.

Second, we can look to the universal church for guidance. For example, in their chapters on John Paul II in this collection, Jennifer Bader and Luke Timothy Johnson note that while there are aspects of his theological understanding of the body and human sexuality that can be critiqued, John Paul helped to focus the attention of the church on questions about the meaning of human sexuality in a new way. Keeping in mind that the need for a renewed theology of human sexuality has been recognized at the highest level of the church can help to sustain our efforts in specific ministerial contexts.

Third, we can look to the future. Callahan begins her chapter by asking, "What are we going to pass on to future generation when it comes to Christian sexuality and morality?"[48] Whenever our efforts in the present begin to get bogged down, thinking in terms of the contribution we are making to a potentially better future can help us to sustain our efforts.

Fourth, and of central importance, is to ground our efforts to develop a renewed theology of sexuality in a biblical spirituality. There is no indication in the gospel that Jesus sought actively to reform or re-envision the Jewish sexual moral standards of his day, and throughout the New Testament established Jewish codes of sexual morality are assumed as givens whenever questions of sex and sexuality arise. However, the New Testament does call for a radical re-envisioning of human relationships, including relationships between men and women.[49] The analysis of sexual morality presented in this chapter can be further developed by examining contemporary concerns about sex and sexuality in the light of the New Testament call for a radical renewal of human relationships. If we are to sustain our efforts to re-envision human sexuality from a Christian faith perspective, such a further development is an absolute necessity.

Fifth, and also of central importance, is to consider concerns about human sexuality in relation to other pastoral concerns. Focusing our pastoral efforts on a single issue can contribute significantly to a sense of tunnel vision. Hence, issues of human sexuality need always to be considered in relation to other concerns about human dignity, human relationships, prayer and worship, and the demands of justice in our contemporary world.

Finally, in working toward a renewed theology of human sexuality in the church it can be helpful to have a clear sense of what is ultimately at stake. In the introduction to this chapter I suggested that we can be swept along by the currents of contemporary culture *or* we can proactively address contemporary changes in how sexuality is understood and contribute to a renewed theology of human sexuality.

In concluding, I suggest that there is even more at stake. If we allow the church to be a swept along by contemporary culture, there will continue to be a confused and confusing babel of voices about sexuality coming from the church. This babel will lend support to the idea that the church cannot speak meaningfully about contemporary issues, and that the confused understandings of sexuality in the church are just another indication that there is no deep meaning and significance to human sexuality.

Of course, if we as a church fail to address questions about human sexuality adequately, there will still be both positive and negative expressions of sexuality in contemporary culture, and the struggle between the two to define the meaning of human sexuality will continue. Our real choice is between adding to the trivialization of sexuality in our contemporary culture by failing to address sexual issues adequately, or to contribute to the development of a renewed theology of sexuality that will enable us to assess the positive and negative dimensions of contemporary postmodern culture, and in the process give witness to the life-giving potential of Christian faith in the world today.

NOTES

1. Information about polyamory can be found on the Polyamory Society at www.polyamorysociety.org (accessed May 15, 2006). The homepage for the Consecrated Virgins in the World Society is: www.consecratedvirgins.org (accessed May 15, 2006). See also Cannon 604 of the new Code of Canon Law.

2. Ferder and Heagle, "Tender Fires," in this volume, 16.

3. In "Sexuality and Relationships in Ministry," in this volume, 75. Callahan remarks, "Unfortunately, the horror and shame of the sexual abuse crisis can turn many Catholics off the whole subject of sexuality. Many of the faithful have given up on efforts to connect human sexuality with Christian discipleship."

4. Gudorf, "A New Moral Discourse on Sexualiaty," in this volume, 51.

5. Ferder and Heagle, "Tender Fires," in this volume, 16; Gudorf, "A New Moral Discourse on Sexuality," in this volume, 52; and Callahan, "Sex and Relationships in Ministry," in this volume, 75.

6. For a fuller description of postmodernity and the ways Christians have responded to it, see Harold Daly Horell, "Cultural Postmodernity and Christian Faith Formation," in *Hopes and Horizons: The Future of Religious Education,* ed. Thomas H. Groome and Harold Daly Horell, 81–107 (New York: Paulist Press, 2002); and Harold D. Horell, "Fostering Hope: Christian Religious Education in a Postmodern Age," *Religious Education* 99:1 (2004): 5–22. For a general philosophical description of postmodernity, see Paul Lakeland, *Postmodernity* (Minneapolis: Fortress, 1997).

7. For accounts of postmodernity that focus on its trivializing dimensions, see Joseph Feeney, "Can a Worldview be Healed? Students and Postmodernism," *America* 177 (1997): 12–16; T. Eagleton, *The Illusions of Postmodernism* (Oxford: Blackwell, 1996); and F. Jameson, *Postmodernism* (Durham, NC: Duke University Press, 1991).

8. The paradigmatic postmodern and deconstructivist analysis of sexuality is, of course, Michel Foucault, *The History of Sexuality: An Introduction,* trans. Robert Hurley (New York: Random House, 1978). Foucault stressed that sexuality is a construct and sought to resist all attempts to evaluate forms of sexuality. He regarded normative evaluations of forms of sexuality as the use of power by one person or group

over and against another person or group. Yet, as Lisa Sowle Cahill points out, "One has the sense that, without quite acknowledging it, Foucault assumes that some power configurations are recognizably bad, and some displacements of power clearly an improvement on the alternatives." Hence, even Foucault's approach is not purely negative. Cahill, *Sex, Gender, and Christian Ethics* (Cambridge: Cambridge University Press, 1996), 23–24.

9. In *Sex, Gender, and Christian Ethics*, Cahill is especially concerned about the dangers of relativistic approaches to sexual ethics. In presenting an understanding of relativism, I also draw from Alasdair MacIntyre, *Whose Justice? Which Rationality?* (Notre Dame: University of Notre Dame Press, 1988), 352–55.

10. Kearney adds that if postmodernist lapses into pure historicism are not to be totally bereft of value, they must acknowledge "the *other* who demands of me an ethical response" and the "inalienable right to be recognized as a particular person whose very *otherness* refuses to be reduced to" a mere historical contingency (emphasis as in original). Kearney, *The Wake of Imagination* (Minneapolis, MN: University of Minnesota Press, 1988), 361–62.

11. In *Sex, Gender, and Christian Ethics*, 29, Cahill writes that, "postmodern ethics is not at bottom nihilistic, but positive and prophetic, for it identifies and seeks to overcome real injustices in the world as 'dominations.'"

12. For example, according to Stanley Hauerwas, the modern era is marked by an attempt "to be historical without Christ" and the "failure of the churches to be faithful." Postmodernity, for Hauerwas, is the "bastard offspring" of modernity and tends to separate us even farther from a God who is made known in the grand narrative of Christian history, tradition, and community. Hauerwas counsels Christians to seek ways of "surviving" postmodernism by seeking refuge in a church that is "unassimilated to the secular world." Hauerwas, *A Better Hope* (Grand Rapids, MI: Brazos Press, 2000), 39, 37, 38, 35, and 45, respectively. I suggest that the adoption of Hauerwas's perspective is likely to foster a Manichaean rejection of the world, rather than a genuine appreciation for the goodness and graciousness of God's presence in our lives and world.

13. My understanding of perspectivism is influenced by Alasdair MacIntyre. See especially *Whose Justice? Which Rationality?* (Notre Dame: University of Notre Dame Press, 1988), 352–55. However, I differ from MacIntyre insofar as MacIntyre recognizes the negative dimensions of postmodernity and fails to see its positive potential. See MacIntyre, *Three Rival Versions of Moral Enquiry* (Notre Dame: University of Notre Dame Press, 1990).

14. A paradigmatic expression of a relativist worldview and ethical position is provided in the early writings of Richard Rorty. See his *Consequences of Pragmatism* (Minneapolis: University of Minnesota Press, 1982) and *Contingency, Irony, and Solidarity* (New York: Cambridge University Press, 1989). However, even Rorty is not able to maintain a consistent relativist position. Throughout his philosophical reflections there is a consistent yearning for transcend meaning and value. This yearning is expressed most clearly in his "Human Rights, Rationality, and Sentimentality," in *On Human Rights: The Oxford Amnesty Lectures 1993*, ed. Stephen Shute and Susan Hurley, 111–34 and notes, 244–48 (New York: Basic Books, 1993).

15. In developing a Christian perspectivist stance I have been influenced by the faith-ethic perspective of Vincent MacNamara. See MacNamara, *Faith and Ethics: Re-*

cent Roman Catholicism (Washington, D.C.: Georgetown University Press, 1985). Noteworthy attempts to develop an explicitly postmodern theological stance that have also influenced my perspective include Kenan B. Osborne, *Sacraments in a Postmodern World* (New York: Paulist Press, 1999) and Stanley J. Grenz and John R. Franke, *Beyond Foundationalism: Shaping Theology in a Postmodern Context* (Louisville, KY: Westminster, John Knox, 2001).

16. David Tracy, "Particular Classics, Public Religion, and the American Tradition," in *Religion and American Public Life*, ed. Robin W. Lovin (New York: Paulist, 1986).

17. John S. Grabowski, *Sex and Virtue: An Introduction to Sexual Ethics* (Washington, D.C.: Catholic University of America Press, 2003). To support his claims, Grabowski cites Andrew M. Greeley, "Sex and the Single Catholic: The Decline of an Ethic," *America* 167 (Nov. 7, 1992): 342–47; and Larry R. Pederson and Gregory V. Donnenwerth, "Secularization and the Influence of Religious Beliefs about Premarital Sex," *Social Forces* 75 (1997): 1071–88 on premarital sex; Andrew K. T. Yip, "Dare to Differ: Gay and Lesbian Catholics' Assessment of Official Catholic Positions on Sexuality," *Sociology of Religion* 58 (1997): 165–80 on homosexuality; John G. Deedy, "Five Medical Dilemmas that Might Scare You to Death," *U.S. Catholic* 53 (April 1988): 6–14 on reproductive technologies; and Michael R. Welsh, David C. Leege, and James C. Cavendish, "Attitudes toward Abortion among U.S. Catholics: Another Case of Symbolic Politics?" *Social Science Quarterly* 76:1 (1995): 142–57.

18. In developing a fourfold framework for pastoral analysis I have drawn insight from the fourfold framework for moral analysis presented by James R. Rest. See James R. Rest, "Morality," in *Manual of Child Psychology*, Vol. 3, vol. eds., J. Flavell and E. Markman, and gen. ed. P. Mussen, 556–629 (New York: Wiley, 1983); and James R. Rest with Robert Barnett, Muriel Bebeau, Deborah Deemer, Irene Getz, Yong Lin Moon, James Spickelmier, Stephen J. Thoma, and Jospeh Volker. *Moral Development: Advances in Research and Theory* (New York: Praeger, 1986).

19. Ferder and Heagle, "Tender Fires," in this volume, 16.

20. See Julia Tier, "Sex and the University: How Does the Church Speak to the Experience of Younger Catholics?" posted on the *Busted Halo* website: www.bustedhalo .com/dimensions/features36.htm (accessed on 12/10/2004).

21. Augustine, *On Marriage and Concupiscence*, in *The Nicene and Post-Nicene Fathers* I:17, ed. Philip Schaff (Grand Rapids, MI: William B. Eerdman, 1971), 270–71.

22. See New Advent, *Catholic Encyclopedia*, "Evangelical Counsels (or Counsels of Perfection)" www.newadvent.org/cathen/04435a.htm/ (accessed June 15, 2006).

23. In their chapter in this collection, Evelyn Eaton Whitehead and James D. Whitehead discuss briefly contemporary efforts to re-envision the counsels of perfection as evangelical councils for today. Their reflections of the evangelical counsels stand in sharp contrast to the view presented in the *Catholic Encyclopedia*.

24. Christine Gudorf, *Body, Sex and Pleasure* (Cleveland, OH: Pilgrim Press, 1994), 3.

25. A recent study indicated that about 90 percent of parents report discussing sex with their teenage children. However, 47 percent of high school students report having had sex, while only 16 percent of parents believe that their children have had sex. Julia Neyman and Julie Snider, "Skewed Views on Teen Sex," *USA Today*, (Dec. 15, 2004).

26. Cecero, "Toward Christian Sexual Maturity," in this volume, 35.

27. For a helpful perspective on fostering sexual maturity in ordained ministry and the dangers of failing to foster sexual maturity see William F. Kraft, *Whole and Holy Sexuality* (St. Meinrad, IN: Abbey Press, 1989). For an organizational perspective on the recent crisis of sexual abuse in the church, see Jean M. Bartunek, Marry Ann Hinsdale, and James F. Keenan, eds. *Church Ethics and Its Organization Context: Learning from the Sex Abuse Scandal in the Catholic Church* (Lanham, MD: Sheed and Ward, 2006).

28. The clearest examples of this countercultural stance are found at the pastoral level. In academic discussion there tends to be more nuanced positions that show an awareness of the temptations to be overly negative about contemporary culture and to be pushed to a premature closure. However, Grabowski comes close to giving into these temptations in his call for a countercultural Christian sexual ethic in *Sex and Virtue*, 156–68. Another example of an approach that leans heavily toward a one-sided counter stance is: Pontifical Council on the Family, *The Truth and Meaning of Human Sexuality: Guidelines for Education within the Family*, issued Dec. 8, 1995. Available at: www.vatican.va/roman_curia/pontifical_councils/family/documents /rc_pc_family_doc_08121995_human-sexuality_en.html (accessed May 15, 2006).

29. See Kieran Scott and Michael Warren, eds., *Perspectives on Marriage: A Reader* (New York: Oxford University Press, 2001), especially Bernard Cooke, "Chapter 2: Christian Marriage: Basic Sacrament"; German Martinez and Lyn Burr Brignoli, "Chapter 3: Models of Marriage: A New Theological Interpretation"; Evelyn Eaton Whitehead and James D. Whitehead, "Chapter 9: The Meaning of Marriage"; and Christine Gudorf, "Chapter 25: Western Religion and the Patriarchal Family." See also Richard R. Gaillardetz, *A Daring Promise: A Spirituality of Christian Marriage* (New York: Crossroad, 2002).

30. Callahan, "Sexuality and Relationships" in this volume, 77; and Gudorf, "Graceful Pleasures," in this volume, 126.

31. Gudorf, "A New Moral Discourse on Sexuality," in this volume, 61; William Masters and Virginia Johnson, *Human Sexual Response* (Boston: Little, Brown, 1966) and *Human Sexual Inadequacy* (Boston: Little, Brown, 1970); and Alan Bell, Martin Weinberg, and S. Hammersmith, *Sexual Preferences: Its Development in Men and Women* (Bloomington, IN: Indiana University Press, 1981).

32. Callahan, "Sexuality and Relationships," in this volume, 76. See also Evelyn Eaton Whitehead and James D. Whitehead, *The Wisdom of the Body: Making Sense of our Sexuality* (New York; Crossroad, 2001); Cahill, *Sex, Gender, and Christian Ethics*, 73–107; and Colleen M. Griffith, "Spirituality and the Body," in *Bodies of Worship*, ed. Bruce T. Morrill, 67–83 (Collegeville, MN: Liturgical Press, 1999).

33. Gudorf, "A New Moral Discourse on Sexuality," in this volume, 65.

34. Cecero, "Toward Christian Sexual Maturity," in this volume, 33.

35. Gudorf, "A New Moral Discourse on Sexuality," in this volume, 56; for her comments on the moral superiority of vowed virginity, see 53.

36. Ibid., 52.

37. In *"Always Our Children?"* in this volume, Daly Horell exemplifies how such discussion forums can be structured.

38. Gudorf, "A New Moral Discourse for Sexuality," in this volume, 61.

39. Ibid.

40. Callahan, "Sexuality and Relationships in Ministry," in this volume, 78.

41. Cecero, "Toward Christian Sexual Maturity," in this volume, 45.

42. Thomas Aquinas, *Summa Theologica* II-II, q. 151, a. 3. (New York; Benzinger, 1947); *The Catechism of the Catholic Church* (Washington, D.C.: USCC, 1983), 561 (no. 2337).

43. Ferder and Heagle, "Tender Fires," in this volume, 24.

44. Scott, "A Pastoral Response to John Cecero," in this volume, 48.

45. See United States Conference of Catholic Bishops, *Renewing the Vision: A Framework for Catholic Youth Ministry* (Washington, D.C.: USCCB, 1997).

46. See Sharon Daloz Parks, *Big Questions, Worthy Dreams: Mentoring Young Adults in Their Search for Meaning, Purpose, and Faith* (San Francisco: Jossey-Bass, 2000).

47. Whitehead and Whitehead, "The Gift of Celibacy," in this volume, 146.

48. Callahan, "Sexuality and Relationships in Ministry," in this volume, 75.

49. See Barbara Jean Daly Horell's chapter in this volume; Gudorf, *Body, Sex and Pleasure*, 55–62; and Lisa Sowle Cahill, *Between the Sexes: Foundations for a Christian Ethics of Sexuality* (Philadelphia: Fortress, 1985): 59–82.

About the Editors and Contributors

Jennifer Bader began writing on the theology and anthropology of Pope John Paul II for her doctoral dissertation at the Catholic University of America, which she completed in 2003. Her scholarly interests include moral theology and ethics, social justice, theological anthropology, and sacramental theology. She is associate director for academic affairs at the Boston College Institute for Religion Education and Pastoral Ministry.

Sidney Callahan, author, professor, and licensed psychologist, holds a Ph.D. from the City University of New York and has written widely on religious, psychological, and ethical questions. For twenty years, she served as a professor of psychology while also teaching moral theology and interdisciplinary studies. She has taught at a number of institutions, including Georgetown in Washington, D.C., and St. John's University in New York. Sidney and Daniel Callahan have been married since 1954 and have six grown children and four grandchildren.

John J. Cecero is a Jesuit priest and clinical psychologist who joined the faculty of Fordham University in September 1998, where he teaches courses in psychotherapy theories and clinical diagnosis. He maintains a part-time private psychotherapy practice and has most recently published *Praying Through Our Lifetraps: A Psycho-Spiritual Path to Freedom.*

Julie Collins has taught religious studies, morality, and spirituality for thirty years at Georgetown Preparatory School in Washington, D.C. She has written numerous articles on youth ministry and sex education in such venues as *America, Review for Religious,* and *The Washington Post.*

Barbara Jean Daly Horell holds an M.T.S. in biblical studies and spirituality from Harvard Divinity School. Her work as a lay ecclesial minister and religious educator spans twenty-five years in the Catholic dioceses of Boston, Massachusetts; Manchester, New Hampshire; Altoona-Johnstown, Pennsylvania; Spokane, Washington; and Bridgeport, Connecticut. Barbara Jean and Harold Daly Horell live in Monroe, Connecticut, with their three children.

Fran Ferder, F.S.P.A., and **John Heagle** are codirectors of Therapy and Renewal Associates (TARA), a counseling and renewal resource in the Pacific Northwest. They also serve as adjunct faculty in the School of Theology and Ministry at Seattle University and are internationally recognized authors and conference speakers. Their most recent book is *Tender Fires: The Spiritual Promise of Sexuality*, about which they write: "*Tender Fires* is more than a book. It is a vision that we invite you to share and claim as your own. It is for anyone who believes that human relationships and sexuality are sacred gifts and responsibilities."

Christine Gudorf is professor and chair in the department of religious studies at Florida International University in Miami. The author of *Body, Sex and Pleasure: Reconstructing Christian Sexual Ethics*, she has published many books and articles on ethics, focusing especially on sexuality and gender, economic development, and the environment. Christine and Frank Gudorf have been married thirty-eight years and have three sons and two grandchildren.

Harold D. Horell is assistant professor of religious education at Fordham University in the Graduate School of Religion and Religious Education, teaching and publishing in the areas of religious education, pastoral theology, Christian moral education, and social ministry. He holds an interdisciplinary doctorate in theology and education from the Boston College Institute for Religious Education and Pastoral Ministry and is coeditor (with Thomas H. Groome) and contributing author to *Horizons and Hope: The Future of Religious Education*. Harold and B. J. Daly Horell have been married twenty years.

Luke Timothy Johnson is the Robert W. Woodruff Professor of New Testament and Christian Origins at Emory University's Candler School of Theology in Atlanta, Georgia. A former Benedictine monk, Luke Timothy earned his Ph.D. from Yale University and is the author of more than twenty books and hundreds of articles. He is currently involved with several projects at the intersection of faith and marriage, including a forthcoming volume in Emory University's Center for the Study of Law and Religion's Sex, Marriage, and Family project, titled *The Loss of the Sexual Body in Christian Theology*.

Kieran Scott is associate professor of religious education at Fordham University in the Graduate School of Religion and Religious Education. He did his doctoral work at Columbia University and now teaches ecclesiology, adult education, curriculum, and religious education. Most recently he has published a third edition of his book (with Michael Warren), *Perspectives on Marriage*.

Evelyn Eaton Whitehead, developmental psychologist, and **James D. Whitehead**, pastoral theologian, are well known in their fields. Evelyn writes and lectures on adult maturity, leadership dynamics, and the social analysis of parish and community life. James's work focuses on contemporary spirituality, leadership in the ministry, and the use of theological methods in the ministry. A married couple, they have jointly authored more than a dozen books and, through Whitehead Associates, they offer courses, seminars, and workshops throughout the United States and internationally. Their newest book, *Christian Adulthood: A Journey of Self-Discovery*, contains chapters on sensuality and self-intimacy.